# Neither Complementarian nor Egalitarian

# Neither Complementarian nor Egalitarian

## A Kingdom Corrective to the Evangelical Gender Debate

Michelle Lee-Barnewall

Foreword by Craig L. Blomberg
Afterword by Lynn H. Cohick

a division of Baker Publishing Group
Grand Rapids, Michigan

Published by Baker Academic
a division of Baker Publishing Group
P.O. Box 6287, Grand Rapids, MI 49516-6287
www.bakeracademic.com

Printed in the United States of America



Library of Congress Cataloging-in-Publication Data
Names: Lee-Barnewall, Michelle, 1966–
Title: Neither complementarian nor egalitarian : a kingdom corrective to the evangelical gender debate / Michelle Lee-Barnewall ; with a foreword by Craig L. Blomberg ; and an afterword by Lynn H. Cohick.
Description: Grand Rapids, MI : Baker Academic, 2016. | Includes bibliographical references and index.
Identifiers: LCCN 2015037203 | ISBN 9780801039577 (pbk.)
Subjects: LCSH: Sex role—Religious aspects—Christianity. | Evangelicalism.
Classification: LCC BT708 .L435 2016 | DDC 270.082—dc23 LC record available at http://lccn.loc.gov/2015037203



Unless otherwise indicated, quotations from ancient classical texts are from editions of the Loeb Classical Library.

Baker Publishing Group publications use paper produced from sustainable forestry practices and postconsumer waste whenever possible.

24 25 26 27 28 29 30 12 11 10 9 8 7 6

To John

---

With deep gratitude for your faithful
and loving presence in my life

# Contents

# Foreword

Craig L. Blomberg,
Distinguished Professor of New Testament,
Denver Seminary

Debates dealing with gender roles in church and the family have been just about as prominent as any other theological controversy throughout my Christian life. Growing up in the old Lutheran Church in America, I met ordained female pastors already in the late 1960s. Coming to evangelical faith through parachurch ministries and being nurtured by them in high school (Campus Life) and college (Campus Crusade for Christ), I discovered a lot of opinions about what men and women should or should not do that were nonissues for the LCA at that time. By the late 1970s in my seminary years, one of my professors at Trinity Evangelical Divinity School opined that Christians who found no timeless restrictions on women's roles in home or church were "either exegetically incompetent or biblically disobedient"! During my doctoral studies in Scotland, a small group of us who were all in the New Testament program decided to study the key passages and the key scholarly sources over a number of months and meet periodically to discuss our findings. Little did I know that this would one day lead to several writing projects of my own on the topic.

By the late 1980s, when I began teaching at Denver Seminary, I discovered that two main sides in the debate had crystallized, referring to their perspectives as either hierarchicalism or biblical feminism. In keeping with secular feminism, the latter group spoke primarily in terms of women's *rights*. In keeping with secular power structures, the former group spoke primarily in terms of men's *authority*. After further study, I came to the conviction that I was a hierarchicalist, but just barely. I saw the only office closed to women in New Testament times as that of elder or overseer, and I saw the twentieth-century functional equivalent of that office restricted to the senior pastor in a church with multiple pastoral staff or the sole pastor in a church too small to have additional pastoral staff. But in keeping with the dominant rhetoric of the day, I still thought largely in terms of rights and authority.[1]

By the 1990s, the two camps had largely adopted different labels for themselves: the hierarchicalists now calling themselves complementarians, and the biblical feminists calling themselves egalitarians. New parachurch organizations had been formed to support each position: The Council for Biblical Manhood and Womanhood (CBMW), representing complementarians, and Christians for Biblical Equality (CBE), representing egalitarians. One of my colleagues, who chaired our counseling department and was active in CBE, suggested that we coedit a book on the topic, inviting four scholars—with a man and a woman on each side—to defend the two positions. This led to the publication in 2001 of *Two Views of Women in Ministry*.[2] Not long before the book was ready to go to press, I had completed a lengthy essay on gender roles in Paul for an anthology of perspectives on various topics in Pauline theology to be published by Brill.[3] I found myself articulating a perspective that did not correspond terribly closely to that of any of the four contributors to our book with Zondervan. I showed it to my coeditor and to the editor at Zondervan with whom we were working, arguing that it was a third position, neither complementarian nor egalitarian. I saw a slightly distinctive role for men in the home and church, but it was something that gave them not added privileges but added responsibilities—to love their wife or their congregation in sacrificial ways as Christ loved the church and gave himself for it (Eph. 5:25). My coeditor and I were convinced that it represented a third approach, but our editor didn't agree. As a strong egalitarian himself, he said I was still clearly complementarian. But he did agree that my piece would make for a good appendix in our book, which is where it appeared.[4]

1. Blomberg, "Not beyond What Is Written."

2. Beck and Blomberg, *Two Views of Women in Ministry*.

3. Due to delays in the project, it would not be published for another five years. See Blomberg, "Neither Hierarchicalist nor Egalitarian."

4. Beck and Blomberg, *Two Views of Women in Ministry*, 329–72. In the revised edition of 2005, I expanded the article to become one of the two complementarian chapters, so that there was a clear difference between the two complementarian options.

A similar exploration in a paper for a conference later in the 2000s led me to suggest that perhaps the key texts in Paul, all of which refer to men and women with terms that could very easily be translated as husbands and wives, prevented only *married* women from occupying the one "buck-stops-here" position in church leadership.[5] Thinking that my respondent would at least be pleased that I was moving so close to her full-fledged egalitarianism, I got a blistering response instead, explaining that this was why evangelical feminism was still necessary, and that there is no such thing as someone who is almost an egalitarian. Either you are one fully or you are the opposition!

The amount of evangelical literature on this topic has tailed off noticeably in the last decade. Most people probably imagine that just about every position that can be articulated has been; all that remains is for them to decide which position they will adopt for themselves. Amazingly, Michelle Lee-Barnewall breathes considerable fresh air into this conversation. She narrates in detail how previous movements within Christianity that gave women greater public prominence stressed their unique *value* and the contributions that only women (or so it was believed) could make to the church and the world and the *responsibilities* they had to fill those roles. Only in the 1970s did biblical feminism emphasize *rights* and *freedoms* to the degree that they did, coming on the heels of the civil rights movement.

Lee-Barnewall focuses also on the key biblical values stressed in the passages so often discussed in conversations about gender roles. When one can sufficiently bracket modern causes and read the text carefully in its original contexts, one sees that *unity* and *inclusion* prove more central than equality or freedom. A concern for love and humility, rather than one of authority and privilege, pervades the scriptural texts and contexts. If it should turn out that there are any roles reserved for men, this is in no way to give them unique *privileges* but rather to require distinctive *responsibilities*. What a contrast with the standard complementarian preoccupation with headship as leadership! Lee-Barnewall also discusses the difference between servant *leadership*, in which leading still predominates, and *servant* leadership, in which service comes first. She notes the typical scenario in which a man first becomes a strong leader and then tempers his exercise of authority in that role with the spirit of a servant's heart. But then she highlights those rare individuals who begin by serving God with their spiritual gifts, no matter how menial a role they play among God's people. Only subsequently, when

5. The paper was subsequently published as Blomberg, "Gender Roles in Marriage and Ministry."

others have admired and imbibed their spirit for a significant length of time, are they then offered leadership roles. This is the model to be sought and commended, whenever possible.

Throughout her book, Lee-Barnewall assiduously refuses to answer the question of whether certain roles or tasks are limited to one gender. She recognizes that eventually one has to answer this question, but she does not want to duplicate past debates over privileges and power. She acknowledges that this will frustrate readers who want more than anything to be able to pigeonhole her as either complementarian or egalitarian. As the book's title suggests, however, she is rejecting both classic options in favor of a different approach altogether.

What would happen if leading proponents of the classic positions could actually come together in a spirit of love, unity, humility, and selflessness, with everyone vowing to study the texts and the issues afresh with commitments to no prior agendas and with no polemic that those who came out in a different place from them are in any sense academically or spiritually deficient? I have no doubt that there would be differing conclusions, but I also strongly suspect that the extremes in each camp would be eliminated. I could hope that people would conclude that there was room in the church of Jesus Christ for multiple perspectives, that at times we would have to agree to disagree in love, but that we could mutually support and encourage one another even when our churches and parachurch organizations differed in their perspectives. Denver Seminary, where I have taught for about thirty years, has far more often than not modeled this ideal and experienced these outcomes, so I know that my vision is not merely utopian.

I also know that readers unacquainted with Dr. Lee-Barnewall will wonder what kind of spirit she personally embraces as she promotes such a beautiful but often absent approach. After knowing her for almost a decade, I can assure readers that she very consistently models exactly what she promotes. She is one of the brightest people I have ever met who does not wear her learning on her sleeve but exudes a spirit of kindness and other-centeredness without vacillating on her core convictions in life. She has perennially been one of the most popular professors at Biola University, where she teaches. I commend her book to you with great enthusiasm. Take it, read it, and be transformed in your spirit on these topics!

# Acknowledgments

This book is the result of a long but immensely rewarding journey. As I look back, it is humbling and gratifying to see how much I am indebted to others for their support, resources, and advice.

First, I want to thank Baker Academic for their willingness to take a chance on yet another book on the gender debate. I am grateful for the skill and efforts of the Baker staff for their various contributions in getting this project to its final stage. In particular, my editor, James Ernest, was instrumental in guiding me throughout the process, and I especially appreciate his insight, wisdom, and willingness to give a hard word when needed.

Thanks go to Koninklijke Brill NV for permission to reprint from my article, "Turning Κεφαλή on Its Head: The Rhetoric of Reversal in Eph. 5:21–33," in *Christian Origins and Classical Culture: Social and Literary Contexts for the New Testament*, vol. 1 of *The New Testament in Its Hellenistic Context*, ed. Stanley E. Porter and Andrew W. Pitts, 599–614 (Leiden: Brill, 2013). The information in the article provided the foundation for chapter 8. Previous versions of chapters 6 and 8 were presented at meetings of the Evangelical Theological Society.

Financial support came from several places, providing me with precious time and other resources to work on the project. I am thankful for a Lilly Theological Scholars Grant from the Association of Theological Schools, which enabled me to work on the first part of the historical chapters and set the entire project in motion. A seventh-semester research leave and a sabbatical from Biola University gave me the time to complete critical portions of the book. These were supported in part by a Biola Research and Development Grant and a grant from the Biola Biblical and Theological Studies Division.

I am very grateful for the support of my administrators: my deans, Clinton Arnold and Scott Rae, and before them, Dennis Dirks and Michael Wilkins; my division dean, Douglas Huffman; and my chair, Matt Williams. Not only did they provide the necessary research leave and sabbatical for me to see this project through to completion, but also their constant encouragement helped me believe that this was something worth pursuing.

My friends and colleagues have contributed much appreciated help and support. Craig Blomberg, Craig Keener, and Mark Strauss provided valuable assistance at the project's early stage, when it was still just an idea looking for a publisher. Numerous Southern California friends and colleagues gave much needed help through prayer, encouragement, and reading and commenting on portions of the manuscript. Thank you Kenneth Berding, Joyce Brooks, Edward Curtis, June Hetzel, Moyer Hubbard, Lisa Ishihara, Joanne Jung, Joy Mosbarger, Ron Pierce, Betty Talbert, and Katie Tuttle. Historians Jonathan Den Hartog and Kristin Kobes Du Mez graciously shared their expertise in American religious history and read the chapters on the background of the evangelical gender debate. Their efforts were especially appreciated since I was moving outside my specialty and very aware of the need for extra help. Of course, any mistakes or misstatements that remain are mine, the result of my own shortcomings.

Finally, I want to thank my husband, John. Not only did he endure days, months, and years with a preoccupied wife, who spent far too much time in her office, but also his constant encouragement, eagerness to discuss the issue with me, and challenge to speak boldly inspired me, kept me going to the end, and taught me much about what it means to live together as men and women in the kingdom.

# Abbreviations

## Old Testament

| | | | |
|---|---|---|---|
| Gen. | Genesis | Song | Song of Songs |
| Exod. | Exodus | Isa. | Isaiah |
| Lev. | Leviticus | Jer. | Jeremiah |
| Num. | Numbers | Lam. | Lamentations |
| Deut. | Deuteronomy | Ezek. | Ezekiel |
| Josh. | Joshua | Dan. | Daniel |
| Judg. | Judges | Hosea | Hosea |
| Ruth | Ruth | Joel | Joel |
| 1–2 Sam. | 1–2 Samuel | Amos | Amos |
| 1–2 Kings | 1–2 Kings | Obad. | Obadiah |
| 1–2 Chron. | 1–2 Chronicles | Jon. | Jonah |
| Ezra | Ezra | Mic. | Micah |
| Neh. | Nehemiah | Nah. | Nahum |
| Esther | Esther | Hab. | Habakkuk |
| Job | Job | Zeph. | Zephaniah |
| Ps(s). | Psalm(s) | Hag. | Haggai |
| Prov. | Proverbs | Zech. | Zechariah |
| Eccles. | Ecclesiastes | Mal. | Malachi |

## New Testament

| | | | |
|---|---|---|---|
| Matt. | Matthew | John | John |
| Mark | Mark | Acts | Acts |
| Luke | Luke | Rom. | Romans |

| | | | |
|---|---|---|---|
| 1–2 Cor. | 1–2 Corinthians | Philem. | Philemon |
| Gal. | Galatians | Heb. | Hebrews |
| Eph. | Ephesians | James | James |
| Phil. | Philippians | 1–2 Pet. | 1–2 Peter |
| Col. | Colossians | 1–3 John | 1–3 John |
| 1–2 Thess. | 1–2 Thessalonians | Jude | Jude |
| 1–2 Tim. | 1–2 Timothy | Rev. | Revelation |
| Titus | Titus | | |

## Other Ancient Sources

### *Aristotle*

*Eth. eud.* — *Ethica eudemia (Eudemian Ethics)*
*Eth. nic.* — *Ethica nicomachea (Nicomachean Ethics)*
*Pol.* — *Politica (Politics)*
*Rhet.* — *Rhetorica (Rhetoric)*

### *Dio Chrysostom*

*Or.* — *Orationes (Discourses)*

### *Dionysius of Halicarnassus*

*Ant. rom.* — *Antiquitates romanae (Roman Antiquities)*

### *Hippocrates*

*Morb. sacr.* — *De morbo sacro (The Sacred Disease)*

### *Josephus*

*Ant.* — *Antiquitates judaicae (Jewish Antiquities)*
*C. Ap.* — *Contra Apionem (Against Apion)*

### *Philo*

*Decal.* — *De decalogo (On the Decalogue)*
*Mos.* — *De vita Mosis (On the Life of Moses)*
*Praem.* — *De praemiis et poenis (On Rewards and Punishments)*
*QG* — *Quaestiones et solutiones in Genesin (Questions and Answers in Genesis)*

| | |
|---|---|
| *Somn.* | *De somniis (On Dreams)* |
| *Spec.* | *De specialibus legibus (On the Special Laws)* |

### *Plato*

| | |
|---|---|
| *Tim.* | *Timaeus* |

### *Plutarch*

| | |
|---|---|
| *Conj. praec.* | *Conjugalia praecepta (Advice to Bride and Groom)* |
| *Cor.* | *Marcius Coriolanus* |
| *Frat. amor.* | *De fraterno amore (On Brotherly Love)* |
| *Galb.* | *Galba* |
| *Pel.* | *Pelopidas* |
| *Praec. ger. rei publ.* | *Praecepta gerendae rei publicae (Precepts of Statecraft)* |

### *Seneca*

| | |
|---|---|
| *Clem.* | *De clementia (On Mercy)* |
| *Ep.* | *Epistulae morales (Moral Letters)* |

### *Xenophon*

| | |
|---|---|
| *Mem.* | *Memorabilia* |

## Bible Versions

| | |
|---|---|
| LXX | Septuagint, Greek Old Testament |
| NASB | New American Standard Bible |
| NIV | New International Version |
| NRSV | New Revised Standard Version |

# Introduction

A large part of the impetus for this book comes from what I have learned as I have talked with numerous men and women about the topic of gender over the years. As I have spoken with both complementarians and egalitarians, I have noticed some things that many of them have in common. First is the conviction on both sides that this is an extremely vital issue for the church, the importance of which is reflected in the energy that is spent defending views and the emotion with which these views are often presented. At the same time, however, there is a growing sense among many that neither position quite encapsulates what they sense is the biblical view, along with the desire to explore the topic beyond the bounds of the current positions.

Since I have increasingly found myself in the same situation, I am proposing that we may find a better solution by going back to the biblical text to see, not which of the two current positions—complementarian or egalitarian—is correct, but rather whether there might be a different way to configure the issue itself. Thus I would like to reexamine the context of gender in Scripture rather than defend one particular view. Like many of the people with whom I have spoken, whether professors, pastors, or laypeople, I have come to believe that the topic cannot be completely defined by either the complementarian or the egalitarian viewpoint, and that there is room, perhaps even a necessity, for an alternative way of conceptualizing gender issues. The goal of this book is to demonstrate why a new viewpoint is needed in evangelicalism today and to present a trajectory for reframing the debate.

## The Evangelical Gender Debate: Complementarian and Egalitarian

The current state is perhaps best seen in the publication of two significant books: John Piper and Wayne Grudem's complementarian contribution, *Recovering Biblical Manhood and Womanhood: A Response to Evangelical Feminism*,[1] and Ronald W. Pierce and Rebecca Merrill Groothuis's egalitarian response, *Discovering Biblical Equality: Complementarity without Hierarchy*.[2] Piper and Grudem present their view as biblical "complementarity," which reflects "both equality and beneficial differences between men and women," the latter including a special leadership role for men in the church and the home. They argue, "The Bible teaches that men and women fulfill different roles in relation to each other" and that these roles, including the unique leadership role of men, are based "not on temporary cultural norms but on permanent facts of creation."[3]

Pierce and Groothuis describe the position of biblical equality, in which "the appropriate outworking of the biblical ideal of equality is for women and men to have equal opportunity for ministry in the church, and shared authority with mutual submission within marriage."[4] Egalitarianism "rejects the notion that any office, ministry or opportunity should be denied anyone on the grounds of gender alone."[5] *Discovering Biblical Equality* was purposely intended to mirror its complementarian counterpart, following a similar format, being approximately the same size, and even presenting a cover that looked much the same except for the orange-brown color intentionally contrasting *Recovering Biblical Manhood and Womanhood*'s blue cover. The books illustrate how the evangelical gender debate has primarily developed as a choice between two sides, the complementarian and egalitarian positions, and highlight the specific questions over which the battle lines have been drawn. In particular they involve issues of male leadership and authority versus the rights of women to participate in all ministry positions and share equally in decision making in marriage.

In this way the debate presents two clearly identifiable sides with two generally distinct positions. Although there may be variations within the positions

1. Piper and Grudem, *Recovering Biblical Manhood and Womanhood*.

2. Pierce and Groothuis, *Discovering Biblical Equality*.

3. These roles, which existed from creation, were then disrupted by the fall. Piper and Grudem, "Vision of Biblical Complementarity," 35.

4. Pierce and Groothuis, *Discovering Biblical Equality*, 19; see also Groothuis, *Good News for Women*, 19.

5. Pierce and Groothuis, *Discovering Biblical Equality*, 13.

themselves,[6] the general situation is characterized by identifying with one of the two positions. The purpose of this book is to question whether this is the best way to frame the discussion and to suggest a different way.

There is no doubt that the current structure has produced many benefits. As the two sides battle, arguments are sharpened, ancient sources are scrutinized more carefully to provide additional supporting evidence, technology enables scholars to access a larger body of evidence more easily, and weaknesses in both positions are exposed, defended, and corrected. However, while this situation has led to some very meaningful gains in understanding, it may have also reached the point where further entrenchment in the respective positions may unintentionally obscure other significant observations and ideas. When the dominant goal is to defend one's position, it is extremely difficult to consider the possibility that answers may not lie exclusively on one side, to see the beneficial arguments on the other side, and to explore new areas.

## The Limitations of Debate

In her book *The Argument Culture*, linguist Deborah Tannen asserts that our culture is permeated by a "pervasive warlike atmosphere that makes us approach public dialogue, and just about anything we need to accomplish, as if it were a fight."[7] While she acknowledges that such an approach is useful in the right context, it has become overemphasized to the point where it often gets in the way of solving problems rather than aiding.[8] The assumption is that opposition is the most desirable option (ibid., 3–4), and Tannen suggests that other means, such as "exploring, expanding, discussing, investigating, and the exchanging of ideas," may yield more fruitful results in some endeavors (8).

The answer may not be the exclusive domain of one side but rather may lie elsewhere. If this is the case, we cannot discover the entire truth in a debate in which the only option is to choose from two positions. Tannen explains,

6. E.g., some egalitarians believe that *kephalē* in 1 Cor. 11 means "source" (e.g., Kroeger, "Classical Concept," 268; Fee, "Praying and Prophesying," 149–55). Others contend that it means "preeminence" (e.g., Cervin, "Rebuttal"). Some complementarians hold that male leadership means only leadership at the "most authoritative level," or the "highest office" in the church, e.g., limiting the position of senior pastor or elder to men (e.g., Blomberg, "Complementarian Perspective," 145, 181). Others place more restrictions on women, including prohibiting them from teaching Bible and doctrine in the church, colleges, and seminaries (Moo, "What Does It Mean?," 186).

7. Tannen, *Argument Culture*, 3.

8. Ibid. Although Tannen wrote in 1998, it does not seem that this trend has abated, and if anything, would seem to have accelerated.

"Opposition does not lead to the whole truth when we ask only 'What's wrong with this?' and never 'What can we use from this in building a new theory, a new understanding?'" (19). Limiting ourselves to an either/or choice does not leave enough room for improving either side or exploring a different understanding.

As Tannen further observes, "When the problem is posed in a way that polarizes, the solution is often obscured before the search is under way" (21). Our methodology should make room for a different kind of answer, but a "culture of critique"[9] does not allow for another position. Although criticism certainly has its place, so do other methods such as integrating ideas from different fields (19).

Some evangelical scholars have expressed similar concerns about the gender debate. Timothy George calls for the pursuit of truth in a context that recognizes individual fallibility and the potential contribution from those of the opposing position. He also states his concerns for the effect of the conflict on relationships among the members of Christ. In searching for a "way beyond the polarization,"[10] George discusses three questions for those involved:[11]

1. "What do I owe to the person who differs from me?" While we are not obligated to agree with that person, we do owe him or her love. As a result, we are to be good listeners, seeking to understand the person's aims and asking whether there is anything valid in his or her position.
2. "What can I learn from those who differ from me?" In recognition of his or her own fallibility, each interpreter should be prepared to learn that he or she is wrong and the other person is right. Seeking after truth is more important than winning discussions or protecting reputations.
3. "How can I cope with those who differ from me?" We must remember that we are brothers and sisters in Christ. Consequently, our goal is not to demolish our opponent but rather "to win him or her over to a new and, we trust, better understanding."[12]

He calls for both sides to recognize their mutual commitment to historic Christian orthodoxy and to allow this greater context to be the basis for a

9. Ibid., 7. Tannen defines "critique" as "not a general term for analysis or interpretation but rather a synonym for criticism."

10. George, "Egalitarians and Complementarians Together?," 267.

11. George attributes the original questions to Roger Nicole from his essay, "Polemic Theology: How to Deal with Those Who Differ from Us," in *Standing Forth: Collected Writings of Roger Nicole* (Ross-shire, UK: Christian Focus Publishers, Mentor, 2002), 10. Cited in George, "Egalitarians and Complementarians Together?," 277–82.

12. George, "Egalitarians and Complementarians Together?," 278–79.

unity under which differences can be discussed.[13] With this underlying unity, perhaps there can then be "honest confrontation of ideas and truth claims as well as a conciliatory spirit that is open to convergence and reconciliation."[14]

As Tannen and George have noted, there are significant limitations in assuming that the truth of an issue is to be found in one of two sides.[15] As a result, the contours of the debate may be in need of reexamination and adjustment. A more fruitful approach at this point may be to expand or redesign the shape of the gender discussion rather than simply reinforcing the two current positions. In searching for the most accurate way to understand the biblical text, we must be open to exploring another way of viewing the issue itself.

## Searching for an Alternative

Recently some evangelicals have made moves to provide a different answer beyond the current complementarian/egalitarian divide. For example, there have been some modifications to both sides. Many complementarians have shifted their position so that the emphasis is on male headship not so much as a position of authority but rather as one of servant leadership. The term "complementarian" moves away from negative connotations linked with terms such as "hierarchical" and "traditionalist,"[16] reflecting an understanding of gender that concentrates on the creation differences between men and women and how Christians are to manifest these differences in the church and the home.[17]

13. Ibid., 285.

14. Ibid., 283.

15. As one historian describes, "Traditionalism and feminism have become the ideological poles which, to a large degree, have set the limits of creative discussion" (Bendroth, "Search for 'Women's Role,'" 122–23).

16. Piper and Grudem say this is why they prefer the term "complementarian." "We are uncomfortable with the term 'traditionalist' because it implies an unwillingness to let Scripture challenge traditional patterns of behavior, and we certainly reject the term 'hierarchicalist' because it overemphasizes structured authority while giving no suggestion of equality or the beauty of mutual interdependence" (*Recovering Biblical Manhood and Womanhood*, xiv).

17. Thus differences in roles, including male leadership, are based on "permanent facts of creation" (Piper and Grudem, "Vision of Biblical Complementarity," 31–59). As Saucy and TenElshof explain, "This complementarity means that two important realities are grounded in the very nature of all men and women: (1) They are different by nature, and (2) they require each other for fullness of their humanity. If such is the nature of man and woman by creation that they exist as co-humanity in a complementary relationship, this truth must find expression in all of life, including church ministry" ("Problem in the Church," 29–30).

On the other side, the stress on the significance of gender differences by complementarians has pushed egalitarians to wrestle with this issue within the context of equality and ministry opportunity based on giftedness. In other words, if ministry is based on calling and giftedness, egalitarians must explain whether and why gender matters. The subtitle of Pierce and Groothuis's book, *Complementarity without Hierarchy*, reflects this desire to show how gender remains relevant in an egalitarian position. In regard to terminology, "egalitarian" or "biblical equality" is often preferred to "evangelical feminist," which helps to avoid negative associations with secular feminism.[18] Furthermore, egalitarians are generally associated with the more conservative part of the movement that split from the progressive evangelical feminists in the 1980s.[19]

Others have proposed finding a "third way" beyond the two positions. Some discuss the importance of restoring relationships between people on both sides and working together. George proposes that as some prominent evangelicals and Catholics worked together to create the Evangelicals and Catholics Together (ECT) statement regarding their common faith commitments and mission, so too might egalitarians and complementarians work together to affirm their shared mission and commit to studying together in a new ECT (Egalitarians and Complementarians Together) project.[20]

Some scholars, like Sarah Sumner, do not explicitly identify themselves with either side. Sumner believes that the debate has been inappropriately reduced to one of roles when it is more fundamentally one of relationships.[21] In this way she challenges evangelicals to approach the issue differently, and her proposed area of relationships may be one in which evangelicals, as Tannen has noted, can do more "exploring" and "expanding."[22]

This study explores how the issue itself might be reframed according to significant biblical categories. Since it is currently set up according to two distinct and opposing sides, it tends to produce questions along preset lines, which then limits the types of answers that can be given and profoundly impacts how we view the issue. These questions revolve around whether men

18. On our use of "secular" and the relationship of religion and feminism, see chap. 1, note 4.

19. See the following chapters for a more detailed account of the evangelical feminist movements. For a specific description of the split in evangelical feminism in the 1980s, see chap. 3, notes 36 and 85.

20. George, "Egalitarians and Complementarians Together?," 282–88. Sumner (*Men and Women*) also speaks in her book about the importance of repentance and restored relationships in the Christian community in regard to this issue.

21. Sumner, *Men and Women*, 30–31.

22. Tannen, *Argument Culture*, 6.

have a special authority or leadership role or whether women have equal access to ministry roles and are equal participants in decision making in marriage.

However, the issue might be helped by applying categories such as love, unity, and holiness. Also there may be considerable implications to seeing the gospel as something that is paradoxical and reverses traditional norms and expectations. The key may be asking not so much whether Scripture promotes equality or authority as how—in a kingdom understanding—gender relates to love and unity between husbands and wives, among the many members of the body, and ultimately between Christ and his bride. We may gain more not from merely asking what rights a person has or who has power but by seeing why unity matters and how it is accomplished by power manifested through weakness (2 Cor. 12:9), such as was exhibited through the cross. This does not mean that questions of rights and authority do not matter. Instead it implies that our perspective on them may shift when we see them within a larger context.[23]

Consequently, the purpose of this book is to demonstrate how the debate as it is presently structured, as a choice between the two current sides, can benefit from a different framework and additional questions. The ways of the kingdom are often at odds with a natural mind-set, since the Christian faith itself is based on the cross as foolishness to the world but the wisdom of God (1 Cor. 1:18). There are compelling reasons to ask whether the New Testament ethic for women and men might follow a similar pattern—something that turns the world's order upside down and is understandable only in light of a kingdom theology.

## Reconsidering a Theology of Gender

In order to begin establishing the need for new categories, part 1 examines some ways in which evangelicals have historically understood gender and how these shifted in ways that reflected larger social trends. This idea about the impact of the larger culture is not new; nor is it limited to our conception of gender. As sociologist Robert Wuthnow explains in reference to the effect of

23. Many of the themes that this study will present are not absent from the current discussion. E.g., complementarians and egalitarians disagree on the implications of "unity" and "oneness" for the new community as seen in passages such as Gal. 3:28 (e.g., Johnson, "Role Distinctions," 156; Bilezikian, "Biblical Community"). However, we will attempt to show how they can reconfigure our understanding of the other categories that have been more prominent in the debate.

society on religion, and here on the widespread changes in American culture following World War II, "to the extent that American religion is a social institution, embedded in and always exposed to the broader social environment, it could not help but have been affected by these changes."[24] To see cultural influence does not necessarily mean that our current categories are not biblical. However, if our definitions consistently reflect the dominant cultural forces in their particular era, then we should seriously consider the possibility that there is still something missing from our current biblical worldview on gender.

Although both egalitarians and complementarians have accused the other of following the larger culture, this book explores how all sides have been impacted by social trends, and more important, how the overall trajectory of the debate aligns with these patterns. Evangelicals in America followed the general movement toward an increasing individualism and preoccupation with personal over corporate concerns. This rising individualism, along with changing conceptions of the boundaries and value of the family, helped to shift evangelicalism from being driven by a core concern for the good of the larger society to the quest for personal fulfillment as seen in the immediate family and then the acquisition of individual rights. In this way social trends influenced the overall movement of conceptions of gender toward an increasingly individualistic concern even as evangelicals seemed to vacillate between more complementarian and egalitarian manifestations.

To illustrate this trend, chapter 1 discusses the mid-nineteenth century to the turn of the twentieth century, dwelling on the influence of the Victorian ideal of womanhood on the first evangelical feminist movement. The connection between domesticity and womanhood characterized a notable period of activity for American evangelical women, as they sought a greater public role based on their identity and corresponding duty as the primary moral guardians of society. Chapter 2 traces how two successive world wars, and World War II in particular, caused Americans to turn to home and family as a refuge. During this period, the typical evangelical home tried to follow the ideal model of the husband as the authority figure and sole provider for the family and the wife as full-time homemaker. Chapter 3 discusses the rise of egalitarianism in the 1970s and its affinities to the secular feminist movement with its emphasis on personal fulfillment and individual rights.

Part 2 turns to the biblical text. Chapter 4 briefly introduces categories that have reframing potential and that are applied in the following chapters. In contrast to an increasing focus on the individual in evangelicalism, the New

24. Wuthnow, *Restructuring of American Religion*, 5.

Testament testifies to a dominant corporate concern for the unified people of God who live as his holy temple and so demonstrate his ways in Christ.

The Old Testament identifies Israel as the people of God, and the New Testament places the spotlight on the church, the temple of God. The body of Christ is not the exclusive province of one race, class, or gender. However, the radically inclusive community is not one in which differences do not exist. Rather it is one that manifests unity in its members' love for one another in the context of such diversity as they are called to build up one another.

This love is characterized and accomplished by a reversal of understanding, for the kingdom values of Jesus—who states that the last will be first, and the first will be last—stand in direct opposition to those of the world. An other-centered orientation by all is crucial to unity, for Paul defines love as following Christ's example as one who did not use his rights but instead laid down his life for others. The continued presence of hierarchies provides the vehicle for exhibiting this aspect of the kingdom of God, as the strong are to be considerate of the weak (1 Cor. 8; Rom. 14–15), the members of the body that seem less honorable are to be given greater honor (1 Cor. 12:23), and leaders such as elders are seen not as those with more privileges but as those called to set an example in suffering like Christ (1 Pet. 5:3).

The relational aspect inherent in the concepts of inclusion and oneness leads to a perspective that is different from and more corporate than the idea of "equality," and the reversal of status and privilege points to a more transcendent understanding of "authority" and "leadership" at stake in the kingdom. While these traditional subjects may still be present, these larger themes may be more representative of kingdom priorities and so provide a more foundational perspective from which to explore biblical concepts of gender.

Consequently, the chapters in this part explore how these themes impact our understanding of gender. Chapters 5 and 6 examine gender in ministry. Chapter 5 investigates the way in which inclusion, rather than equality, may be more relevant for understanding the new relationships among the people of God and the impact of passages such as Acts 2 for gender. Once people are included in the body of Christ, the priority is a willingness to sacrifice for one another rather than individual benefits for members of the group. Chapter 6 considers how the concept of "reversal" challenges our understanding of authority and leadership in the New Testament, including the meaning of the popular term "servant leadership." "Servant" describes not merely the manner of leadership but also a critical part of its essence. Furthermore, leaders are to imitate Christ, not only as a "servant" but also as a "slave," for the sake of promoting unity in the church as the believers follow their example of self-giving love.

Chapters 7 and 8 examine the biblical view of marriage, focusing on Gen. 2–3 and Eph. 5:21–33 and their relationship to each other. Egalitarians and complementarians argue about whether or not the Genesis passage presents a hierarchical relationship between Adam and Eve. This part demonstrates that it is better to see their relationship as characterized by differences that are to lead to unity in their "one flesh" relationship and that also illustrate their shared obligation to obey God.

In considering the connections with Paul's discussion of marriage in Eph. 5, we will examine how Paul views marriage as being exemplified by the Genesis "one flesh" relationship, as related to the husband's role as the "head." Examining the head metaphor in its ancient context will reveal that the passage should be understood according to a reversal that follows the example of Christ. While the head is the "leader," it unexpectedly forgoes the privileges and benefits of headship and instead loves the body by sacrificing for it. This humility is key to the desired unity between husband and wife, as well as between Christ and the church.

God's unified church, the holy temple of his Spirit, thus provides a critical and underutilized component for the discussion. A natural desire is to concentrate attention on personal good and individual roles, leading to well-intended questions that highlight rights or proper positions of authority. But this method can have the unintended consequence of reinforcing our conception that the individual is the central concern. However, if we begin from the perspective of God's purpose for the church as a whole, we see that these concerns are transcended and put into larger perspective as the members are called to love one another following the example of Christ, who purposely relinquished his rightful privileges for our sake.

## Conclusion

While this book tries to present some fresh ideas for the gender debate, there are some things it does *not* attempt to do. First, it does not present a detailed and systematic examination of all the passages traditionally associated with the debate. To engage every text is beyond the scope of this book, especially when the main purpose is to argue for the need for an alternative perspective.

Second, I offer a proposal for moving in a different direction, rather than outlining specifics of what the end result might look like. Because the discussion can be so contentious, it seems more fruitful at this point not to present something that may appear to favor one "side" over the other. Rather, I attempt to be as evenhanded as possible in critiquing both positions for the sake of a larger goal, which is for both sides to reconsider the nature of the debate and to examine critically their own positions while not having to surrender present concerns.

Third, I am not trying to propose a way that is entirely different from the complementarian and egalitarian positions since I am not denying that equality and authority can be valid categories. However, since the greater purpose of the book is to consider our orienting perspective, I argue that the dominant categories may not be the most appropriate ones with which to ground our understanding of gender. While these issues may be present, they must be viewed within a larger kingdom perspective, and I try to point out the way in which this other framework impacts these categories.

Since the kinds of questions we bring to the text determine the kinds of answers we receive, we will reconsider those questions. The principle aim has generally been to define what women can or cannot do. Approaching the issue in this way with the primary goal of determining what is allowable can cause us to miss another explanation of gender that could reframe the way we understand the issue, in particular as it relates to God's greater purposes for his people.

The apostle Paul knew the importance of formulating proper questions. In his discussion in Romans on the gift of grace in Christ Jesus, he proclaims, "where sin increased, grace abounded all the more" (Rom. 5:20). Paul anticipates that one can draw the conclusion that there could be an advantage to sin in that it leads to more grace, so he asks preemptively, "What shall we say then? Are we to continue in sin so that grace may increase?" (Rom. 6:1). But Paul does not address the question by merely answering yes or no. Instead he changes the trajectory of the discussion by exhorting, "May it never be! How shall we who died to sin still live in it?" (Rom. 6:2).

By responding in this way, Paul demonstrates the need to see the implications of grace in Christ in a different way. One view begins from the perspective of sin and presumes a somewhat mathematical relationship between sin and grace. If sin leads to grace, and increased sin leads to increased grace, why not simply keep sinning more to get more grace? But Paul says that such a question is misleading, perhaps even dangerous, because it misunderstands the nature of sin and grace and the believer's new life in Christ. Christ's followers not only receive grace, resulting in justification, but also are freed from slavery to sin. If they are no longer under sin's tyranny, why would they consider wanting to sin more?

Instead of asking how much a person can sin, a better perspective considers the nature of grace, what believers have become in Christ, and the subsequent implications for how they are to live. To see grace in terms of what it allows one to do (i.e., to sin) is to live according to the old mind-set. The new mind-set reorients them toward how their new identity in Christ has transformed their relationship to sin and so enables them to live properly in relation to God.

Thus the answer to the question is essentially no, but it does not come simply as a prohibition ("Do not sin!"). Instead Paul sets it in the context of the believers' new life and identity. His goal is not just to provide a command to be followed but also to help them understand that rather than being something desirable, sin is a slave master from whom they have been freed, and grace transforms as well as pardons. The proper perspective, therefore, is not to ask whether one can still sin but to see implications of being someone who has been freed from the power of sin through Christ and how this impacts one's desires and goals.

Consequently, Paul's answer does not concentrate on a rationale for a prohibition as much as it fundamentally reorients believers to view their lives in a different way. His concern is not simply on behavior (to stop sinning) but for them to be people who see sin for what it truly is and how Christ has freed them from its merciless grasp. Paul's answer is intended to shift their perspective, so he answers the original question, "Are we to continue in sin that grace might increase?" in light of their newfound freedom from sin. Since sin is the enemy from which they want to be freed, of course they should not continue in sin. To ask that question means that they have not fully understood the ramifications and nature of God's grace.

We can learn from Paul's answer in contrast to what could have happened if he had simply replied yes or no as we consider gender. As evangelical Christians, we often want to know what we can or cannot do, or what we should or should not do. As the gender debate has concentrated on specific activities, it runs the same risk of creating a theology defined by an external pattern of prohibitions and allowances. Various biblical and theological arguments are brought to bear to support a theology that concentrates on form and praxis, and in particular, as related to individuals. As a result, the discussion is dominated by practical questions such as "Can women be elders?" "Can women teach men?" and "Do men make the final decision in marriage?"

I understand the need to address the practical questions, but I also ask whether there is room to suspend them for a moment to reexamine Scripture without these predetermined goals. To use a modern analogy, we can easily see the problems of a theology of spiritual formation grounded on a question such as "Can Christians drink/smoke/gamble and so on?" These questions are formed by our desire to know precisely how to live, but if we present them as our *starting* point, we take a shortcut that causes us to miss the larger picture and perhaps do more harm in the long run. Not many people would say that Christian spirituality is defined simply by conformity to external rules, and the same is true in a theology of gender.

The focus on authority, leadership, equality, and rights tends to lead to yes or no answers that do not prompt deeper questioning. It is not that these do not matter, but rather that there is a way to reconsider them. The New Testament can reorient us in the purpose and implications of our new identity in Christ, including the corporate dimension as the people of God in relationship with him and with one another.

In this book, I propose the need to step back for a moment from the pressing questions of the day to ask whether they represent the best way to approach the issue. I also present some other possibilities. While our current questions have a definite practical value, are there other questions we should be asking, ones that are more foundational to the topic? In other words, can we gain a more robust understanding of the role of gender in the kingdom of God, which may then help us answer our specific questions?

A principal point of this book is that more transcendent kingdom concerns can profoundly challenge how we view the current debate. For example, Paul asserts that the critical topic is not our rights, important as they are, but how the giving up of rights can be necessary for the gospel and for the sake of unity (e.g., 1 Cor. 9; Phil. 2:1–11). While rights can be a legitimate issue, there is a kingdom value that supersedes rights and is more representative of kingdom ways. On the other side, the gospel redefines considerations of power and authority in terms of humility, sacrifice, and suffering, not simply as qualifiers but as essential components, even starting points. I suspect that the full implications of Christ's example of giving up the benefits of his status for our sake are yet to be discovered.

Thus this study seeks to provide the rationale for enlarging our perspective by reconsidering gender according to categories that are more transcendent. In various ways God is presenting a witness to the world through the life of the church, called to unity and holiness, and so issues of rights, authority, individual benefit, and duties must flow out of this larger understanding. As a result, we may gain new insights on old topics as we interact with essential kingdom themes that speak of our corporate identity in Christ in the new age and how the church is to glorify God as the body of Christ.

# PART 1

# Gender in Evangelical History

# 1

# Evangelical Women and Social Reform

In order to argue for the need for a new framework, the next three chapters examine some of the historical contours of the evangelical gender debate and how the dominant concerns reflected general cultural ideas. The point is to show how the types of issues that captured the interest of evangelicals corresponded to larger social trends. We will see how the specific concerns and values of a certain period impacted perceptions of appropriate ideas of gender.

The purpose of this section is not to indicate approval or disapproval of a particular view but rather to note its existence and historical context. Furthermore, while each period might contain a variety of thoughts on the topic, the main attention here is on the ideas that dominated the discussion or at least were successful in gaining a substantial foothold so we can consider why they were accepted.[1] Also, these chapters are not meant to be comprehensive but rather are intended to demonstrate a pattern of striking similarities between

1. E.g., at the turn of the century, Katharine Bushnell was strongly critical of the notion of a woman's sphere (Du Mez, *New Gospel for Women*, 144) and traditional gender relations (130–31). Her book, *God's Word to Women*, received enthusiastic endorsements from places such as *Moody Bible Institute Monthly*. However, the book's influence was hindered by changes in the evangelical theological culture, including a shift from social reform to personal morality and "soul-saving revivalism" (152–58).

evangelical gender discussions and the cultural context in which the gender debate was formed.

In this way we are interested in the larger contours of the discussion and the overall trajectory. Issues of authority and equality existed throughout these periods but took on different forms and found different levels of acceptability according to how well they fit into these greater concerns. We will note the impact of a general movement from a more corporate concern to an individualistic ethos and also of changing views of family and the home. Thus we will see how the priority of male authority waned in a more pragmatic age that was fueled by the concern to send as many people as possible to the mission field and saw the benefits of women's leadership in social reform. This study also investigates how, despite the early appearance of arguments for women's equal rights, the subject was mostly rejected as too focused on the self until it found more fertile ground in a later era that was more accepting of the importance of civil rights. We will note the variety of views on the family and consequently the acceptable type of women's activity. These views shifted from seeing the entire world as a woman's home and so her sphere of influence, to a narrowing to the immediate household of the nuclear family, to finding a sharp distinction between home and work that identified a woman's "role" as including the world of "work" beyond home and family.

In order to illustrate the framing impact of these larger social issues, this section discusses three time periods in American history: (1) the mid-nineteenth century to the turn of the twentieth century, a period dominated by the Victorian ideal of womanhood but one that also produced the first evangelical feminist movement as evangelical women played a major public role in social reform; (2) the post–World War II era of the 1940s–1950s, which saw a reversal in evangelical openness to women's public ministry and was characterized in large part by a definition of ideal womanhood in terms of marriage and motherhood that reflected to some degree a return to the Victorian model but in a greater sense the home-oriented culture of postwar America; (3) the 1970s, which saw the rise of egalitarianism, the second evangelical feminist movement, which differed from the previous one in its stress on individual "rights" over women's roles in larger social issues.

This section intends to outline a few significant phases in American evangelical history in order to demonstrate ways in which ideas about gender fluctuated according to cultural shifts and so draw attention to the way in which our framework for the gender debate can be influenced by larger social ideas and concerns.[2] The subject of this chapter, the mid-nineteenth to the turn of the twentieth century, has been seen as providing evangelicalism's first feminist movement, but the movement was also based on very strong ideas about a feminine nature that not only separated women from men but also considered them morally superior.

Consequently, this period provides a unique window into the topic because ideas of gender in this early period did not reflect our contemporary categorization of gender according to "authority" and "equality." Although these aspects were not absent, they did not dominate the discussion as they would later. Instead ideas about gender for the most part reflected the interests of the era in expediency, the relationship between feminine nature and virtue, and the need for a moral foundation for a rapidly changing country. Perhaps most of all, an overriding corporate perspective meant that women's domestic nature thrust them out of their immediate homes into the larger "household" of the world.

## Women and Social Reform at the Turn of the Century

One of the more remarkable features of post–Civil War America through the turn of the century was the vigorous activity of American evangelical women in social reform and missions. Fueled by a millennialism that led them to believe that their work could help usher in the kingdom of God on earth, evangelical women had major leadership roles in numerous benevolence society and reform movements.[3] The work of these women was so pioneering that numerous scholars have connected their activity to the beginnings of the secular[4] feminist

2. Unfortunately the limitations of the study also mean that we will not be able to focus on the contribution of working-class or African American women but will study primarily white, middle-class women who figured more prominently in evangelicalism during this time.

3. Gallagher, *Evangelical Identity*, 33. It can be pointed out that American culture at this point was profoundly influenced by evangelicalism, so much so that it "infused the world view of America's educated classes" and "molded the way Americans lived their private lives and the way they thought about their nation's destiny." William G. McLoughlin's statement—"the story of American Evangelicalism is the story of America itself in the years 1800–1900"—has been called by Watt a "stark expression of a historian's commonplace" (*Transforming Faith*, 37).

4. In order to distinguish the larger feminist movements from their evangelical counterparts, we will use "secular" to refer to "that which is not controlled by formal or organized religion" (Marsden, *Religion and American Culture*, 6). At the same time we can recognize that religious women often played important roles in these movements, although historians at various times have downplayed their contributions. E.g., when Elizabeth Cady Stanton wrote *The History of Woman Suffrage*, she recast the movement as focusing on political and constitutional rather than religious issues (Braude, "Religions and Modern Feminism," 1:14; Braude, "Religious Feminist," 570; G. Lerner, *Creation of Feminist Consciousness*, 269). The bias was then carried into the work of subsequent historians who focused on women like Stanton and Susan B. Anthony

movement, including the suffrage movement.[5] Women also were accepted as preachers by prominent evangelical leaders such as Dwight L. Moody and A. J. Gordon and played key roles in the foreign missionary movement.[6]

This period is an intriguing moment in evangelical gender relations. The influence of the Industrial Revolution and Victorian ideology created a mix of ideas that assigned women to the domestic realm while simultaneously propelling them into the public arena. While complementarians and egalitarians may argue over, for example, whether women's place is primarily in the home or whether they should have equal opportunity for public leadership roles, this era saw a blurring of the private versus public distinction precisely because women's domesticity meant that they had a duty to bring their domestic values to influence the corrupt larger society. Women did not argue for their "right" to public ministry as much as they felt compelled and were urged to act because of their superior moral and spiritual nature.

### Women, Virtue, and Extending the "Sphere"

Industrialization and urbanization caused a significant shift in the structure of the family. Men became more distant from domestic activities as they began to work outside the home, and the household became primarily the woman's realm.[7] Since women were no longer as involved in economic production, their work concentrated on child rearing, housework, and making the home a "refuge" for men when they returned home from work.[8] In this way industrialization and urbanization helped to create a distinction between the genders, with each being associated with a "separate sphere of activity and expertise." Women were the keepers of the home and domestic sphere, and men were linked with the realm of business, labor, and politics.[9] Religion also became the province of women at this time as the church was connected with the private domestic realm and the man's world became the battlefield

---

rather than Frances Willard, the influential president of the Woman's Christian Temperance Union (Braude, "Religions and Modern Feminism," 1:14; Braude, "Religious Feminist," 570).

5. See, e.g., Dayton, *Discovering an Evangelical Heritage*, 85–98; Harrison, "Early Feminists," 46; Hardesty, *Women Called to Witness*; Bendroth, *Fundamentalism and Gender*; Berg, *Remembered Gate*.

6. Hassey, *No Time for Silence*; Hassey, "Evangelical Women in Ministry."

7. McDannell, *Christian Home in Victorian America*, 7.

8. Epstein, *Politics of Domesticity*, 2. She summarizes, "Female domesticity was linked to the destruction of an agrarian economy and the development of commercial and industrial capitalism and the town life that accompanied it" (7).

9. DeBerg, *Ungodly Women*, 17–18.

of business and industry.[10] The view of woman's sphere has been called the "cult of true womanhood," in which there was a "sharp dichotomy between the home and the economic world outside that paralleled a sharp contrast between female and male natures, the designation of the home as the female's only proper sphere, the moral superiority of women, and the idealization of her function as mother."[11]

In the cult of true womanhood, women became associated with virtues such as "purity, piety, and domesticity."[12] In comparison the highest Puritan virtues for women included industry, modesty, and good stewardship.[13] This moral elevation of women contrasted sharply with other aspects of Puritan thought. For the Puritans, both men and women were considered sinful, but women were often particularly so since they were associated with Eve, who had tempted Adam and was responsible for the fall.[14] However, women were now seen as the guardians of the nation's virtue. They were the moral superiors of men, who had been corrupted through their involvement in the world and needed their guidance.[15]

This connection of virtue with women has been linked with the founding of the country and the republicanism of the 1780s and 1790s.[16] As the citizenry drew together in their opposition to England, they also realized the necessity of social cohesion. But rather than tyranny, they would form a collective government by combining the individual liberty of each person. This "pooling of each man's liberty into a common body" is what would enable them to avoid both slavery and anarchy.[17] Since such an undertaking would

10. Ibid., 18–21.

11. B. J. Harris, *Beyond Her Sphere*, 33. The term was first introduced by Welter, "Cult of True Womanhood."

12. McDannell, *Christian Home*, 7. As Gallagher notes, factories took away many of women's opportunities for productive labor as they manufactured the items, such as clothing and soap, that had previously been made in the home. As a result women found their duties focusing more on housecleaning and child rearing so that "what remained for women by the mid-1800s were those elements of sentiment, piety, and tenderness that were coming to be seen as characteristics of true womanhood" (*Evangelical Identity*, 31).

13. Gallagher, *Evangelical Identity*, 20–21. E.g., Puritan theologian Cotton Mather described the importance of women's labor by saying, "The Actions of even the meanest Milk-maid or Cook-maid, when done in the fear of God, are in the Account of God more noble Things than the Victories of a Caesar!" (*Daughters of Zion*, 47).

14. Epstein, *Politics of Domesticity*, 41–42.

15. Degler, *At Odds*, 26.

16. Noll defines republicanism as "the conviction that power defined the political process and that unchecked power led to corruption even as corruption fostered unchecked power" (*One Nation under God?*, 38).

17. Wood, *Creation of the American Republic*, 23–25.

require one to surrender some of one's own liberty, the cultivation of virtue took on a political role.[18] The safety of the government and the people's morals were intimately connected, so that public virtue would promote a flourishing government, while vice could lead to tyranny.[19]

However, the concept of virtue also underwent an important transition during this period. During the Revolutionary War, public virtue was a masculine trait, defined by one scholar as "active self-sacrificial service to the state on behalf of the common good."[20] At the end of the war, interests shifted to state building. As government became more institutionalized, there was less perceived need for a citizenry that would be held together by the common good. At the same time, factors such as the greater association of virtue with the emotions in moral philosophy and literary sentimentalism caused people to see virtue as more a feminine trait.[21] Since virtue was still regarded as essential to the state, the responsibility for public virtue fell to women, only now it was connected more with "private benevolence, personal manners, and female sexual propriety."[22] Motherhood became the moral foundation of society, and the main civic duty for women was to instill civic virtues in their children.[23]

In Victorian America, the home was not only its own realm separate from society but was also the starting point from which to shape the larger world. Although the father was still the leader of the family, women played the primary role in nurturing the children.[24] The home was seen as the cornerstone of society,[25] and since the home was the province of women, these values were also associated with them.

Although women made few gains in terms of legal and political status, the emphasis on a virtuous citizenry gave them a new importance in the public realm since "public-minded women were supposed to be the guarantors of their husbands' and children's attachment to the new frame of government."[26] Women were responsible for instilling virtue in their husbands and children, but they were also expected to impact the larger society directly as virtue assumed a new political and public significance. This connection between

18. G. Matthews, *Rise of Public Woman*, 55.
19. Noll, *One Nation under God?*, 38.
20. Bloch, "Gendered Meanings," 42.
21. Ibid., 49–53.
22. Ibid., 56.
23. Gallagher, *Evangelical Identity*, 31.
24. McDannell, *Christian Home*, xv.
25. Ibid., 77.
26. G. Matthews, *Rise of Public Woman*, 61–63.

the private and public realms led to a new discussion about women and family, and women began to be influential not just in religion but also in public moral discourse. In this way what became known as the notion of "Republican Motherhood" overcame the traditional separation between the female domestic realm and the male political community. Linda Kerber characterizes it as "revolutionary" because it "justified women's absorption and participation in the civic culture."[27]

Ebenezer Rogers, a pastor in Augusta, Georgia, describes a woman's role in impacting both her family and all of society. She was first of all the keeper of the home:

> Christianity . . . crowns her as the lawful queen of the little world of home. The bosom of the family is her undisputed empire. . . . She is the guide and companion of her children, whose influence shapes their characters and directs their destiny. . . . This is emphatically woman's place, a place fitted for the display of those peculiar talents and graces with which God has invested the female character.[28]

At the same time, however, she was compelled to leave the boundaries of the home and impact the world directly.

> She was not made to be secluded from life and shut up within the narrow limits of a cloister. . . . There is work for her to do here in the actual world. . . . Children in want and sorrow, suffering in the cottage of the poor and sorrow laden. Pour out the streams of your benevolence into the abodes of poverty and sickness. Be an ornament and a blessing to our native land . . . one of God's richest gifts to earth.[29]

As Sally Gallagher notes, "Women's purifying influence, in time, would increasingly be called on to elevate the lives of those outside the household."[30] While associated with the domestic, women did not remain limited to the immediate boundaries of the household. Rather, the entire world was seen as an expansion of women's domestic realm, and it was precisely the concern to preserve those virtues associated with their domestic role that compelled

27. Kerber, *Women of the Republic*, 284.

28. Ebenezer P. Rogers, *The Obligations and Duties of the Female Sex to Christianity: An Address Delivered at the Annual Examination of the Washington Female Seminary* (Augusta, GA: McCafferty, 1849), 5–7, cited in Gallagher, *Evangelical Identity*, 31.

29. Rogers, *Obligations and Duties*, 13–15, cited in Gallagher, *Evangelical Identity*, 32.

30. Gallagher, *Evangelical Identity*, 32.

them into the public arena. Thus, while domesticity led to a narrower understanding of women's roles, at the same time it enlarged their moral influence.

Industrialization affected the national consciousness in additional ways. The possibilities it created helped to forge a national mind-set that emphasized the equal opportunity available to all, as long as one was willing to work for it. Thus older religious ideas were replaced by ones that emphasized the freedoms the United States offered. Children learned these ideas from their textbooks, as the authors described a free society where all people had the chance to become rich and powerful if they were only willing to work hard enough to attain their goals. The purpose of children's textbooks was to train a new middle class to seek success.[31] The difference between success and poverty came through merit and exertion, and although not everyone would achieve the same level of success and wealth, America was nonetheless seen as the land of equal opportunity.[32]

In the new industrial culture, "Independence and worldly success had taken the place of pious self-abnegation and obedience to superiors; ambition had taken the place of humble acceptance of one's lot."[33] America's greatness lay in the opportunities it offered everyone to become rich and famous. Even though girls did not have the same economic opportunities as boys, they still learned about liberty and independence as the highest social values.[34]

Women in this period were caught between two conflicting impulses. On the one hand, the division of labor brought on by industrialization reinforced and even increased their subordination and dependence on a superior authority. Under the agrarian economy, men and women were more economically interdependent, and women were producers as well as men.[35] Now the husband worked for wages, with the family dependent on him to earn enough for them to buy the mass-produced goods they no longer made themselves.[36] On the other hand, women grew up learning the importance of self-effort and the "need to take action on behalf of cherished values."[37] The new liberalism stressed human capabilities and helped the people caught in the middle of an expanding commercial system to feel a new optimism and self-confidence in their own power.[38] Pragmatism characterized the age for

31. Epstein, *Politics of Domesticity*, 72.
32. Ibid., 69.
33. Ibid., 71–72.
34. Ibid., 74.
35. Gallagher, *Evangelical Identity*, 19.
36. McDannell, *Christian Home*, 7.
37. Epstein, *Politics of Domesticity*, 87.
38. Ibid., 83.

both Christians and non-Christians, and the expectation was that knowledge would lead to action.[39]

With this attention on human potential and the connection between action and success, the nineteenth century was an "age of doing good, of extensive and intensive reform."[40] According to Douglas Frank,

> [Evangelicals] were caught up in a flurry of activity. . . . They were racing madly ahead with schemes for personal piety, for church growth, for social improvement and moral reform, for missionary enterprise—ultimately for the inauguration of the millennium in America. In their intoxication with human action, they were simply mirroring the spirit of the age.[41]

Barbara Cutter further describes how this emphasis on action and accountability influenced views on women. She argues that the dominant ideology of the nineteenth century was "redemptive womanhood," because the key was woman's use of her superior "moral, religious, and nurturing nature to redeem others."[42] America viewed events through a moral lens, so one was obligated to act on one's knowledge. The action-oriented perspective meant that the choice was whether to perform or shirk one's duty, and the virtuous person was the one who did what was right, no matter the obstacles.[43]

Women were encouraged to "perform heroic actions as part of their duty to preserve the moral and religious health of the nation."[44] While various aspects of these actions might seem to contradict the stereotypical Victorian image of the woman as homebound and passive, the entrance of women into the public realm in this way was actually a continuation of a gender ideology that sharply defined women as those who could preserve domestic values. The acceptance of women's public action "was not a breakdown of antebellum gender ideology, but its culmination."[45]

Thus we see that ideas about gender corresponded well with the complex nature and changes of the era, such as the division of labor brought by the Industrial Revolution and the growing acceptance of emotions and their connections with virtue. However, they do not fit neatly into twenty-first-century categories of leadership and equality. In many aspects, women were

39. Frank, *Less than Conquerors*, 20.
40. Hardesty, *Women Called to Witness*, 86.
41. Frank, *Less than Conquerors*, 20.
42. Cutter, *Domestic Devils*, 7.
43. Ibid., 11.
44. Ibid., 17.
45. Ibid.

considered to be the moral and spiritual "leaders" of the home and society since they were the ones with the superior moral and religious nature. They were to be the primary reformers in a world in which men were viewed as having succumbed to the temptations of the marketplace, which caused them to value individual success and competition over community and virtue. At the same time, one could hardly say that women had achieved equality in an era in which men were still the unquestioned patriarchs of the family and authorities in the church and women had little political or economic power.

In this era, the drawing of these parameters of women's roles reflected many of the dominant cultural concerns of the day. We will examine three areas—public speaking, missions, and temperance work—for what they further reveal about conceptions of gender in this era.

## Propriety and Public Speaking

Although women were expected to take the lead in social reform, deep questions remained about what constituted an acceptable public appearance and how this related to male authority. The general public did not seem to think that women should be limited to the immediate domestic realm, but what was proper for a woman outside that realm was an important subject. While there might be general agreement about woman's nature, there was much disagreement about what actions were appropriate for that nature.[46]

Conceptions of gender both restricted and propelled women into the larger society. Although the woman's "household" might extend into the entire world, at the same time she was still to remain within the boundaries of what was considered proper for her sex. According to the "cult of true womanhood," women were believed to have a distinct female nature that both made them morally superior and imposed limitations. For example, they were not to dirty themselves by participating in the male arena of politics and economics. While their moral purity and special nature provided fertile ground for benevolence and social reform, they were still barred from pursuing activities seen as naturally belonging to the sphere of men.[47]

A major point of contention over what was acceptable and proper was public speaking. Female public speakers faced the charge that the activity "unsexed" them, made them "masculine," and was an act of "usurping" a role

46. Or, as Cutter describes, "what actions such a nature would require or prevent" (ibid., 121).
47. Gallagher, *Evangelical Identity*, 33.

that belonged to men.[48] Early pioneers such as Quaker abolitionists Angelina and Sarah Grimké faced severe opposition. What has been described as "the antebellum era's most famous debate over woman's sphere"[49] occurred over the Grimké sisters' antislavery lectures in New England in 1837. Although they were originally to speak only to women, men began to attend. The Massachusetts Congregationalist clergy responded by condemning female lecturing in a "pastoral letter," in which they asserted that a woman's influence should be "unobtrusive and private," "as becomes the modesty of her sex," and that female lecturers such as the Grimké sisters are "unnatural," "threaten the female character with wide-spread and permanent injury," and open the way for "degeneracy and ruin."[50] On another occasion, a mob rioted outside while Angelina spoke; later that night the mob burned down the building.[51]

However, female public speakers found increasing acceptance in the 1840s and 1850s. Fewer than twenty years after the Grimké sisters were denounced for speaking in public, women were regularly speaking to mixed audiences in the Northeast and could even expect to support themselves through their public speaking on issues.[52] By the end of the century, female temperance workers often spoke from the pulpit.[53] Cutter proposes several reasons for this. Many people changed their minds about the propriety of female public speakers when they viewed the women themselves. When they realized that in their demeanor the women were actually quite feminine, it became harder to believe that the growing number of female speakers were the "Jezebels" they had imagined them to be. The more people became exposed to the speakers who fit their image of femininity, the more they became accustomed to them.[54] In other words, concerns about whether their actions were improper and usurped male authority were overridden when people realized that the women conformed to their ideas of what the feminine character or demeanor should be.

48. Cutter, *Domestic Devils*, 117. Catherine Beecher, an ardent supporter of women's benevolent societies, opposed women's participation in the abolitionist movement "on the grounds that such public activity would undermine the basis of women's domestic power—the God-given character that marked her as different from men" (Gallagher, *Evangelical Identity*, 35).

49. Cutter, *Domestic Devils*, 113.

50. "Pastoral Letter of the . . . General Association of the Massachusetts Congregationalist Clergy," quoted in Kraditor, *Up from the Pedestal*, 51–52.

51. G. Matthews, *Rise of Public Woman*, 113; Porterfield, *Mary Lyon*, 13.

52. G. Matthews, *Rise of Public Woman*, 115.

53. Bendroth notes that they described themselves as "teaching" rather than "preaching" (*Fundamentalism and Gender*, 28).

54. Cutter, *Domestic Devils*, 121–25.

Also, the ideology of redemptive womanhood proved to be persuasive. As Cutter says, "a growing national crisis made women's duty to save the nation seem increasingly vital."[55] This mind-set also revealed a practical consideration that fit in well in an era that emphasized activity. While doctrinal purity might be a priority in the later fundamentalist period, duty and action were now prime concerns.[56]

The practical orientation of the age was reflected in the way the church justified the women's work as preachers and general Christian workers on the grounds that such actions were necessary, and indeed it was incumbent on them to use their gifts to fulfill the needs of the church. Charles H. Pridgeon, founder of the Pittsburgh Bible Institute, stated, "The question of the ministry of women is more than just an academic question. The force of men who offer for His service is inadequate. Souls of men are perishing. There is no time to argue whether it be a man or woman that performs the service. The need must be met."[57] In speaking about female evangelists, Fredrik Franson noted that the need to save souls took precedence. "Brothers, the harvest is great and the laborers are few. If the ladies want to help out in the fields during the harvest time, then I think we should let them bind as many sheaves as they can. It is better that women bind the sheaves, than that the sheaves get lost."[58] The question of the proper arena for women was still in question but occupied a lesser position to the extreme need. There was a feeling that the "fine points of theology might have to be settled on the basis of whether they furthered or hindered what Christians had decided was God's program of action on this earth."[59]

In sum the debate was not so much over the appropriateness of women's participation in private versus public life as much as what type of public activity was acceptable. Eventually the protests gave way as people experienced the women's feminine demeanor. Even more revealing was how the issue itself, at least temporarily, could be decided in terms of the era's need for action.

55. Ibid., 124.

56. Experience and a sense of "calling" also played key roles in justifying women's ministries during this time, particularly among Pentecostal and Holiness movements. See Hardesty, *Women Called to Witness*.

57. Charles H. Pridgeon, "The Ministry of Women" (Gibsonia, PA: Pittsburgh Bible Institute, n.d.), 26–28, cited in Hassey, *No Time for Silence*, 127.

58. From Edvard P. Torjesen, *Fredrik Franson—a Model for Worldwide Evangelism* (Pasadena, CA: William Carey Library, 1983), 47, cited in Hassey, *No Time for Silence*, 126.

59. Frank, *Less than Conquerors*, 25. DeBerg writes that women's leadership in the church was tolerated "only because it was needed and could be justified within the boundaries previously established by the ideology of separate spheres and virtues" (*Ungodly Women*, 83).

## Missions and Temperance: Fulfilling a Need and Doing One's Duty

In regard to missions, women's activity also reflected the tenor of the times. One of the keys to understanding the large numbers of women on the mission field lay in Victorian ideology itself. People believed that the conversion of "heathen mothers" was the most effective means of Christianizing foreign lands since mothers were seen as crucial to an enduring church, due to their influence in raising up their children in the faith.[60] They also believed that only women could reach these mothers and that woman's nature made her especially suitable for the task.[61] As Patricia Hill summarizes,

> Like the other mass women's movements of the nineteenth century . . . , the woman's foreign mission movement was rooted in ideologies of domesticity that defined a "public" dimension of appropriate female influence in society. Victorian women were encouraged to exert themselves in moral and religious causes. In the Progressive era, women were applauded for involving themselves as "public housekeepers" in campaigns for civic reforms and the enactment of social legislation.[62]

For these women, missions work did not take them out of the domestic sphere but just enlarged it.[63] At the turn of the century, Maud Wotring Raymond would speak of missions as "the logical climax to the American woman's program of service."[64]

The foreign mission crusade has been linked to the imperialistic mood of the age.[65] In the missionaries' fervent desire to see the gospel preached in the farthest lands, they were in line with the national mood of "expansiveness and optimism about world conquest."[66] Hill also notes that the women themselves,

60. Tucker, *Guardians*, 117. Porterfield speaks of the "belief that the women and children of those cultures must be reached in order for religious and cultural transformation to occur" (*Mary Lyon*, 21–22).

61. Hill, *World Their Household*, 5. Porterfield writes, "They had access to the women of other lands as missionary men did not. . . . It was widely agreed that heathen and infidel women could only be taught by other women" (*Mary Lyon*, 21–22).

62. Hill, *World Their Household*, 6–7.

63. Parker notes that the women followed the ideas of Catherine Beecher, who believed that women should apply themselves in "appropriate places in the public sphere, such as teaching and nursing" (*Kingdom of Character*, 51).

64. Raymond, *King's Business*, 8–9.

65. E.g., Schlesinger, "Missionary Enterprise." Hill (*World Their Household*, 199n29) notes that Neill includes a chapter titled "The Heyday of Colonialism, 1858–1914" in his *History of Christian Missions*, 273–334.

66. Hill, *World Their Household*, 1–2.

as much as the national mood, contributed to the popularization of foreign missions as they found themselves with increased time and energy due to technology.[67] Furthermore, the Civil War opened their eyes to their potential and responsibilities, since during the war they filled many of the roles usually taken by men. They had grown accustomed to a greater use of their talents and energy and now sought to fill that void in their lives.[68]

Raymond speaks of the women's missionary enterprise as

> more than a crusade; it is the established campaign of a great army, whose ranks . . . gather strength and volume as they march; an army which combines the science of a highly organized and Divinely equipped warfare with the dignity and sagacity of a civil service . . . and under the direction of a General whose ultimate victory waits only on implicit obedience to His commands.[69]

Although such military language might seem to be the province of men more than women, there was "an increased acceptance of women's public action and even violence in the defense of righteousness."[70] The exemplary woman of the age was not only willing to leave her home and country to further the kingdom, but also she herself was part of an army, marching forth to warfare and conquest.

However, while the emphasis of the age was on the need and the special responsibility of women in fulfilling the need, what was not prominent was the argument over rights. Although rights were a prominent concern for some reformers such as the Grimkés and some in the suffragist movement, they were not the most dominant arguments. Furthermore, as Glenna Matthews notes, "many of the ideas *about* women's rights were being developed to justify a woman's right to speak in public about important issues."[71] Instead, the role of women as social reformers was the prevailing concern.

The temperance movement is an example of a cause in which moral reformation counted more than equality. The movement "provided the basis for a demand for public recognition of women's values and for action by society . . . in defense of these values and the family life in which they were embedded."[72] Led by Frances Willard, the Woman's Christian Temperance

67. "When domestic demands upon them lessened, family boundaries widened to include the community, the state, the nation of which their individual homes were a part" (Raymond, *King's Business*, 6).

68. Hill, *World Their Household*, 37.

69. Raymond, *King's Business*, 48.

70. Cutter, *Domestic Devils*, 17.

71. G. Matthews, *Rise of Public Woman*, 115, italics original.

72. Epstein, *Politics of Domesticity*, 90.

Union (WCTU) worked for the defense of the family, particularly against the destructive effects of alcohol on women and the home.[73] Willard's slogan of "Home Protection" was the crucial link.

Early biographer Mary Earhart writes that Willard was successful because she knew to base her arguments on the two areas in which women were most interested: home and church.[74] Moreover, Willard was able to convince numerous evangelical women who had shunned the suffrage movement to join the cause only because she made the issue a matter not of "rights" but of Christian duty and motivated the women by appealing to their interest in the home. Willard wrote in her *Home Protection Manual*:

> During past years the women who pioneered the equal suffrage movement, and whose perceptions of justice were keen as a Damascus blade, took for their rallying cry: "Taxation without representation is tyranny." But the average woman, who has nothing to be taxed, declines to go forth to battle on that issue. Since the Crusade, plain, practical temperance people have begun appealing to the same average women, saying "With your vote we can close the saloons that tempt your boys to ruin"; and behold! they have transfixed with the arrow of conviction that mother's heart, and she is ready for the fray. Not rights, but duties; not her need alone, but that of her children and her country.[75]

In this the rationale for women's activity in many ways mirrored the beliefs of the times. Acting on one's knowledge was a moral duty, and therefore women could and should be moral reformers because they were the moral guardians of society. Women engaged in public activity and led the crusade for reform because they believed it was in their nature and their responsibility to do so.[76] This set the evangelicals apart from the early secular women's rights movement, which spoke more forcefully about rights, at least in the beginning.[77]

73. Ibid., 116.

74. Earhart, *Frances Willard*, 194.

75. Frances Willard, *Home Protection*, in Leeman, *"Do Everything" Reform*, 130.

76. In her manuscript "Women and the Temperance Movement," Maria T. Hale Gordon supported the women's activity because it belonged in the category of "moral suasions" ("Women and the Temperance Movement," n.d., Gordon College Library, cited in Hassey, *No Time for Silence*, 22).

77. Fletcher writes, "The political purpose of the Crusade, as much as the sensibilities of the temperance men involved, necessitated Crusaders behave as victims or moral authorities, that their work at least *appear* apolitical, and certainly that it not be connected with anything controversial like women's rights" (italics original). The women made sure they maintained "gendered propriety" and "assured their audience that they acted strictly out of moral obligation and had no intention of revolutionizing gender roles" (*Gender and the American Temperance Movement*, 97).

Similarly, the women involved with foreign missions did not always support and more often dissociated themselves from the women's rights movement.[78] An 1871 editorial from *Woman's Work for Women*, the journal of the Woman's Foreign Missionary Society of the Presbyterian Church, demonstrated the way in which many women opposed the language of "rights":

> One [of the movements] insists upon what its promoters call the equality of woman with man. It seeks to give to her whatever advantage in the battle of life is supposed to belong to man; to afford her the opportunity (and more than this, to lay it upon her as a duty) to push her way into public life, to the polls and rostrum. . . . They insist upon *rights*, they talk of the down-trodden position of women in this free and happy land, and call upon her to take the place which these dissatisfied few claim to be rightly hers.

The writer scolds such women for being willing to abandon their "womanliness and delicacy" in order to gain these rights. Instead, she calls women to take the gospel to "heathen lands," a task more in accord with their female nature.

> So they . . . reach forth to the other side of the world to bring love and hope to those who are wasting their lives in idle ignorance of the capabilities of true womanhood . . . the blessings of wifehood . . . the holy responsibility of motherhood.[79]

Taking action on behalf of cherished values and extending one's moral influence in the world were seen as the duty of women. More middle-class women found themselves in accord with women like Catherine Beecher, who argued that women should exercise their influence within a more limited scope in areas such as temperance and benevolent societies, than with those like Angelina and Sarah Grimké, who advocated for rights.[80] As Hill notes,

> The egalitarian rationale underlying the woman's rights crusade challenged the very assumptions about the sanctity of the Christian home that fueled other nineteenth-century female benevolent and reform movements. It is scarcely

78. E.g., Lindley, "*You Have Stept out of Your Place*," 86; Hill, *World Their Household*, 35.

79. *Women's Work for Women* 1 (1871): 24–26, italics original, cited in Hill, *World Their Household*, 35–36.

80. Hill, *World Their Household*, 34. Cutter similarly notes that Beecher's criticisms seemed to come from her beliefs that women should not participate in "divisive" political causes such as abolition (*Domestic Devils*, 119).

surprising that the woman's foreign mission movement would adjure a crusade for woman's rights.[81]

Thus, while women extended their sphere of action and influence in the mid-nineteenth to the turn of the twentieth century, the rationale for their activity was strikingly different from the evangelical egalitarian movement in the 1970s. Rather than promoting equal rights, Victorian morality led to an extension of women's influence in a more broadly defined area, while presenting "a defense of women's interests only within the framework of an acceptance of male dominance."[82]

## Conclusion

In many ways the mid-nineteenth to the turn of the twentieth century was filled with seeming contradictions. Women were domestic but not homebound. They were virtuous but not passive or fragile. They were under the authority of the men in the church and their husbands at home at the same time that they were to be moral and spiritual leaders and reformers.

Some of the beliefs that created this intriguing situation came from the unique age in which women found themselves. Industrialization, urbanization, expansionism, and Victorian ideology, among other factors, combined to create an environment in which women and men found their identities in flux, with women being closely connected with the domestic sphere. However, the need for moral and social stability cast women into the public arena and helped to redefine what was considered proper for women in relation to that sphere. In this environment religion itself exerted a profound influence on the larger culture as the drive for kingdom building helped to thrust evangelical women into reform and missionary activity.

One key to the era was the importance of virtue. Women may not have been limited to a geographical "sphere" as much as they were associated with different values. They were connected with virtue, morality, and self-sacrifice, while men were associated with the "values of the market," such

81. Hill, *World Their Household*, 54. Tucker cites the writing of Sue McBeth, whose work among the Nez Perce Indians included planting churches and preaching: "Dr. Lowrie must not think for a moment that she is what is called a 'Women's Rights Woman.' (I am afraid she is not even among the strong minded.) She has no affinity for such. Has more 'rights' now than she can make good use of—and aims to try to be with God's help a true woman" (cited in *Guardians*, 38).

82. Epstein, *Politics of Domesticity*, 149.

as greed and ambition.[83] With virtue seen as a foundational value for society, women's activity extended into the public sphere as people viewed their reform activities as fitting their unique moral nature. Thus the most prominent and influential voices would be those that spoke along the lines of moral duty rather than rights. While the concern for rights was certainly not absent in this time, it would not dominate the discussion until the civil rights era, when evangelicals would join their secular counterparts in making this a central aspect of their appeals.

But another aspect is the corporate perspective and assumptions that helped frame the discussion. This perspective meant that a woman could consider the world, and not just her immediate home, as her household and object of concern. The need for women to work in behalf of this larger "home" helped to propel them into the public arena of reform and also to shape perceptions of what was acceptable for women. As in other eras, women were largely defined by the home, so it was an essential component of their identity. However, enlarging this understanding of "home" provided a compelling justification, indeed an obligation, for women's involvement in larger social issues.

As we continue with the next chapters, we will see that the gender discussion shifted in line with social developments involving a move away from this corporate perspective and changes in the understanding of the home. Growing individualism and changing conceptions of what constituted a home and also the value of the home in terms of women's identity would exert a profound influence on how evangelicals viewed gender.

83. Fletcher, *Gender and the American Temperance Movement*, 13.

# 2

# Returning Home after World War II

In the previous chapter we saw that the position of evangelical women at the turn of the century cannot be neatly characterized as either "equal" or being under "authority." Instead evangelical women energetically participated in and led social reform activity and missions. As exemplars and promoters of virtue, their influence was not only allowed but encouraged and even urged in the public realm. They were not predominantly concerned with rights as much as with fulfilling their duties, which obligated them to enter the public realm to effect needed social change. The impetus behind their actions reflected a combination of Victorian ideology, the impact of the Industrial Revolution, and the practical and imperialistic mood of the age. A more corporate perspective led them to view their domestic duties in terms not of their immediate homes but of the world as their household of concern. As we turn to another period, the post–World War II era, we will see a different way in which larger cultural priorities may have impacted evangelical conceptions of gender.[1]

1. We can also note that, at least in one aspect, evangelical concepts of gender seemed to develop in opposition and in reaction to larger social trends. Beginning in the 1920s, the threat of liberal theology placed more focus on the defense of Christian orthodoxy, leading to an "assertive masculinity" in which men were the defenders of orthodoxy (Bendroth, *Fundamentalism and Gender*, 62–68). (See below on the relationship between evangelicalism and fundamentalism.) Fundamentalists also reacted strongly to the change in morals after 1910. The "corruption of

## A Culture Seeking Peace

The end of World War II caused Americans to turn inward, seeking peace and security in their homes and with a new focus on the individual. William Graebner argues that the 1940s can be divided into two halves, separated by, among other things, the bombing of Hiroshima and Nagasaki and the end of World War II. The first half was a "culture of war," that is, "public, nationalistic . . . championing the group and its political equivalent, democracy; committed to production and to the new roles for women it required." The second half was a "culture of peace," characterized as "private, familial . . . favoring the individual and its political equivalent, freedom; committed to consumption and the consequent reversion to traditional gender roles."[2]

The 1940s were a period of great change, which also led to great uncertainty and so a desire for security and order. Graebner writes,

> The trauma of war and cold war, the shattering revelation of the murder of millions of European Jews, the discovery of nuclear fission and the use of an atomic bomb on civilians at Hiroshima and Nagasaki, the Great Depression that threatened to return any day—these were the events that held Americans in a decade-long state of anxiety. Never before had progress seemed so fragile, history so harmful or so irrelevant, science so lethal, aggregations of power so ominous, life so full of contingencies, human relationships so tenuous, the self so frail, man so flawed. (Ibid., xi)

Americans had an intense desire for security (19), and after the long years of war, they "turned to peace with an almost desperate self-consciousness" (101).

Central to the feelings of anxiety was a problem of identity, which was viewed as the problem of the fragmented self and the rootless self. Social scientists often understood the fragmented self in terms of role theory, which was "a way of explaining what people do by the positions (roles) they occupy in a social structure" (105–6). The war and its aftermath presented numerous challenges to the sense of identity for both men and women and turned attention to the home.

---

traditional morality" was a common theme in fundamentalist literature, and the "flapper" figured prominently as someone who threatened the established convention of women as the guardians of public morality and so "the very fabric of private life and public virtue" (DeBerg, *Ungodly Women*, 99–117). Bendroth notes, "Evangelicals have often merely reacted to changing social practices instead of influencing their direction" ("Search for 'Women's Role,'" 122–23).

2. Graebner, *Age of Doubt*, 1.

## Women Refocus on the Home

World War II had necessitated a substantial influx of women into the workforce to fill the jobs left open by the men who joined the armed forces. According to one estimate, 36 percent of women between the ages of sixteen and sixty-five worked outside the home at the height of the war.[3] However, after the war, many women left the workforce or returned to the lower-paying work they had before the war. For some the transition was voluntary, while others were forced out as priority was given to the returning servicemen.[4] Public opinion surveys revealed that Americans believed men should earn a living and make the "big" decisions and women should take care of the home.[5] The head of the National Association of Manufacturers declared that, despite women's wartime contributions, "From a humanitarian point of view, too many women should not stay in the labor force. The home is the basic American institution."[6] The messages to women were to go back to the home and take care of the needs of husbands and children.[7]

Other factors also facilitated the move toward increasing gender distinctions, including the association of women, particularly white, middle-class women, with the home and the nuclear family. War highlighted the differences, as the men had fought on the battlefield while women did mostly the supporting work on the home front.[8] The economic prosperity of the 1950s also made it possible for women to stay home and rely on their husbands economically. As a result, "the idea that women and employment are by nature not meant to mix became the ethos of the decade."[9]

According to Susan Hartmann, another factor that increased the distinctions was the emphasis on helping the returning servicemen readjust to life after the war.[10] She describes the enormous body of literature, in a variety of

3. Dicker, *History of U.S. Feminisms*, 62–64.

4. Ibid. Other reasons for the decline in women in the labor force have also been noted, e.g., a decrease in financial motivation due to wartime savings and the favorable labor conditions for men in the postwar economy. Hartmann says, "It is probable that many married women did not so much reject paid employment itself as they calculated that the kinds of jobs available in the postwar economy would not compensate for the strains involved in handling double roles" (*Home Front and Beyond*, 91).

5. Chafe, *American Woman*, 178.

6. Quoted in Mezerik, "Getting Rid of the Women," 81. However, it has also been noted that wives and mothers began to work in large numbers in the 1950s. One reason for this was the necessity of increased purchasing power for the abundance of household comforts available after the war (Coontz, *Way We Never Were*, 38).

7. Breines, *Young, White, and Miserable*, 33.

8. Groothuis, *Women Caught in the Conflict*, 16.

9. Ibid.

10. Hartmann, "Prescriptions for Penelope."

forms including books, novels, movies, government pamphlets, professional journals, and women's magazines, that conveyed what were seen as the challenges to the returning men. These challenges involved not only their employment but also social aspects.[11] The home was seen as crucial to successful social readjustment, and in this women had the primary role. They were told to balance their newly found competence and independence with what was seen as the possibility of the men's loss of self-confidence. Rightly or wrongly, there was an expectation that a woman would put a man's needs and desires ahead of hers and help him restore his position as head of the household.[12]

In this period of uncertainty and transition, the home played a vital role in grounding Americans. In contrast to the more corporate concerns and assumptions at the turn of the century, Americans now began to turn inward to view their homes as their main source of identity and concern. The home was the place to gain a sense of identity, as Americans looked to the home for happiness and satisfaction.[13] The drive to put women back into the home came not only from policies that gave the highly desired jobs back to the returning GIs, but also from men and women who desired to have a bountiful private life free from the sacrifices of war and the struggles of the Great Depression.[14]

In addition, the home provided a place of security.[15] For example, historian Elaine Tyler May argues that Americans' embrace of the domestic ideal was connected with their fears of the atomic age. She states, "Amid a world of uncertainties brought about by World War II and its aftermath, the home seemed to offer a secure, private nest removed from the dangers of the outside world. . . . The self-contained home held out the promise of security in an insecure world. It also offered a vision of abundance and fulfillment."[16] Although, of

11. Ibid., 224–25.

12. Ibid., 231–32.

13. Gurin, Veroff, and Feld, *Americans View Their Mental Health*, xvi.

14. Stansell, *Feminist Promise*, 183.

15. As Hartmann observes, "The vast social change and insecurity accompanying the war put a high premium on the preservation of social order. And, typically, the family seemed the one institution which most effectively could provide a rudder for this rapidly changing society" ("Prescriptions for Penelope," 224).

16. May, *Homeward Bound*, 1. She refers to this perspective as one of "containment." Although the term generally referred to the policy of preserving national security by "containing" the Soviet Union within a "clearly defined sphere of influence," she argues that there was also a domestic version in which the "sphere of influence" was the home. She writes, "Within its walls, potentially dangerous social forces of the new age might be tamed, so they could contribute to the secure and fulfilling life to which post-war women and men aspired. . . . More than merely a metaphor for the cold war on the homefront, containment aptly describes the way in which public policy, personal behavior, and even political values were focused on the home" (ibid., 16). This view is echoed by others, such as Breines, *Young, White, and Miserable*.

course, the family could not actually prevent nuclear destruction, it could represent "a source of meaning and security in a world run amok," so the family was the place where people could feel in control of their destinies.[17]

As a result of the tremendous expansion of the economy that had begun during World War II, Americans aspired to live the "good life," which included "a well-equipped house in the suburbs, a new car or two, a good white-collar job for the husband, well-adjusted and successful children taken care of by a full-time wife and mother."[18] Stephanie Coontz notes that in the 1950s less than 10 percent of Americans believed that someone who was not married could be happy.[19] The highest calling for women now became attached to their homes and their roles as wife and mother.[20] The 1950s were a period in which the dominant expectation was that a mother would be the homemaker in a household where the man was the breadwinner.[21]

An important factor in shaping this view of what was "normal" for women was women's magazines. Although some magazines such as *Harper's* and *Atlantic Monthly* ran articles disputing this portrayal of "normal" womanhood or profiled working women, there was a marked increase in articles promoting the traditional view of marriage and gender roles, including ones on women sacrificing their aspirations outside the home.[22] At the same time, working mothers were portrayed by politicians, psychiatrists, and social workers as the cause of childhood ills such as delinquency, insanity, and criminality.[23] Many observers saw women's continued presence in the workforce as a direct threat to the stability of the nation's social institutions.[24]

17. May, *Homeward Bound*, 26.

18. Breines, *Young, White, and Miserable*, 2.

19. Coontz, *Way We Never Were*, 25.

20. This is the situation Friedan described in *The Feminine Mystique*, which is widely seen as having started second wave feminism. Friedan's work came under subsequent criticism for, among other things, focusing on white, middle-class women and not reflecting the diversity among American women. See, e.g., the collection of essays in Meyerowitz, *Not June Cleaver*. Historians, Meyerowitz says, have reexamined postwar concepts of gender as they were influenced by race, ethnicity, and class, as well as women's involvement in politics, labor, and civil rights activism. In contrast to Friedan's depiction, women were recognized as "legitimate public actors" (*Not June Cleaver*, 4–5, 9). However, as Coontz notes, even though "there were more mixed messages, exceptions and contradictions in the media's depictions of the ideal feminine life than Friedan admitted in her book . . . many women never heard the exceptions and caveats to the feminine mystique. . . . And the few who did hear them seem to have found them all the more confusing" (*Strange Stirring*, 74).

21. Coontz, *Strange Stirring*, 64.

22. Ibid., 67.

23. Ibid., 68.

24. Chafe, *American Woman*, 176.

The emphasis on the nuclear family led to the increased priority of individual fulfillment,[25] and a woman's life in the home was seen as her route to that fulfillment.[26] Often it was seen as part of her nature, so it should be considered before other things such as employment. Margaret Mead predicted that the women who wanted to continue working after the war were those without children or who had to work from financial necessity. Otherwise, "far from wanting to get out of the home, during the years when they are needed in it, more women want, if possible, to devote themselves to their homes and children."[27] Furthermore, if a woman was unhappy with her life as a homemaker, the solution was not to change her life but to change her feelings so that she could reconcile herself to her role as wife and mother.[28]

## Rebuilding the Christian Home

Gallagher notes that evangelicals reflected the larger culture in their ideals of the husband as breadwinner and the wife's focus on domestic life.[29] On the one hand, many women were employed in the 1940s.[30] On the other hand, conservatives (often called "fundamentalists" in this period)[31] "enthusiastically

25. Cherlin, *Marriage, Divorce, Remarriage*, 38.

26. E.g., in her study of data involving surveys of six hundred white middle-class men and women who formed families during the Cold War era, May found that "both men and women mentioned the responsibilities of married life as sources of fulfillment rather than sacrifice" (*Homeward Bound*, 32).

27. Mead, "Women in the War," 278–83.

28. Coontz, *Strange Stirring*, 73. The application of Freudian psychoanalysis also meant that women who did not fit into this pattern could be labeled as psychologically maladjusted (Groothuis, *Women Caught in the Conflict*, 16). Berger and Berger write, "Women were to find their mission at home, as mothers and as the intelligent, emotionally sensitive companions to their husbands—and if they did not accept this mission, the psychologists were ready to treat this reluctance as a neurotic ailment" (*War over the Family*, 15).

29. Gallagher, *Evangelical Identity*, 12.

30. It is also interesting to note the high rate of employment for fundamentalist women in the 1940s. Bendroth says their rate of employment even went beyond the national trend for female employment (*Fundamentalism and Gender*, 75). In various ways, fundamentalists let women know that their work was an important part of their expected duties. The book *God's Ideal Woman* states that "every girl should make the proper preparation to be self-supporting" and discourages women from marrying too soon (Lewis, *God's Ideal Woman*, 22). The influential evangelist John R. Rice told his daughter that she should pursue "full-time Christian service" rather than being a banker's wife (cited in Bendroth, *Fundamentalism and Gender*, 75).

31. For an outline of the development of evangelicalism and its relationship to fundamentalism, see the chart in Marsden, *Fundamentalism and American Culture*, 234–35. In the 1920s, "fundamentalism" characterized a coalition of militant evangelical Christians who "opposed both modernism in theology and the cultural changes that modernism endorsed" (ibid., 4). After the Scopes trial, the fundamentalists withdrew and until the 1940s were characterized by their

participated in postwar celebrations of motherhood and nuclear family life."[32] Rev. Carl Sweazy wrote in *The Baptist Bulletin* that married life is "God's plan of building a society," while "single life and promiscuity is the devil's plan for destroying society."[33]

Wuthnow presents a detailed description of how the mood of religious leaders across the country after World War II reflected that of the general society. The aftermath of both the war and the Great Depression left many longing for their children to have a more peaceful life. The comments of this mother in an article published in *Bible Magazine* in 1946 likely reflect the thoughts of many in that period:

> We long to think of peaceful years ahead, normal days with fullness of living, and with little girls marching gaily into kindergarten and not through snowy, war-torn streets, and bigger girls marching to the platform to receive their school diplomas. We want to dream of little girls grown to womanhood and marching down the bridal aisle and from there to years of happiness and sheltered, joyous living. . . . We desire for our children a normal life, peace and plenty throughout their life span, achievement, and fulfillment.[34]

Alongside the optimism of a "time of new beginnings filled with opportunities,"[35] there was also a strong sense of uncertainty and foreboding like that articulated by May. Unlike after World War I, the mood following World War II was one of doubt that peace would last.[36] Concerns about communism and moral decay only added to the sense of peril.[37] Evangelicals, like the larger culture, seemed to turn to the home to provide this sense of peace.

American religion following World War II also moved away from the corporate dimension of faith to a more individualistic emphasis. The spiritual growth and empowerment of individuals became more valued than constructing the

---

separation, in stark contrast to their status in the 1920s as a movement that attempted to exert a controlling influence on the culture (Marsden, "From Fundamentalism to Evangelicalism," 127). In the 1940s and 1950s, a group of fundamentalists worked to reengage culture, calling themselves the "new evangelicals" and then simply "evangelicals" (Marsden, *Fundamentalism and American Culture*, 235; Sweeney, *American Evangelical Story*, 170–77). Bendroth notes that despite their differences with fundamentalism, evangelicals essentially held to fundamentalist views on gender (*Fundamentalism and Gender*, 105).

32. Bendroth, *Fundamentalism and Gender*, 105.

33. Sweazy, "Christian Home," 3.

34. Doris Coffin Aldrich, "Our Children and the Next War," reprinted in *Religious Digest*, June 1946, 55–58, cited in Wuthnow, *Restructuring of American Religion*, 45.

35. Wuthnow, *Restructuring of American Religion*, 53.

36. Ibid., 40.

37. Ibid., 41–42.

moral community.[38] The home was the critical component in this shift because it was seen as primary to individual personality development.[39] Consequently, the church became secondary to the family, and "the corporate body became subtly transposed into a service agency for the fulfillment of its individual members."[40] As one author wrote in 1962, "Too often the home has been used as an agency of the church. There is a need to remember that the church was not established to be ministered to but to minister. It is the responsibility of the church to help families build strong Christian homes."[41]

Thus, in this period the calling of women was considered in terms of individual fulfillment and was tied to their roles in the home as wives and mothers, providing a marked difference with the expectations for women at the turn of the century. While the woman was still seen as the more domestic partner, there was a marked change in the perception of her realm of influence. At the turn of the century, a woman's duty extended directly to the larger culture because the world was her household. Now her sphere of influence was her immediate household, and her main impact on the world came through the support she gave to her husband and her ability to train godly children.

As a 1956 editorial in *Eternity* magazine states, "A true Christian woman has her first duty under God to her husband; her second duty is to her children. Only in third place does she have any duty to church work."[42] An article that appeared in the June 1955 issue of *Moody Monthly* describes how one woman learned from her friend that her "first responsibility" was to her home. The author recounts, "I decided that I, too, should be first of all a housewife, and I made up my mind . . . not to think so much about outside service."[43] This was portrayed not only as the natural inclination of women but also as something that would ultimately cause them to be dissatisfied with being in the workforce. As one editorial proclaimed, "Many a modern woman has found that the petty annoyances and the feelings of frustration that arise from modern emancipated living are dissipated by the tremendous satisfaction that comes from going back to her right place as wife, as homemaker, and as mother."[44]

The wife was responsible for providing the proper environment for her husband so that he could be prepared to go out into the world and for Christian

38. Ibid., 56.
39. Scudder, *Family in Christian Perspective*, 91.
40. Wuthnow, *Restructuring of American Religion*, 55.
41. Scudder, *Family in Christian Perspective*, 147.
42. *Eternity* 9, May 1956, 11.
43. Kiel, "Just a Housewife," 15.
44. Howard, "What Right Has a Woman?"

service. As one woman described it, "I realized more clearly how much a husband's success and also his Christian service and leadership in the church depends upon his home life—the cheerfulness, the restful atmosphere, punctuality, good food, and little attentions meant for him alone."[45] An article in *Moody Monthly* makes clear that the housewife's job revolved around her husband and children and was considered her form of Christian service: "Her job—making a happy home for her husband and training her growing children—is every bit as important in God's scheme of things as are the more obvious forms of Christian service."[46]

Marriage was to be a woman's career.[47] For example, May cites a woman who stated that while she gave up financial independence and a career, "these [had] been replaced by the experience of being a mother and a help to other parents and children. Therefore the new career [was] equally as good or better than the old."[48] One woman wrote in the *Saturday Review*, "Being a good wife, a good mother, in short, a good homemaker, is the most important of all the occupations in the world."[49]

This sentiment was echoed in prominent Christian publications. As John R. Rice maintained, "With a man, marriage is only a part of his life. . . . A man does not change his life work, usually does not change his residence, and does not change his name when he marries. But when a girl marries, that means a change of all of her life, her career, her plans. Marriage and home are a whole career for a good woman."[50] Similarly Elton and Pauline Trueblood stated in 1953, "Marriage is a career for a woman as it can never be for a man,"[51] which means for the woman "the career of homemaking."[52] In the article "If I Were a Mother," by the superintendent of women of Moody Bible Institute, the author finished the title by stating that she would "concentrate on bringing up" her family and make it her "full-time" job. She ended by declaring, "Mothers, yours is the grandest, biggest, most important job in the world."[53] This attitude provided a contrast to an article in the same periodical in 1909, in which the author complained about the emphasis

45. Kiel, "Just a Housewife," 15.

46. Shaw, "Finding Time for God's Best," 22.

47. Bendroth, *Fundamentalism and Gender*, 96.

48. May, *Homeward Bound*, 32.

49. Montagu, "Triumph and Tragedy," 14.

50. Rice, *Home*, 116, 122.

51. Trueblood and Trueblood, *Recovery of Family Life*, 58.

52. Ibid., 73.

53. Dantuma, "If I Were a Mother." Similarly Howard described a "woman's true right" as "the right to marry, bear children, to guide and guard the little ones entrusted to her, and to

on a woman's duties in the home. She charged that in their exhortations of proper motherhood, the male teachers and preachers were overbalancing "the effeminacy of woman rather than her humanity."[54]

Evangelical women were called to see the home as their job and ministry, and having a job outside the home was seen as endangering the family. As one woman stated, it would be impossible for a woman to be a successful mother if she were also a career woman: "I put it down as an axiom that no woman with a husband and small children can hold a fulltime job and be a good homemaker at one and the same time."[55] Scudder described the dangers of a two-income family. Because of the confusion of roles, "Making of marriage and the family what God intends seems almost impossible where both husband and wife work outside the home."[56] Instead the wife should "share the vocational interest of her husband."[57] This was the view of the larger culture as well, as "charges were made that women had 'forgotten their place' during the war and had endangered the home and their children's lives because they had worked."[58]

Thus, in contrast to the earlier period when evangelical women felt the obligation to have a moral impact on the larger society, women's new domestic role was limited to the private, household sphere. The home was still central for doing God's work, but a woman's expected area of influence no longer stretched to the world as her household but rather concentrated on the immediate home. According to P. B. Fitzwater, a professor of systematic theology at Moody Bible Institute, "Man is organized to operate in the affairs of science, commerce, and the state. The woman is organized to regulate the affairs of the home and family." This was how one could cultivate either "manliness" or "true womanliness."[59] While women were "mentally and spiritually fitted to develop and mold [children's] lives," the man's responsibility was "as the breadwinner and the controller of the affairs of the state."[60] The Truebloods stated that part of the requirements for the wife in the 1950s "may be the willingness to forgo

---

produce by her influence and teaching men and women of true Christian character" ("What Right Has a Woman?," 633).

54. Foster, "Work for Women." This was the original title of the magazine, the official publication of Moody Bible Institute. In 1909 the title changed to *The Christian Workers Magazine*, in 1920 to *Moody Bible Institute Monthly*, and in 1938 to *Moody Monthly* (Hassey, *No Time*, 227).

55. Montagu, "Triumph and Tragedy," 34.

56. Scudder, *Family in Christian Perspective*, 13.

57. Ibid., 14.

58. Dubbert, *Man's Place*, 250.

59. Fitzwater, *Woman*, 30.

60. Ibid., 83.

much of public life."[61] In the words of Donald Gray Barnhouse, "The Christian wife is happiest when the interests of her entire life are those of her husband: his work, his problems. While he is fighting the battles of life at his job, she should be supporting him in spirit while she works at home." Because she is the "center of the home, he is strengthened to go on in the work that God has given him to do." This work of the wife constitutes "the highest service to her Lord."[62]

## Appropriate Women's Ministry

The 1950s emphasized clear distinctions between the public world of men and the private, home-oriented world of women rather than allowing for a certain blurring of the public/private boundaries because of the perceived need for expediency and social reform as in the previously discussed era. The nature of appropriate women's ministry reflected this distinction. Charles Ryrie, who served as dean at Dallas Theological Seminary and president of Philadelphia College of the Bible, maintained that "women should not lead in any way in public worship."[63] H. A. Ironside asserted that women were not to participate in the "public ministry of the Word," although the "public prayer" and "public testimony" of women described in 1 Corinthians was allowed because it had occurred in less formal meetings.[64]

The acceptable forms of service could extend beyond a woman's family but revolved around her own home and her immediate neighborhood. Home Bible classes were one such ministry. Interestingly, one article on Bible classes in Dallas describes them as being taught by either laymen or laywomen. At the same time, the classes also highlighted the domestic duties of women in that they required a "hostess" who could "produce chairs somehow to seat from two to one hundred people all at the same time; who [was] willing to spend the next morning collecting pencils, straightening rugs, and putting away chairs, and who [had] the capacity to greet with sincere Christian love and charm anyone at all who [might] come to her home for the class."[65] Another article promoted the home as "one of the richest sources of potential for God's service" and described activities such as child evangelism, neighborhood visitation, and intercession as ways of

61. Trueblood and Trueblood, *Recovery of Family Life*, 83.
62. Barnhouse, "Bible Way," 3.
63. Ryrie, *Place of Women*, 80.
64. Ironside, "Ministry of Women."
65. Bailey, "Texas Grows a GIANT Bible Class," 18.

"serving the Lord at home."[66] In this way the duties of women centered on the more individualistic work of personal evangelism and ministry to their families and neighborhoods in contrast to the more corporate aspect of social reform.

Finally, the rationale for arguing that a woman's principal domain and sphere of influence was her household had a different emphasis from that of the turn of the century, one that also reflected the tenor of the times. The social changes and accompanying insecurity that characterized the larger culture led to a "high premium on the preservation of social order."[67] In the home this was manifested in the idea of the husband's "headship." Friedan quotes a 1954 issue of *McCall's*: "For the sake of every member of the family, the family needs a head. This means Father, not Mother."[68] In particular, this reflected a cultural value that Groothuis describes as the wife as the keeper of the house and the husband its "chief executive."[69]

Similarly, for evangelicals the theological discussion revolved around the concept of "order" rather than the need for women to be the moral guardians of society. The differing roles of men and women in the church and the home represented God's order, and to disrupt this order was to invite chaos. One periodical said that for women to assume the place of "minister" would be "out of order."[70] Another spoke of the necessity of the husband as the head of the home: "The wife cannot function in her feminine role if her husband's masculine role is taken from him. The family group cannot function as a family if its natural head is dethroned."[71] Rice argued pointedly:

> This does not mean slavery for the wife. Rule, government, authority, is of God. The only alternative to government and authority is anarchy and chaos. It is not slavery that we have a president and congress of the nation and governors for states, sheriffs in counties, mayors and councils and police forces in the cities. It is not slavery for a teacher to have authority in the schoolroom or a pastor in the church. So it is only law, order and government for God's man to be the head of the home, the head of the wife, and to rule over his wife.[72]

66. Enlow, "Ministries on Your Doorstep." In *HIS* magazine, a homemaker included as her home-based activities teaching vacation Bible school, working with missionary societies, teaching Sunday school, assisting in "city-wide Christian enterprises," and leading her children to Christ (Jacobsen, "Marriage—A Career?," 6).

67. Hartmann, "Prescriptions for Penelope," 224.

68. Friedan, *Feminine Mystique*, 49.

69. Groothuis, *Women Caught in the Conflict*, 18.

70. "Women as Ministers."

71. Scudder, *Family in Christian Perspective*, 13.

72. Rice, *Home*, 89–90.

Not all portrayed their positions as strongly as Rice. One writer talked about "headship" as meaning that the husband had the "chief responsibility for the home and family," including for the economic well-being and spiritual growth of the family, along with the "emotional tone" or "emotional climate" of the home.[73] Overall, however, the shift was from the social value of gender roles to an "order of creation" that required male leadership and female submission. As Margaret Bendroth notes, this idea was not new. However, in the postwar era, evangelicals proposed a stricter hierarchy, which they also pursued with more insistence.[74] In the period of transition and uncertainty following two world wars, a creation order helped in "reducing the world to manageable proportions" as the Christian home was seen as a microcosm of the hierarchy of the cosmos.[75]

## Conclusion

In the 1950s evangelicals turned to the home. Whereas at the turn of the twentieth century, evangelical attitudes toward women reflected an emphasis on their virtue and subsequent obligation to be the moral guardians of society, now women's sphere of influence was mostly contained in the immediate home and nuclear family, without the duty to impact the larger "household" of the world. As the country turned inward during the post–World War II years and became more individualistic in its focus and values, evangelical women were primarily child centered, placed priority on their marriages over jobs, and concentrated on their own homes. The husband was the one who went out into the world, had the "authority," and made the "big" decisions for the household.

While the home was still considered the most suitable place for a woman because of her nature, a different understanding of the woman's "home" and its relationship to her identity shaped the view of expected ministry. In line with the growing value of individualism in the culture, personal evangelism and neighborhood ministry took precedence over social reform, and the home was seen as the place of a woman's primary ministry and where she would find the most personal satisfaction.

73. Granberg, "Husbands Hold the Key," 14, 35.

74. Furthermore, the idea of female submission was now grounded in creation, whereas previously it had been justified by the fall. This intensified the notion of male and female spheres because it rooted the order in creation itself (Bendroth, "Search for 'Women's Role,'" 131).

75. Ibid., 132.

In the next chapter we will see how the growing trend toward individualism and another change in the understanding of the home and its relationship to women, including a backlash against women's confinement to the home, impacted evangelical notions of gender. The rise of evangelical feminism provided a stark contrast to the domestic emphasis of the 1950s, but in a larger sense it was part of the next step in America's and subsequently evangelicals' increasing preoccupation with the individual and personal fulfillment.

# 3

# Egalitarianism and Equal Rights

The 1960s saw a strong reaction against the domestic expectations placed on women. However, unlike at the turn of the twentieth century, this time concerns about rights and equality predominated. The increased emphasis on the individual and personal fulfillment in the larger culture seemed to provide a fertile environment for the feminists who would in turn provide a vital catalyst for the evangelical egalitarian movement.

A watershed moment for feminists was the publication of Betty Friedan's *The Feminine Mystique*, the book that is widely credited with starting what is called "second wave feminism." Friedan identified what she called "the problem that has no name" that afflicted millions of women who stayed home and were supposed to be content taking care of the household and raising their children. Instead of contentment, Friedan portrayed a widespread malaise among these middle-class, suburban women. Whereas the popular, although not universal, sentiment of the 1950s was that women would find their fulfillment in being housewives and mothers, "Friedan depicted a mass of women who had fallen into catatonia or hysteria under the totalitarian pressures of neo-domesticity."[1]

1. Stansell, *Feminist Promise*, 204.

*The Feminine Mystique* was a critique of the role of the 1950s housewife.[2] Women had been told that taking care of the household and the family was the path to personal fulfillment as well as their duty as women. However, Friedan noted that many of her college classmates who had followed this prescribed path had expressed much dissatisfaction with their roles in their later years. Second wave feminism focused on scrutinizing and freeing women from this tightly defined role.

As second wave feminism concentrated on the rights of women and the abolition of roles based on gender so did the second evangelical feminist movement. Whereas the first evangelical movement saw a push for women's influence in the public sphere due to the belief in their greater moral influence, the second movement tried to help Christian women free themselves from what many said were the burdens of a patriarchal church culture. As a result, they would have the opportunity to claim their rightful positions in the church and in marriage and so fulfill their potential and "enjoy the full benefits" of being in Christ.[3] Thus one early evangelical writer discussed the challenge that the women's movement posed to the church in terms of allowing women to pursue the "fulfillment" of their "individual gifts" and "the power of making their own decisions."[4]

A major issue is the relationship between second wave feminism and evangelical feminism, along with the possible impact of the nineteenth-century reform movements on both. Consequently, we will need to analyze the distinctive features in each period. It will also be important to examine other trends that might have impacted these movements.

Scholars have noted the ways in which the first feminist movement emerged from the nineteenth-century evangelical reform movements. Some roots of feminism are seen in the revivals of Charles Finney and the reform movements that grew out of them.[5] Women discovered parallels between the antislavery argument and their own situation and also parallels in the interpretation of Scripture. As Donald Dayton explains, "The basic egalitarianism of evangelicalism that supported abolitionism was also extended to women."[6] However,

2. Although the book came under sharp criticism, for example, for its focus on white, middle-class women, as Stansell notes, "For the moment the simplistic account got [Friedan's] message across" (ibid.).

3. Hull, *Equal to Serve*, 122.

4. Mollenkott, "Women's Movement Challenges the Church," 298, 301.

5. E.g., Dayton, *Discovering an Evangelical Heritage*, 85–98; Harrison, "Early Feminists," 46; Hardesty, *Women Called to Witness*.

6. Dayton, *Discovering an Evangelical Heritage*, 89. Thus the abolitionist Angelina Grimké wrote a letter to her critic Catherine Beecher, explaining, "The discussion of the rights of slaves

as noted in chapter 1, the most prominent arguments for the Christian reform movements revolved around Victorian ideas of women's moral superiority rather than their right to equality.[7] As will be shown next, this would become the case for the secular feminist movement as well.[8] In both cases the argument based on rights, although not absent, did not capture the public imagination and was insufficient to produce the desired changes. However, the larger acceptance of the argument based on rights for second wave feminism in the 1960s would have a profound impact on the second evangelical feminist movement in the 1970s.

## Rights, Duty, and the First and Second Feminist Movements

The first feminist movement eventually coalesced around one political issue: the right to vote. The Seneca Falls Convention, which is commonly seen as the origin of the women's rights movement, took place in 1848.[9] At the convention, the lack of the right to vote was one of the chief grievances,[10] but by 1910 only four states had voted for female suffrage, and women did not receive the vote until 1920. While the Civil War was a critical interruption of the activists' goals, there were other reasons for the prolonged delay. As noted previously, many Christian women opposed the efforts of the early women's rights advocates on the basis that the fight for rights was too oriented to themselves rather than the larger concerns of society, and their beliefs echoed those of other women of those times. It was not until the suffragists changed

---

has opened the way for the discussion of other rights, and the ultimate result will be most certainly the breaking of every yoke . . . emancipation far more glorious than the world has ever yet seen" (cited in Storkey, *What's Right with Feminism*, 142).

7. The lack of prominence given to equal rights also appears to have been a characteristic of the prior time as well. E.g., Chaves notes, "Before the Civil War, proponents of female preaching almost always based their arguments more on the extraordinary abilities of the few women who wanted to preach or on the special religious sensibilities of women or on the practical need for effective workers for Christ than on the principle of gender equality" (*Ordaining Women*, 66).

8. As mentioned in chap. 1, we are using the term "secular" to distinguish the larger women's movements from the evangelical ones, recognizing that the former were not exclusively secular. E.g., Braude has discussed the role of Catholic and liberal Protestant women in the early years of the National Organization for Women ("Religious Feminist," 555–72). She distinguishes between religious feminists and their secular counterparts ("Religions and Modern Feminism," 14). However, since the dominant view still seems to be that feminism is not explicitly tied to religion and often that it is incompatible with religion ("Religious Feminist," 555–77), especially in comparison with the evangelical movement, for the purposes of this study, we will continue to use the term in this way here.

9. Kraditor, *Woman Suffrage Movement*, 1.

10. Dicker, *History of U.S. Feminisms*, 30.

their argument, a shift that corresponded to social priorities, that they were able to achieve their goals.

The original basis for suffrage was directly opposed to some dominant social values. The early rationale was that "votes for women symbolized their individuality, their sense of self-interest, their need to be able to speak politically as individuals" and that "no man could speak for a woman."[11] Thus there was strong emphasis on the individuality of woman and her separateness as a person. As one woman wrote in 1851, "Our right to individuality is what I would most assert."[12]

However, these individualistic and self-interested aspects were perceived as conflicting with the traditional understanding of a woman's roles as mother, wife, and "sustainer of the family"[13] and led to much of the hostility to woman suffrage from both women and men. When women eventually did receive the vote, it was because of some significant changes that brought the movement more in line with accepted social conventions.

One of the leading changes was that women overcame their apprehension of what would happen to the family because of a fundamental shift in rationale by the suffragists. By the early twentieth century, the original leaders such as Elizabeth Cady Stanton were gone, and so too were most of their arguments based on individual rights. Because that strategy had not worked, the next generation of activists promoted a different appeal. The justification was that women, in their character as wives and mothers, had a special contribution that men could not make.[14] The move away from arguments based on rights and equality to a view of the moral superiority of women, which conformed to the popular late-Victorian view of women, helped to mainstream the suffrage movement.[15] As a result, the suffragists succeeded because they were able to adapt to the ethos of the times that the world was an extension of the home and so a primary arena for women's activity. As Carl Degler explains, "Suffrage now became a way of extending women's special sphere to society, rather than being a way of providing political expression for women's self-interest as individuals."[16] The vote came to be seen as the means by which women could accomplish their goals of impacting society through their superior moral nature. It was not individual rights or equality for women but

11. Degler, *At Odds*, 357.
12. Smith, *Woman and Her Needs*, 27, cited in Degler, *At Odds*, 343.
13. Degler, *At Odds*, 349.
14. Ibid., 357–58.
15. Dicker, *History of U.S. Feminisms*, 46.
16. Degler, *At Odds*, 357–58.

rather a reinforcement of their familial role as mothers and wives that led to the acceptance of the suffrage argument in society.[17]

The connection between suffrage and temperance further illustrates the change. As noted in chapter 1, temperance was a more popular early cause because it fit better with the traditional view of woman, which included helping the weak, being oriented to the home, and reforming society rather than changing her own position.[18] Its "other-serving" orientation stood in contrast to the "individualistic and admittedly 'self-serving'" aspect of the early arguments for suffrage.[19] However, many temperance women began to advocate for the vote on the rationale of what they could accomplish through it. They believed that their votes would be the means to accomplish prohibition through legislation. The WCTU's justification in 1883 for enfranchisement was that it was necessary to protect the home and the women in it.[20]

An argument presented for woman suffrage was often that the "intrusion of the state into all areas of life weakened families and women's position within them" and that suffrage would rectify this balance.[21] However, Frances Willard and other members of the WCTU did not view rectifying the balance of power as an end in itself. Rather it was a way to create a higher morality, one based on the values of family life, instead of a vision of equality between women and men.[22] As Aileen Kraditor describes it, "The new era saw a change from the emphasis by suffragists on the way in which women were the same as men and therefore had the *right* to vote, to a stress on the way in which they differed from men, and therefore had the *duty* to contribute their special skills and experience to government."[23] The argument that women could change society through their vote meant that suffrage could be the means to reform as well as the reform itself.[24]

17. As Dicker summarizes, "Whereas early thinkers such as Wollstonecraft and the Grimkés believed that women deserved the vote because of their natural rights as citizens, women in the early twentieth century didn't make arguments about women's equality. Instead, they claimed that women were different from men and superior to them: as a result, they deserved the vote. This notion of the moral superiority of women conformed with popular late-Victorian views of women and contributed to the mainstreaming of the suffrage movement, which was no longer seen as a radical or fringe movement but as acceptable work for middle-class women to undertake" (*History of U.S. Feminisms*, 46).

18. Degler, *At Odds*, 348.

19. Ibid.

20. DuBois, *Woman Suffrage*, 39.

21. Epstein, *Politics of Domesticity*, 129.

22. Ibid., 147.

23. Kraditor, *Woman Suffrage Movement*, 52, italics original.

24. Ibid., 51–52.

The dominant concern of these movements was that women should have a voice for the good of society because they had a duty to contribute. The common good was a much more compelling argument than personal rights. In contrast the feminism of the 1960s emphasized the rights of women as individuals and the impact of these rights and equality on the needs of women.

## Evangelicals and Feminism

Just as broader social expectations appeared in the arguments of both the secular and evangelical feminists in the earlier period, so too were the particular types of concerns that energized both of the second movements found in prominent social developments of their day. Furthermore, this time secular feminism played a key role in conveying its ideas to an evangelical audience.

Historians generally acknowledge that an important catalyst for second wave feminism lay in the social turmoil and civil rights movement of the 1960s. The society that was seen to discriminate against blacks, the poor, and others was seen to discriminate against women as well.[25] Thus the civil rights movement helped to create a favorable environment for feminist concerns. As William Chafe notes, "It is unlikely that feminism could have gained the energy that it did during the 1960s had not Americans been preoccupied with the demand to eliminate prejudice and discrimination."[26]

This time concerns for equality and freedom from discrimination impacted the general population, and the argument for individual rights dominated the feminist movement. The more moderate liberal feminists, as opposed to radical feminists, were particularly instrumental in spreading these ideas to mainstream America. As Christine Stansell observes, "It was liberal feminism . . . that modified and transmitted ideas that originated with women's liberation through a network that reached deep into the heartland."[27] Even if their legislation was not always successful, their ideas spread throughout the nation. Indeed, from early on, the leading evangelical writers spoke of how their encounters with feminist ideas had caused them to rethink their theology.

For example, the original subtitle of Nancy Hardesty and Letha Scanzoni's book, *All We're Meant to Be*, called "the most influential work in helping

25. See, e.g., Stansell, *Feminist Promise*, 221–72; Groothuis, *Women Caught in the Conflict*, 46; Dayton, *Discovering an Evangelical Heritage*, 89. The word "sexism" to identify the problem first appeared in 1968 (Stansell, *Feminist Promise*, 257).

26. Chafe, *American Woman*, 232.

27. Stansell, *Feminist Promise*, 276.

launch the evangelical feminist movement,"[28] was *A Biblical Approach to Women's Liberation*. In the preface, Scanzoni states that she began to think about writing on the issue after observing that Christians were "sitting on the sidelines" in regard to the "woman question" raised by the feminist movement.[29] Elaine Storkey describes how the initial and failed push of the radical feminists and the Women's Liberation Movement was replaced by a far-reaching "*quiet* revolution" that led to the replacing of "offensive material." It was in the midst of this "quiet revolution" that "most women [were] called upon to make some response in their own lives to the ideas of the feminists," and that "not least among these [were] Christian women," the people to whom Storkey said she was writing.[30] Patricia Gundry relates that while she had long wondered about the interpretation of biblical passages on women, it was the activities of feminists and the church's response to them that prompted her to study and write on the subject.[31]

The connection between the nationwide spread of feminist ideas and evangelical feminism is documented in the book *Our Struggle to Serve*, in which fifteen evangelical feminists share their testimonies. The testimonies are remarkable in how freely the women mention the impact of feminism on their journeys. In the preface the editor, Virginia Hearn, thanks one of her husband's students because she gave Hearn her "first insights into the 'women's movement' . . . and parked her extensive feminist library on [their] living room mantel."[32] Others explicitly reported how the women's movement had caused them to reevaluate their beliefs. One woman recounts, "The 'women's movement,' as it came to focus for me during the late sixties, made me come to grips with what I believe is the fundamental social change of our time: full equality for all women. It made me see the implications of this belief . . . in my participation in the church."[33] Another describes the profound personal change that happened as she was exposed to feminist ideas and literature: "I knew I would never be the same again. Too much had happened. The complacent Christianity that I had known was inadequate."[34] The secular feminists were the catalyst for Christian women to recognize how their faith

28. Cochran, *Evangelical Feminism*, 25.

29. Hardesty and Scanzoni, *All We're Meant to Be*, 7, 206–7.

30. Storkey, *What's Right with Feminism*, 2, italics original.

31. Gundry, *Neither Slave nor Free*, 2.

32. Hearn, *Our Struggle to Serve*, 11. Another woman lamented, "Those years in college could have been so much more fruitful had I known what I know now about 'women's liberation' and had society's consciousness been raised as it is now" (ibid., 32).

33. Ibid., 102.

34. Ibid., 79.

related to their freedom. As one woman summarizes, "The women's movement . . . encouraged me to appropriate the freedom for which Christ has set us free (Gal. 5:1)."[35]

Although biblical feminists worked to ground their beliefs in Scripture, it was the ideas of secular feminists that first prompted them to reexamine their own situation and interpretation of Scripture.[36] As Ina Kau summarizes,

> The [evangelical] feminists did not carefully examine the biblical texts, consult theology books and their ministers, and then declare themselves feminists. Rather, there was something about the [secular] feminist articulation of what it means to be a woman in American society that seemed true to them. They took . . . a leap of faith, claiming to be feminists despite the teachings of their church. Their biblical and theological work came after this leap.[37]

The evangelical feminists said that secular feminists helped them to see how they were being treated unfairly in the church and in the home and sought to claim the rights of their position in Christ.[38]

The greater acceptance of the concern for individual rights, as compared to the situation at the turn of the century, helped both movements. As women reacted to what they saw as the confinement of their domestic roles, the arguments for individual rights took central place in the feminist movement. Now the argument was more that women should not be victims of injustice and should receive their basic individual rights and privileges, particularly in comparison with men. This was also the approach that evangelical feminists adopted, in contrast to the earlier period in which evangelicals denounced advocating for personal rights. Thus, for example, Gretchen Hull decries the "injustice" of

35. Ibid., 52.

36. The role of Scripture as the basis for their beliefs became a prime dividing point. Cochran (*Evangelical Feminism*, 111) differentiates between the more traditional evangelical feminists, or those who hold a strong belief in biblical authority, and progressive evangelical feminists, who also consider personal experience authoritative. In 1986 biblical feminists split into two movements, with traditional feminists represented by Christians for Biblical Equality (CBE) and progressive feminists staying with the original organization, the Evangelical Women's Caucus (EWC).

37. Ina J. Kau, "Feminists in the American Evangelical Movement" (MA thesis, Pacific School of Religion, Berkeley, 1977), 111, as cited in Quebedeaux, *Worldly Evangelicals*, 125.

38. Although feminism seems to have been a critical catalyst for the evangelical feminist movement, particularly in its more widespread influence on evangelical culture, there were some, particularly in the Methodist tradition, who supported women's rights before the 1960s and 1970s. Georgia Harkness, described as "very much a product of the Social Gospel of the 1920s and early 1930s," supported ordination and was deeply concerned with the issue of women's rights, although she did not write a major book on women's issues until 1971 (Keller, *Georgia Harkness*, 24–27).

"teaching that men could enjoy the benefits of their earthly citizenship and their heavenly standing right now, while women would have to wait until the Hereafter."[39] A particular concern of egalitarians was that the exclusion of women from any part of ministry represented discrimination. Hull defines discrimination as "treating oneself or one's group as entitled to certain human rights and other persons as unentitled or not entitled to the same degree and basing this unequal treatment on the proposition that the unentitled have different characteristics or belong to a different group from the entitled."[40]

One of the major considerations that second wave feminism contributed to the biblical feminists was an understanding of what they came to view as the influence of cultural patterns and attitudes in an unjust subordination of women. The feminists helped evangelical women identify prejudice against them as the result of a "patriarchal social system" rather than legal inequality, the focus of the earlier feminists. Groothuis asserts, "The most helpful insight of the modern (late twentieth century) feminism is that patriarchy—that is, culturally rather than legally instituted male domination of women—is at the root of women's traditionally subordinate place in society."[41]

Groothuis notes similarities with the black civil rights movement in her understanding of what happened. In the nineteenth century, goals primarily centered on legal outcomes. Slaves were emancipated in 1865, and black male citizens received the vote in 1870. Similarly, the first feminist movement was successful in obtaining the right to vote for women in 1920. However, after realizing that legal rights did not end "systemic social discrimination," blacks fought against segregation and women resisted "patriarchal custom" in the 1960s.[42] They fought against "a deep-seated attitude" and an "intangible, ineluctable creation of culture called prejudice."[43]

Thus a critical issue for evangelical women was whether they could see, based on what they learned from feminism, the "patriarchal premise of gender roles." Second wave and evangelical feminists differed in the solutions to the problem they proposed.[44] But feminism had given evangelical women a

39. Hull, *Equal to Serve*, 122.

40. Ibid., 86.

41. Groothuis, *Women Caught in the Conflict*, 65. In the preface to the 1992 edition of their seminal work, originally published in 1974, Hardesty and Scanzoni described their journey in this way: "We began to realize how women have been made captive, blinded, and oppressed through the centuries. Nearly all cultures have been patriarchal, ruled by the patriarchs" (*All We're Meant to Be*, x).

42. Groothuis, *Women Caught in the Conflict*, 47.

43. Ibid.

44. Ibid., 67.

means to understand the nature of their situation, and the insights of this new movement had a profound impact on the character of evangelical feminism in this period.

### New Roles for Women

Evangelical feminists were responding to the frustrations of women who felt confined in their domestic roles and limited opportunities in the church, just as Friedan documented the lives of women who felt trapped in their lives at home and unfulfilled in their personal growth and potential. Whereas men were free to use their individual talents to work in the world or for the church, women were compelled to fulfill their predetermined roles of wife and mother. As Hardesty observed, "What women really want is a *choice*."[45]

Some taught that women should see the importance of learning to meet their own needs.[46] Gundry expresses how women were first of all trained to be good mothers. As a result they care about other people's needs first, and "*then* try to catch up on their own needs if and when the opportunity comes." However, women must learn to take care of their own needs, even if they need to be convinced that this is acceptable. "They have a right to life, a life that is theirs alone."[47]

In comparison with earlier times, the types of concerns that provided the fundamental basis for the second wave of evangelical feminism were more individualistic than those at the turn of the century or even in the 1950s. In this way the second movement reflected the ascendance of individualism in American culture[48] as well as the rise of a consumerist and therapeutic culture and its emphasis on the perceived needs of the individual.[49] While evangelicals were not unaware of the inherent dangers of a theology focused on the self,[50] they continued to emphasize applying the Bible to meet these perceived needs.[51]

45. Hardesty, "Women and Evangelical Christianity," 70, italics original.

46. E.g., Gundry, *Neither Slave nor Free*, 17.

47. Ibid., 16–17, italics original.

48. E.g., Cochran, *Evangelical Feminism*, 4.

49. Ibid., 5.

50. E.g., Hestenes describes how Christian freedom must be understood in terms of submission to Christ: "Freedom for the Christian woman is an opportunity to become the person that God intends her to be. This finding of self is not possible without self-denial (Matt. 10:39) and self-giving through the power of the Spirit (Gal. 5:13–26). . . . We must not conform to the counterculture with its excessive emphasis on personal freedom and self-fulfillment" ("Culture, Counterculture and Christian Transformation," 282).

51. Cochran, *Evangelical Feminism*, 5.

Sociologists Brigitte Berger and Peter Berger saw feminism as reflecting what they called "hyper-individualism," or an increased focus on the individual over all collective entities, including the family.[52] Hyper-individualism derived from a "bourgeois-Protestant mentality" that came to dominate the Western world and that emphasized individualism and effort as opposed to the "supernatural interventions" of medieval Catholicism. This mind-set highlighted virtues that were accessible to all, such as hard work, diligence, and discipline and so led to an ethic that emphasized "individual responsibility and performance of duty." In this way it was from the very beginning "a democratic and egalitarian" morality. There were to be no barriers to individual advancement, and so all were liberated to advance themselves.[53]

A critical component of this mentality was the maintenance of a balance between individualism and social responsibility, but the balance became radicalized.[54] The Bergers conclude that feminism, in its emphasis on the individual woman and her individual identity, could be understood in this context of hyper-individualism. As James Davison Hunter summarizes, "The rise of contemporary feminism takes on meaning in this regard. The *individual* woman (her rights, her needs, her occupational and political interests) is now emphasized over against every social context in which she finds herself."[55]

This provides a critical context for understanding how the second evangelical feminist movement differed markedly from the first movement in its driving concern. The first movement dealt primarily with social issues and moral reform and was occupied not with personal gain but with helping others. Storkey writes,

> One thing which remained constant in this early Christian feminism was a commitment to *others*. Mostly, these women were not fighting for their own case. It was not *their* rights, employment, need for justice which drove them, but concern for those who were weak and oppressed: those at the fag ends of respectable society who could not present their own case.[56]

Even when women such as the Grimké sisters spoke of rights in the mid-nineteenth century, there was an intimate connection between rights and responsibility, for they were arguing for their right to speak on behalf of

52. Berger and Berger, *War over the Family*, 120.
53. Ibid., 107–12.
54. Ibid., 117.
55. Hunter, *Evangelicalism*, 90, italics original.
56. Storkey, *What's Right with Feminism*, 140–41, italics original.

others. Thus Sarah Grimké argued for rights based on shared moral obligations, saying in her *Letters on the Equality of the Sexes*, "WHATSOEVER IT IS MORALLY RIGHT FOR A MAN TO DO, IT IS MORALLY RIGHT FOR A WOMAN TO DO; and . . . confusion must exist in the moral world, until woman takes her stand on the same platform with man, and feels that she is clothed by her Maker with the *same rights*, and, of course, that upon her devolve the *same duties*."[57] Sarah's sister, Angelina, held the same sentiments. As Hardesty describes, she believed that "women had every right—and responsibility—to think, speak, and act on all the great moral questions of the day."[58]

This view was seen in Charles Finney's theology, especially his belief that every Christian must be "useful." For Finney, whose ideas had a profound impact on reformers such as the Grimkés,[59] salvation entailed turning from selfishness to benevolence, which would be manifested in good works.[60] Finney believed that the job of the church was nothing less than "the universal reformation of the world," so the church should "never rest until . . . every form of iniquity [should] be driven from the earth."[61] As a result, he helped create an environment that encouraged women to use the advantages of their particular nature to work for the good of the greater society. Such good works were a matter of duty, not choice, and the spirit of benevolence of the age eventually moved from philanthropy to reform.[62]

The importance of the moral obligation of women also figured into thoughts on equality in the battle for woman suffrage. The temperance workers fought for the defense of the home against what they believed was the irresponsibility of male culture. Many joined the suffragists' cause because they believed that "only female equality would ensure responsible male behavior and give family issues their proper place in public life."[63] They held that "female suffrage and female equality in public life generally would be the means by which moral reformation and defense of the home would be achieved."[64] "Equality" itself

57. Grimké, "Letter XV," in *Letters on the Equality*, 100, emphasis and italics original.

58. Hardesty, *Women Called to Witness*, 98.

59. See the detailed description in Hardesty, *Your Daughters Shall Prophesy*; and Hardesty, *Women Called to Witness*.

60. Hardesty, *Women Called to Witness*, 86.

61. Charles G. Finney, "The Pernicious Attitude of the Church on the Reforms of the Age," *Oberlin Evangelist* 8, January 21, 1846, 11, cited in Hardesty, *Women Called to Witness*, 87.

62. Hardesty, *Women Called to Witness*, 86–88. See also the chapter "On Being Useful," in Hardesty, *Your Daughters Shall Prophesy*, 113–29.

63. Epstein, *Politics of Domesticity*, 128–29.

64. Ibid., 4.

was based on a continuance of the "separate spheres" ideology and a traditional morality that defended the values of the home.[65] The early Christian feminists advocated equality not in order to pursue the opportunity for their own fulfillment, especially as it related to their identity as women, but as a moral and religious imperative to help those in need.

Ideas about the home in evangelical thought also underwent profound revision during this time. Both second wave and evangelical feminists focused on work as a response against the strict definition of womanhood according to women's domestic roles in the 1950s. The charter for the National Organization for Women (NOW) states, "We do not accept the traditional assumption that a woman has to choose between marriage and motherhood, on the one hand, and serious participation in industry or the professions on the other."[66] Women's place was no longer just in the home but in the world. However, it was not, as in the earlier era, a bringing of the domestic sphere into the world. Rather there was a sharp division between the two, and the home was now the source of women's weakness rather than their strength.[67]

Evangelical feminists also articulated clear distinctions between work and home to support their position. Friedan had written of the women who believed the feminine mystique and so made their "only dream" to be "perfect wives and mothers" and "wrote proudly on the census blank: 'Occupation: housewife.'"[68] Now evangelicals such as Gundry distinguished between "*wife*" and "*mother*"

65. Hassey, *No Time for Silence*, 132. Degler notes, "Simply because of the doctrine of the two spheres, in the name of which the women undertook the temperance crusade, it was difficult, if not impossible, to object to women's increasing participation in the war on liquor" (*At Odds*, 317).

66. Charter of the National Organization for Women, http://feminist.org/research/chronicles/early1.html.

67. Whitehead and Blankenhorn, "Man, Woman, and Public Policy," 33. Whitehead and Blankenhorn also offer a reason for the disconnection between women, virtue, and the home:

> The values and language of the marketplace are invading the family realm and, more broadly, the realms of church, neighborhood, and community. Activities once assigned to families—child care, meals, even outdoor play—are increasingly monetized: converted to services that are bought and sold in the marketplace. As one part of this trend, mothers, who have traditionally dominated the realms of family and community life, now pursue, or at least are strongly expected to pursue, regular paid employment outside the home. As a result, the separate sphere of family and community life is both shrinking and losing its distinctive character. Increasingly, this sphere no longer constitutes an independent moral realm containing relationships and values different from those of the commercial realm. This trend helps explain why women are no longer considered—nor, at least in the dominant discourse, would they want to be considered—more virtuous or innocent than men. More importantly, this trend tells us why home and family are no longer expected to serve as the essential base of women's power and self-esteem. (Ibid., 32)

68. Friedan, *Feminine Mystique*, 18.

as referring to "*relationships*" rather than "occupations" or "job roles."[69] Hull similarly defined marriage and "child-related activities" in terms of relationship rather than career, stating, "A woman does not have an occupation in life to bear children, any more than a man has an occupation in begetting children."[70] Thus evangelical feminists sought to uphold the importance of the family while not limiting women to the roles of mother and housewife.

As evangelical feminists sought equality by demonstrating an essential distinction between the two areas, they spoke of women's "roles" rather than women's "sphere."[71] Women should be free to pursue any role in the church and should not be prevented from doing so based on gender. Consequently, publications of this era did not speak of the need to recognize the moral duty of women to better society, as in the earlier period, but rather spoke of the moral right of women to pursue the same opportunities as men, whether in the church or in the larger working world.

The evangelical egalitarian movement that started in the 1970s represented the desire for women to have equal opportunities in church roles and shared decision making in their marriages. The common concerns with second wave feminism were reflected in their language. The evangelical feminists proposed that God is "an Equal Opportunity Employer,"[72] and the concern was not gender but "qualification to do a job."[73] Equal opportunity in ministry was a "biblical principle" because "the God who created the sexes did not discriminate between them."[74] The earlier writings in particular used the language of feminists, speaking also of limits,[75] restrictions,[76] injustice,[77] unfairness,[78] oppression,[79] liberation,[80] and equal rights.[81] As Kau explains, "They . . . learned from the feminist movement to articulate the pain and struggle of those lives in a feminist way."[82] Feminism inspired Christian women to seek what the Bible might say about how their faith could fulfill their needs, give

69. Gundry, *Woman Be Free*, 89–90, italics original.
70. Hull, *Equal to Serve*, 161, 174.
71. Gallagher, *Evangelical Identity*, 43.
72. Gundry, *Woman Be Free*, 107; Hull, *Equal to Serve*, 128.
73. Gundry, *Woman Be Free*, 107.
74. Hull, *Equal to Serve*, 126–27, 230.
75. Groothuis, *Good News for Women*, 19.
76. Gundry, *Woman Be Free*, 9.
77. Hull, *Equal to Serve*, 231–32.
78. Scanzoni, "Feminists and the Bible," 10.
79. Hull, *Equal to Serve*, 100.
80. Hardesty and Scanzoni, *All We're Meant to Be*, 11.
81. Bilezikian, *Beyond Sex Roles*, 36.
82. Kau, "Feminists," 108–9, in Quebedeaux, *Worldly Evangelicals*, 125.

them autonomy in their lives and equality in ministry, and help them to reach their personal potential in Christ.

## Conclusion

As the 1960s and 1970s focused on cultural patriarchy, the identification of traditionalism with discrimination became an integral part of the message for evangelical feminists. The unfairness of a church order that limited ministry opportunities for women was seen to deny their full personhood in Christ. Evangelical feminists set out to correct what they saw as the wrongs of patriarchy in the church, at times doing so self-consciously in imitation of the civil rights movement. Hull summarizes this sentiment: "As Americans have done in the civil rights movement, we must face the injustices of the past and must begin to apply the lessons of the past to the future."[83]

The concern was for equal opportunity and rights for women, the chance for women to fulfill their potential in Christ and to be able to use the gifts that God had given them. The language and concerns of the egalitarians bore a striking resemblance to their secular counterparts, and from the very beginning they expressed how the secular feminist movement had given them the impetus to reexamine their beliefs. The type of equality they fought for concentrated on what benefited the individual, as opposed to earlier arguments centered in a more corporate context.

Historians have noted that throughout American history, public thought and religious life have consistently impacted each other, and evangelicals are no exception.[84] The correspondences between larger cultural trends and evangelical movements do not necessarily negate the significance of the latter since there is nothing inherently contradictory about holding a biblical belief that is also reflected in some way in the contemporary culture. However, they should at least give us pause to ask whether this influence is hindering our ability to see other ways of understanding gender.

These chapters have tried to show that cultural values have had a profound impact on the way evangelicals talk about gender. The impact of culture in setting the interpretive framework is important because the questions and concerns with which one approaches the Bible play a large role in deciding what types of answers one finds.

83. Hull, *Equal to Serve*, 100.

84. E.g., Cochran (*Evangelical Feminism*, 192) cites the work of scholars such as Nathan Hatch, Mark Noll, and William McLoughlin.

At the turn of the century, the importance of male authority waned as concerns for the moral good of society and the salvation of the world propelled women to the forefront of the very public arenas of social reform and missions. In the post–World War II period, as part of a homebound and peace-desiring nation, evangelicals emphasized a gendered order based strongly on male leadership centered on the nuclear family and the individual household. In the 1960s and 1970s, heightened concerns about justice and civil rights created a fertile environment for egalitarians to challenge this situation and advocate for equal rights.

Thus, on the one hand, we see a fluctuation of concerns about male authority. When larger concerns such as evangelizing the world and reforming society took hold, women faced less opposition to their leadership in these corporate matters. When the country was no longer consumed by these greater concerns, evangelicals turned to the family as a source of identity and paid more attention to the structure of the home. On the other hand, while the argument for equal rights appeared early on, it did not take hold until the broader culture provided an environment in which its more individualistic concerns could be accepted.

Rising individualism in America seemed to play a dominant role in these changing values. When America was occupied with more corporate concerns, such as global evangelism and social reform, evangelicals paid less attention to a gendered order. Belief in male authority never disappeared but was less relevant in the everyday lives of evangelicals more consumed with changing the world for the better. As Americans turned inward and desired peace and security, evangelicals also looked to the immediate family for their identity and sought individual fulfillment there. As the trend toward individualism and self-fulfillment continued, a growing concern for individual rights took root, and the individual superseded the family as the locus of identity.

There was also a change in the conception and value of the family. At the turn of the century, the woman's domain was not merely her immediate household but the entire world, reflecting the corporate assumptions and values of the period. The duty of the church and the women (and men) within it was to exert a positive Christian influence on the world. In the 1950s the household was that of the immediate family, and the priorities of its inhabitants likewise centered on this limited sphere. In this period the church was not so much the instrument to bring Christian good into the world, but rather it existed to serve its members. In the 1970s the home became something from which women needed to be freed so that each woman could take her rightful place in the world and not be limited to the confinement of domestic duties.

I have highlighted these specific aspects of evangelical conceptions of gender to show how key elements varied in different time periods in correspondence with larger trends. If we can see how this rising individualism impacted the way that evangelicals thought about gender, it is worth considering whether we have adequately examined the biblical view of gender. Perhaps we should ask whether there are other aspects of understanding gender that we have not yet considered fully because we have focused our attention too narrowly on issues related to these social trends.

Therefore, we must be mindful of both the corporate and the individual aspects of the saved community and whether we have mistakenly prioritized the latter at the expense of the former. The church is the body of Christ, an entity in which each one of the parts has been placed by God (1 Cor. 12). Since the church is the family of God, we should consider the boundaries and nature of this new family and its individual members. Even more so, however, we must understand the community in light of the overall plan of God. The church is God's holy temple, in whom the Spirit of God resides, and the eschatological bride, to be joined with Christ at the end of the ages.

Consequently, the areas that are of immediate concern in today's discussions of gender must be seen in this greater context. These issues are often viewed as central to human life, making them especially important and explosive in traditional evangelical discourse. However, there may be larger kingdom issues that transcend and so provide the essential context for understanding these concerns. The way in which one asks questions and subsequently finds answers is critical to the ethos of any group. As mentioned in the beginning, a framework that is essentially decided prior to analysis, not surprisingly, leads to answers that fit that framework. To a large degree the questions determine the answer, or rather the type of answer. For example, if the question is "Is it A or B?" then there is no option to answer "C," or perhaps even "5," or "blue." As a result there is little room or inclination to explore areas that may provide a different or more nuanced answer. If we ask only "Who has authority?" or "Is there equality?" we may miss deeper and more foundational aspects of understanding gender in the kingdom.

In recent years there have been modifications on both sides, indicating dissatisfaction with the status quo. Terminology has changed, with "complementarian" generally replacing the use of "traditionalist" or "hierarchical," and evangelical feminism more often referred to as "egalitarianism" or "biblical equality."[85] Complementarians began to emphasize the concept of "servant leadership" to refer to male leadership in the home and church. Some complementarians qualified their position by agreeing that women can have leadership roles, with the exception of the "highest" ones, such as elder and senior pastor.[86] As a result the argument that women can have leadership roles is not a distinctively egalitarian position. Egalitarians also modified their position by insisting that they too were "complementarian" in that they believed in differences between the sexes that went beyond physical traits.[87] However, complementarity did not necessitate hierarchy.[88]

Ultimately, however, the current debate still comes down to whether there are any restrictions for women in ministry, and in terms of marriage, whether women are to "submit" to their husbands in a unique way or whether there is only "mutual submission" in marriage. Thus the themes of "authority" and "equality" remain the critical points. In other words, do women have equal opportunity in the church and equal decision-making power in the home, or are some positions restricted to men, who also have a particular authority in the home? Within this essential structure, research has focused on answering these basic questions in support of the respective sides.

However, these questions, while important, may reveal cultural rather than biblical priorities. For example, how central is equality when Paul talks more about not using rights than having or fighting for rights? Is more time and energy spent trying to establish male authority and leadership or wrestling with what that might actually look like since Christ talked about the first

85. As noted earlier, in 1986 evangelical feminism split into two movements, with the traditional biblical feminists, represented by Christians for Biblical Equality, focusing on equal opportunity, and the progressive side, represented by the Evangelical Women's Caucus, focusing on larger justice concerns (Cochran, *Evangelical Feminism*, 111). As Ingersoll relates, one result of the split is that the more conservative egalitarians fought more for functional equality in the church and society, whereas the others concentrated on sexism and challenging "the patriarchal system that undergirds society" (*Evangelical Christian Women*, 45). In general, the references to egalitarianism in this book refer to the traditional and conservative biblical feminist side.

86. E.g., Blomberg, "Complementarian Perspective," 145, 181.

87. E.g., Kimball, "Nature, Culture and Gender Complementarity."

88. It can be noted that many of these ideas are not completely new to the contemporary debate. E.g., in a review of Hardesty and Scanzoni's book, one person wrote of the need to go beyond "role interchangeability" to talk about "*her* uniqueness, *his* uniqueness, how these cooperate in a union, and what that 'union' is all about" (Barcus, "Milestone for Christian Women," italics original). Another woman coming from a more traditional perspective wrote that the role of the husband as head was to "die to himself in order to meet the needs of others," which included "assessing (his wife's) needs, physical and emotional, and trying to meet them" (Howe, "Husbands, Forget the Heroics!," 12). However, such ideas do not seem to have been as prominent a part of the discussion in the early stages, which was dominated rather by the larger concerns outlined here.

being last and leaders being slaves? The way in which Scripture presents these issues represents a larger structure of kingdom living and morality that has come into the world with the coming of Christ. Our current concerns are not unimportant but are redefined in the kingdom, and our goal as students of the Word is to understand how the redeemed community is to exemplify this kingdom way of life. In this light it is worth reexamining the way we approach the very debate itself.

The following chapters will offer an alternative answer by presenting different categories with which to understand gender. While the traditional ones remain relevant, I will argue that Scripture reveals other and more overarching categories, such as the unity of the body of Christ, a theology of "reversal," and the holiness of the people of God. I will try to show that these are more transcendent and more fundamental to the topic. I will attempt to demonstrate that a robust application of God's purposes for his people as a whole, his church, which is to glorify him and be his bride in the eschaton, provides a better overall perspective from which to understand how women and men fit into his plans. In this way we may find a larger point of view that includes insights from both positions yet does not fall neatly into either side in structure or rationale. If nothing else, I hope at least to communicate the need to examine Scripture to find different categories with which to consider the topic. These categories do not necessarily negate the old ones but may help illuminate the message in the biblical text concerning this critical issue.

PART 2

# Reframing Gender

# 4

# Kingdom Themes

"Modern scholarship is quite unanimous in the opinion that the Kingdom of God was the central message of Jesus."[1] Although George Eldon Ladd originally wrote these words decades ago, his assessment of the vital importance of Jesus's message of the kingdom of God is timeless. In proclaiming the kingdom, Jesus announced the coming of the reign of God. The implications of the kingdom have been a pivotal point in the gender debate as interpreters have wrestled with the question of what Jesus's message means for women.

However, we must consider the corporate as well as the individual sphere. We have seen evangelicals' tendency to follow the larger social trend toward defining gender according to more individualistic considerations. While not denying the importance of the individual, we must also recognize the centrality of the identity of the people of God in Scripture. As one scholar describes it, the church is "the community of Christ's kingdom."[2] In addition, we must be careful that our theology centers not on people but on God, to whom we belong. To this end, we will briefly discuss two themes that will be foundational for our discussion of gender: (1) unity and the corporate identity of God's people and (2) the way in which "reversal" demonstrates the power and glory of God in the Christian community.

1. Ladd, *Theology of the New Testament*, 54.
2. Clowney, *Church*, 16.

### Unity and the Corporate Identity

In the Old Testament, the role of Israel, God's people, was understood corporately. Israel was to be God's representative to the nations, and so faithfulness was of paramount importance. As Derek Tidball summarizes, "As a 'holy nation' they would have a unique role in the world of being God's showcase and displaying God's glory among the nations."[3] The nations were to see God's presence in Israel, which would lead them to worship him.[4] The nation's holiness was related to the community as a whole and not just as individuals.[5]

However, Israel failed, and in the New Testament, the church is to accomplish what Israel could not. Once again God has created a people of his own (Deut. 7:6–8; Titus 2:14), but now it is the church that God calls "my people" (Rom. 9:25; 2 Cor. 6:14–16).[6] As Raymond Ortlund observes, "Paul assumes continuity between the covenanted peoples of the Old and New Testaments, such that Israel's destiny as the bride of God, frustrated through her own harlotry, is to be realized in the Christian church."[7]

The church is not to be like Israel, which committed spiritual adultery and acted immorally (1 Cor. 10:1–13). Instead, the Christian community is to be "built up as a spiritual house for a holy priesthood . . . a chosen race, a royal priesthood, a holy nation, a people for God's own possession" (1 Pet. 2:5, 9–10). Peter applies the titles, which originally refer to Israel and come from Exod. 19:5–6 and Isa. 43:20–21, to the church.[8]

Israel was called to be "a kingdom of priests and a holy nation" in Exod. 19:6, even before the institution of the priesthood was established. Thus the point of 1 Peter is not the priestly role of individual believers but the "priestly identity of God's people" and the "role of the community of believers in the

3. Tidball, *Message of Holiness*, 173.

4. Routledge, *Old Testament Theology*, 172. Thomas summarizes,

> The outcome of the sanctification of Israel will be the accomplishment of God's missionary purpose for Israel. God's glory will be revealed throughout the whole world (Isa. 11:9; 40:5). All nations will acknowledge His authority and will participate in the worship of Him (Mic. 4:1–4; Isa. 66:18–21). In other words, the corporate sanctification of Israel is expected to lead to the corporate sanctification of the nations, and therefore to a universal state of righteousness, justice and peace. ("Holy God," 63)

5. Levine, *Leviticus*, 256.

6. Saucy, *Church in God's Program*, 20.

7. Ortlund, *Whoredom*, 151–52.

8. E.g., Carson, "1 Peter," 1030–31; Clowney, *Church*, 29; Davids, *First Epistle of Peter*, 90–91; Fung, "Some Pauline Pictures," 89.

world-at-large."[9] As a holy nation (1 Pet. 2:9), the community is set apart for God, as Israel was.[10] It is not the individual that is in view, including the possession of a type of spiritual authority similar to that of the Levitical priests, but rather the Christian community as a whole.[11] While the passage is often used to support the doctrine of the "priesthood of all believers," it rather describes the holy character of the eschatological community and its missionary responsibility.[12] The passage reflects "not the qualities of individuals but rather the special nature of the community as a single cohesive unit with a common origin, character, and purpose."[13] It reflects the identity of the community in which God's people stand out and are different because they belong to God.[14]

Karen Jobes summarizes the thought of the passage:

> An ancient priesthood was to be sanctified and set apart from the people at large for their ministry to the deity, to whom they had special access. Accordingly, the entire nation of ancient Israel was to be set apart from the nations of the world to serve God through obedience to the covenant with him, which obedience constituted Israel's holiness. Peter now declares similarly that collectively Christian believers are to perform that same function with respect to the nations among which they are scattered. By obedience to the new covenant in Christ's blood (1 Pet. 1:2), they are to be sanctified and set apart from the peoples of the world. . . . This is the priesthood that serves the King of the universe.[15]

As with Israel, the believers are to realize the way in which they are distinct because they belong to him.[16] When they realize how they belong to God, this will impact the way they live. God demands holiness of his people because he is holy (Lev. 11:44–45; 19:2; 20:26; 1 Pet. 1:15–16). Furthermore, when

9. Green, *1 Peter*, 61. So as Tidball notes, "Although the doctrine of the priesthood of believers is a true New Testament doctrine, to build the doctrine on the foundation of these verses is to miss Peter's meaning" (*Message of Holiness*, 175).

10. Davids, *First Epistle of Peter*, 92.

11. "It is not the concept of clerical authority but rather the theme of obedience and holiness that Peter has in view, concepts that were also present in the original context of Exod. 19" (Jobes, *1 Peter*, 161).

12. Elliott, "Ministry and Church Order," 370. For an extended defense of this position, see Elliott, *Elect and the Holy*.

13. Elliott, *1 Peter*, 444.

14. Wells, *God's Holy People*, 229.

15. Jobes, *1 Peter*, 161.

16. As Wells states, "The priority is to understand themselves in terms of belonging" (*God's Holy People*, 244).

others see their holiness in their worship and daily lives, they will be drawn to God's holiness.[17]

Thus the corporate holiness of the church is critical. In John 17:11–22 Jesus prays for the disciples to be sanctified and to be one as he and the Father are one so that the world will know that the Father has sent him, thus indicating the oneness of believers as a sign of God's "sanctifying presence."[18] The idea of corporate holiness is perhaps most explicitly seen in the image of the temple of God. The temple was the dwelling place of God[19] and so was where one came "before" or "into the presence of" God.[20] Because the temple was God's dwelling place, it was holy.[21]

In 1 Cor. 3:16 Paul explicitly calls the church God's temple, where God's Spirit resides.[22] He emphasizes the temple as the dwelling place of the deity, since he uses *naos*, which referred to the actual sanctuary, as opposed to *hieron*, which referred to the temple as a whole.[23] Second Corinthians 6:16 states that the Corinthians as a whole are "the temple of the living God," and that God "will dwell in them and walk among them." In Eph. 2:11–22, the oneness of Jew and gentile is explicitly seen in terms of holiness as the two groups form one "holy temple," a place where "God himself is present as Spirit."[24]

However, holiness requires obedience. Stephen Barton describes the two main components of holiness as being worship and obedience. The community celebrates God's holiness not only in worship but also "in lives devoted to doing God's holy will."[25] A central passage in regard to Israel describes this connection, "Now then, if you will indeed obey My voice and keep My covenant, then you shall be My own possession among all the peoples, for all the earth is Mine; and you shall be to Me a kingdom of priests and a holy nation" (Exod. 19:5–6).

17. Ibid.

18. Barton, "Dislocating and Relocating Holiness," 211–12.

19. See, e.g., Renwick, *Paul*, 26–46.

20. Nickelsburg and Stone, *Faith and Piety*, 56.

21. McKelvey, *New Temple*, 183.

22. For the argument that the church is part of the actual eschatological temple and not simply "like" a temple, see Beale, *Temple and the Church's Mission*, 245–52; Newton, *Concept of Purity*, 58–60.

23. Fee notes, "The distinctions between the two words do not necessarily hold in all the Greek of the NT period, but the usage in the LXX, where the distinction is common, seems to have influenced Paul here" (*First Epistle to the Corinthians*, 146–47).

24. Barton, "Dislocating and Relocating Holiness," 210.

25. Barton sees the key text here as Exod. 19:4–6 ("Dislocating and Relocating Holiness," 195–96). Israel is rescued from slavery in Egypt and commanded to obey God's voice and keep the covenant to become a holy nation.

As God's holy temple, believers are to abstain from idolatry and maintain purity. The imperatives in 2 Cor. 6:17 and 7:1 reflect how the community as a whole must respond to this identity as God's temple.[26] They are to separate themselves from idolaters, which they can do if they "Come out from their midst and be separate," "not touch what is unclean" (2 Cor. 6:17),[27] and cleanse themselves "from all defilement of flesh and spirit, perfecting holiness in the fear of God" (2 Cor. 7).[28] When Paul expels the man caught in immoral behavior, he says the purpose is not only for the sake of that person but also for the entire congregation, because it is necessary to "clean out" the "new lump" (1 Cor. 5:7).[29]

There were other aspects of holiness as well. J. Ayodeji Adewuya argues that Israel's holiness is "first and foremost, relational."[30] Israel's holiness is based on the nation's call to be the people of God. Yet it is based not only on a special relationship with God but also on the way in which that relationship impacts the Israelites' relations with other people and nations and among themselves. Leviticus 19, for example, outlines their expected conduct toward their families, their neighbors, and strangers.[31] "The call for Israel to be holy is the call for the community to concretise the divine life in the world," so holiness includes the way it is manifested in and through the life of the people in their relationships.[32]

In the New Testament, the importance of relationships among the believers and the sanctity of the whole is readily evident. For example, believers are to love one another (Rom. 12:10), take care not to cause another believer to stumble (1 Cor. 8:13), and exhort and encourage one another (1 Thess. 5:11). Paul also explicitly states the importance of maintaining unity among the people of God with a dire warning. The context of Paul's passage about the church as the temple of God in 1 Cor. 3:16 is his instructions to a congregation

26. "Paul elaborates the community's identity as the temple of God and challenges it to live out the implications of that identity" (Thompson, *Moral Formation*, 52).

27. Thompson (*Moral Formation*, 52–53) notes that Paul uses these imperatives to identify the church's experience with Israel's since they are foundational for Israel's identity as the holy people of God.

28. Thus the temple image "depicts the church under its divine aspect as the society of the redeemed, which through sanctification by the Holy Spirit constitutes the inviolable dwelling-place of God" (McKelvey, *New Temple*, 92).

29. As Newton summarizes, "Paul calls on the Corinthians to remove, from the Church, the man who has been polluting the community, a community which has to be kept pure if it is to remain the sanctuary in which God's spirit dwells" (*Concept of Purity*, 88).

30. Adewuya, *Holiness and Community*, 57.

31. Ibid.

32. Ibid., 72.

divided among leaders. The extreme threat that disunity poses is seen as Paul warns that if anyone destroys God's holy temple, God will destroy that person (1 Cor. 3:17). Causing division in the church is a desecration of God's temple.[33]

Gordon Thomas observes that "a holy God among a holy people in a holy place" is "the enduring eschatological hope of the Scriptures."[34] The people's holiness reflects God's holiness, so they are a witness to the world. This testimony of the church in the New Testament means that unity was a critical aspect for preserving the sanctity of the dwelling place of God's Spirit, and the relationships within the community were a supremely important way to manifest the divine life. Consequently, as we examine gender in the life of the church, we will consider it from the perspective of holiness and unity in the church's obedient response to God's saving grace. This results in the corporate witness of the church, and not simply in terms of rights or privileges given to individuals or groups of individuals.

## Reversals and the Power of God

One notable feature of the Old Testament is the presence of "reversals," in which God works in unexpected ways that upend traditional expectations. For example, God chooses the elder Esau to serve the younger Jacob (Gen. 25:23) and selects David as the Lord's anointed rather than his older brothers because "man looks at the outward appearance, but the Lord looks at the heart" (1 Sam. 16:7). It is through reversals that God demonstrates that his ways are not human ways (Isa. 55:8–9). The Lord has Gideon winnow his men from thirty-two thousand to three hundred to defeat the Midianite army (Judg. 7:2–8) to make clear that God is the one who delivers Israel. Thus these reversals of expectations often teach a larger lesson of God's sovereignty and human inadequacy.

The presence of these reversals and the lessons they impart continue in the New Testament. The rich man goes to Hades, while Lazarus, the poor man, is carried away by the angels to blessings with Abraham (Luke 16:19–31). The widow's mite counts more than the large contributions of the rich (Mark 12:41–44). The news of the birth of the Messiah is given to lowly and humble shepherds (Luke 2:8–20), and it is the women, not the twelve male apostles,

33. And likewise, profaning God's temple was a capital offense in the Old Testament (1 Sam. 5; 2 Sam. 6:6–7); see McKelvey, *New Temple*, 101–2.

34. Thomas, "Holy God," 55.

who are the first witnesses to the resurrection (Matt. 28:1–10; Mark 16:1–8; Luke 24:1–10; John 20:1–18).[35]

The principle of reversal also characterizes the very nature of the church. In 1 Corinthians Paul speaks of God's calling of the Corinthians in their low state, in which "there were not many wise according to the flesh, not many mighty, not many noble" (1:26). For the most part, the church did not consist of the elite and those considered influential in society.[36] However, God used them instead of the powerful. "God has chosen the foolish things of the world to shame the wise, and God has chosen the weak things of the world to shame the things which are strong, and the base things of the world and the despised God has chosen, the things that are not, so that He may nullify the things that are" (1:27–28).

What is lowly or despised in the world may be esteemed in the kingdom. Those of low status perform great deeds for God, contrary to the expectations of their society, in which they may be rejected, ignored, or marginalized. In this way the reversals show God's power and supremacy and the futility of human ways. Mary praises God for choosing her despite her low status (Luke 1:48–49) and speaks of how the humble are exalted and God brings down rulers from their thrones (1:52). Those who think they are self-sufficient will see their error as the rich are sent away empty, but God will fill the hungry (1:53). God chooses those who were considered low in the world's eyes so that "no man may boast before God" (1 Cor. 1:29). What matters is not human strength or power, but dependence on God. John Drury describes this pattern in this way: "God's judgement and mercy always form the classic prophetic message, worked out in the annihilation of the achievements of disobedient human pride and the rebuilding of a new life in obedient humility."[37]

The reversals must also be understood in the context of the kingdom of God. According to Jewish apocalyptic, in the age to come God would establish his final and undisputed reign, and the coming of the kingdom would bring a reversal of Israel's fortunes in which Israel would exercise lordship over the

35. See the many examples in Elliott, "Jesus Was Not an Egalitarian," 75–91. The use of this theme has been particularly noticed in Luke's Gospel; see, e.g., York, *Last Shall Be First*; Drake, "Reversal Theme in Luke's Gospel."

36. As Fitzmyer states, "For few among them would have been philosophers or even members of the educated classes; few would have been influential people or even politically adept; few were wellborn or of the upper class of Corinthian society" (*First Corinthians*, 162). Thiselton points to the Corinthians' "relative *lack of public esteem, political power, and family status, and influence from a sociopolitical viewpoint*" (*First Epistle to the Corinthians*, 181, italics original).

37. Drury, *Tradition and Design*, 53–54.

kingdoms that had formerly oppressed and humiliated the nation. The end could be brought about not by any human activity but only through God's decisive act, "the apocalyptic, world-shattering, and world-renewing act of God, which brings both final judgment and final salvation."[38]

However, the kingdom that Jesus announced did not bring about the transformation of Israel's fortunes as expected. Instead the kingdom is characterized by a reversal of the existing order as the eschatological blessings are given to the ones least expected to receive them—the poor, the hungry, the outcast, the sinners, the gentiles—and woes fall on the rich and the religious leaders. This is the "great reversal," in which the present order and its rules of prestige and privilege are questioned and values are transformed.[39]

Thus Jesus makes pronouncements such as "many who are first will be last, and the last, first" (Mark 10:31; Luke 13:30; Mark 9:35; Matt. 20:16); "whoever exalts himself shall be humbled; and whoever humbles himself shall be exalted" (Matt. 23:12; Luke 14:11; 18:14; cf. Matt. 18:4); and "the one who is greatest among you must become like the youngest, and the leader like the servant" (Luke 22:26). He proclaims that instead of the ethic of reciprocity, which marks the present age, his disciples are to love their enemies, do good to those who hate them, and pray for their persecutors (Luke 6:27, 35; Matt. 5:44). The ethic of Jesus "spells an end to self-assertiveness and self-glorifying and the beginning of the self-forgetfulness that already submits to God's sovereignty and serves the neighbor."[40]

As will be explained more in the following chapters, Christ himself is the prime example of the reversal of the kingdom, especially as seen in his incarnation and death. He is the one who, "although he existed in the form of God, did not regard equality with God a thing to be grasped," and so took the form of a "bond-servant" and became "obedient to the point of death" (Phil. 2:6–8). Instead of exercising his privileges as God, he took the opposite course and became a servant or slave.

The cross is the most prominent place where notions of wisdom and power are reversed, setting up a paradoxical situation. Paul says, "The word of the cross is foolishness to those who are perishing, but to us who are being saved it is the power of God" (1 Cor. 1:18). The Jews would have considered a crucified Messiah to be an oxymoron, since "cursed is everyone who hangs on

38. Verhey, *Great Reversal*, 13.

39. Ibid., 15. Thus York (*Last Shall Be First*, 55) notes that the reversals articulated in the Magnificat (Luke 2:51–53) indicate that the new order has been inaugurated.

40. Verhey, *Great Reversal*, 16.

a tree" (Gal. 3:13; Deut. 21:23).[41] In the Greco-Roman world, where people sought a "mastery" of life characterized by esteem, honor, and success, the crucifixion would have signified failure, dishonor, and shame.[42] Consequently, Jesus is a "stumbling block" to Jews and "foolishness" to the gentiles, but to those whom God has called, he is "the power of God and the wisdom of God" (1 Cor. 1:23–24). God has called people to believe that one who was cursed by God and who died as a crucified criminal is the Savior and that the death of Christ leads to life. To see the truth of the cross, one must be able to comprehend the reversal inherent within it.

As citizens of the kingdom, Christ's followers are also to emulate his example of humility and self-sacrifice for the sake of others. They are to learn from Christ's example to "regard one another as more important than [themselves]" (Phil. 2:1–11). Instead of striving for their own honor, they are to "give preference to one another in honor" (Rom. 12:10). Jesus states in John's Gospel, "He who loves his life loses it, and he who hates his life in this world will keep it to life eternal" (John 12:25). The sacrifice of those who follow Christ will result in humble service to others, which will then result in their being considered "great" in God's eyes.

Significantly, one of the main results of such a "reversal" is to increase unity. In Phil. 2:1–11 Paul tells the Philippians that they can achieve the "same mind" and "same love" and be "united in spirit, intent on one purpose" by following Christ's example of humility and so looking out for the interests of others. The community is bonded together as the members care for one another. Paul elsewhere says that God reverses the status of the members of the body, so that the less honorable ones receive more honor and the less presentable ones become more presentable "so that there may be no division in the body, but that the members may have the same care for one another" (1 Cor. 12:22–25).

Another example occurs in 1 Cor. 12:31, where Paul urges the Corinthians to seek the "greater gifts." That Paul would exhort the church to seek what is greater has caused some interpreters to conclude that the statement is a

41. Garland, *1 Corinthians*, 70. As Savage states, "Far from manifesting divine glory, he seemed to bear a divine curse. Far from purging the nation of pagan domination, he succumbed to a pagan cross" (*Power through Weakness*, 140).

42. Thiselton, *First Epistle to the Corinthians*, 170. As Hengel states, Jesus "had suffered a particularly cruel and shameful death, what as a rule was reserved for hardened criminals, rebellious slaves and rebels against the Roman state. That this crucified Jew, Jesus Christ, could truly be a divine being sent on earth, God's Son, the Lord of all and the coming judge of the world, must inevitably have been thought by any educated man to be utter 'madness' and presumptuousness" (*Crucifixion in the Ancient World*, 83).

description of what the Corinthians are doing rather than a command.[43] However, Paul's instructions can be understood according to the paradoxical nature of the "greater" gift. As explained in more detail in an earlier work, the Corinthians sought the gift of tongues because in their society it gave the individual a higher status, since it was considered heavenly speech, as opposed to prophecy, which was normal human speech. But Paul tells the Corinthians that prophecy is the gift they should seek because it edifies the church rather than the individual (1 Cor. 14:1–4). Paul speaks ironically, so that if the Corinthians truly want the "greater" gift, they will seek the one that benefits the church as a whole, not the one that benefits the individual. In other words the "greater" gift is actually the one that makes them "lesser" in the world, and they can understand this only if they accept that it is better to seek what is good for others—to love—rather than pursue gain for themselves.[44]

In light of the importance of "reversal" as illustrating important ideas about the kingdom of God, we will need to consider how it would apply in what would seem to be an area of great potential fruitfulness: leadership. It comes as no surprise that Jesus himself speaks of this:

> But Jesus called them to Himself and said, "You know that the rulers of the Gentiles lord it over them, and their great men exercise authority over them. It is not this way among you, but whoever wishes to become great among you shall be your servant, and whoever wishes to be first among you shall be your slave; just as the Son of Man did not come to be served, but to serve, and to give His life as ransom for many." (Matt. 20:25–28)[45]

The symbol of the servant "expresses the antithesis of power, status and domination."[46] Such an example of lowering would be both striking and perplexing in the ancient Mediterranean world, which was "a markedly agonistic society in which the quest for public honor dominated the behavioral priorities of males of nearly every social rank."[47] However, according to the values of the kingdom, the leaders of the community are directly called to

43. E.g., Iber, "Zum Verständnis von 1 Cor. 12:31"; Bittlinger, *Gifts and Graces*, 73–75; R. Martin, *Spirit and the Congregation*, 35, 57, 75; Wischmeyer, *Der höchste Weg*, 52.

44. Lee, *Paul*, 192–96. For a more detailed description of the philosophical background to the evaluation of prophecy versus tongues, see D. Martin, *Corinthian Body*, 88–92; D. Martin, "Tongues of Angels."

45. Also Mark 10:42–45; Luke 22:25–27.

46. Chilton and McDonald, *Jesus and the Ethics*, 88.

47. Hellerman, *Reconstructing Honor*, 165.

be servants because of their "higher" and more powerful position. As will be explained in more detail below, they, above all others, are to be concrete manifestations of Christ's example of humility and service so that the rest of the church might learn from them (1 Pet. 5:3).

Thus the concept of reversal speaks to issues of identity found not in oneself, one's position, or personal power, but in dependence on God. It refers to a profound willingness to sacrifice what gives people status and meaning in their current context for a value that comes from God alone. As such it causes the credit to be given to God rather than to flawed and sinful humanity. When applied to the community, it results in the deep unity of his people as they consider others before themselves and challenges leaders to be primary examples of this submission to God.

## Conclusion

Believers are to reflect God's holiness and be a witness to the nations. G. K. Beale summarizes, "God's ultimate goal in creation was to magnify his glory throughout the earth by means of his faithful image-bearers inhabiting the world in obedience to the divine mandate."[48] A part of this obedience that glorifies God relates to the foundational value of our existence as the people of God, called to corporate unity in our relations with one another. We are also called to complete dependence on the sovereign God, who illustrates through the cross and the lives of his people how his ways confront and oppose the self-centered and self-glorifying ways of humanity. In the following chapters, we will explore these ideas in more depth to consider how they impact our understanding of gender and conceptions of authority, leadership, equality, and rights.

48. Beale, *Temple and the Church's Mission*, 82.

# 5

# Ministry, Part 1

## *Rethinking Equality and Rights in the Body of Christ*

Both egalitarians and complementarians assert that there is equality in Christ. For complementarians it is an equality in Christ that includes differences in role and function.[1] For egalitarians it is an equality in which there are no restrictions on women's roles in ministry and leadership and they share equally in decision making in marriage.[2] The issue has not necessarily been whether there is equality in the church as much as what kind there is. However, less attention has been paid to reexamining the basic notion itself. In this chapter we will ask whether Scripture leads us in a different direction, one that may still include "equality" but produces more foundational categories with which to understand the significance of gender in our new life in Christ.

1. E.g., House, *Role of Women*, 118–19, who says it is an "heirship." Johnson ("Role Distinctions," 164) calls it "an egalitarianism of privilege in the covenantal union of believers in Christ." Knight describes it as "spiritual equality as joint heirs of life" (*Role Relationship*, 8–9).

2. Pierce and Groothuis, *Discovering Biblical Equality*, 17. Grenz and Kjesbo summarize, "Egalitarians . . . assert that equality of soteriological *position* in Christ must receive an appropriate outworking in the *practice* of the church" (*Women in the Church*, 101, italics original).

## The Kingdom of God, Unity, and the Inclusive Community

Although they draw different implications, both complementarians and egalitarians remark on how Jesus treated women with great dignity.[3] This is seen in many ways. Jesus has significant conversations with women, in contrast to the traditional practice of men not speaking with women in public. For example, he speaks to the Samaritan woman at the well, an action that causes his disciples to be "amazed" (John 4:27). This woman, furthermore, is the first person to whom Jesus reveals his identity as the Messiah. Women are praised for their faith (Matt. 15:28; Luke 7:36–50). Jesus calls a woman whom he heals a "daughter of Abraham" (Luke 13:10–17), as he similarly calls the redeemed tax collector Zaccheus a "son of Abraham" (Luke 19:9).[4] Furthermore, he fully accepted women as disciples, breaking down traditional barriers between the genders in the process.

Egalitarians argue that this is a reflection of how Jesus promoted full functional equality between men and women. However, while Jesus's treatment of women was indeed groundbreaking, the notion of "equality" may not be the most accurate lens through which to try to understand the importance of his actions. Several scholars have demonstrated that Jesus's concern was not to establish an egalitarian community.[5] Instead it may be more important to understand the issue according to the idea of "inclusion."

We will see that Paul also affirms a kingdom community characterized not so much by equality as by a "oneness" in which all could be included, regardless of factors such as gender, race, or socioeconomic status, and, even more, could love one another as brothers and sisters in Christ despite these traditional barriers. While such inclusion might have social ramifications such as equality, it was the love of the believers for one another that was to be a hallmark of the body of Christ. Rather than structural change, "the issue for Jesus was one of attitude and perception of the relation between self and others."[6]

This means not that equality could not be a feature of the New Testament community but rather that it is not the primary guiding point. The key to Paul's ethic is the "mutual upbuilding" of the members of the body, so

3. As Spencer says, "Recognizing that Jesus both affirmed and elevated the status of women has now become commonplace on both sides" ("Jesus' Treatment of Women," 127).

4. For more detailed summaries, see Spencer, "Jesus' Treatment of Women," 127–33; Wilkins, "Women in the Teaching"; Borland, "Women in the Life," 113–20.

5. E.g., Elliott, "Jesus Was Not an Egalitarian"; Elliott, "Jesus Movement Was Not Egalitarian"; Corley, "Egalitarian Jesus."

6. Elliott, "Jesus Was Not an Egalitarian," 84.

individual rights are ultimately subservient to love, because one may need to sacrifice a right in order to help another.[7]

### *Finding the Transcendent Perspective*

It is important to define what is meant by "equality" and to understand its implications in order to see the subtle but important differences in the biblical account. John Elliott suggests a number of possibilities. "Equal" or "equality" can denote "sameness." It can also have the sense of "fair," or "equitable," using a social standard of measurement.[8] It can refer to a certain quality, including age, social rank, economic status, talents, or rights. Finally, in social-scientific discussion, the idea that equality could be a possibility for all of society arose beginning in the eighteenth century with its optimism regarding possible social transformation. The idea of the "basic equality of membership in a society" in the eighteenth century extended to include political rights beginning in the nineteenth century and then social rights in the twentieth.[9]

The concept that all people are created equal and endowed with certain inalienable rights comes from the Enlightenment and would have been "thoroughly alien" to the ancient world. The predominant belief instead was that people were by nature created unequal, as evidenced physically (males as dominant and females as inferior), socially (parents would be superior to children, freeborn superior to slaves), and ethnically (Greeks vs. barbarians). Furthermore, social status was apportioned by nature or God, so in this sense it was permanent and unchangeable.[10]

Where concepts of equality were considered, they were often different from our contemporary version. For example, Aristotle discusses "equality" according to the principle of "assignment by desert," but the concept of what is deserving varies so that the criterion for democrats is "free birth," for oligarchs "wealth," and for aristocrats "virtue."[11] Thus Dennis Duling cautions, "Ancient society was not 'egalitarian' in the modern Enlightenment, individualist, political-philosophical sense in which equality is a self-evident human right and/or social goal for everyone."[12]

7. Clarke, *Pauline Theology*, 136.
8. Elliott, "Jesus Was Not an Egalitarian," 76.
9. Ibid., 76–77, citing Halsey, "Equality," 261–62.
10. Elliott, "Jesus Was Not an Egalitarian," 77.
11. Aristotle, *Eth. nic.* 5.3.1131a.
12. Duling, "'Egalitarian' Ideology," 126.

What Jesus promotes is inclusion in that he made it possible for all people to become disciples and members of the new covenant community. Rather than an egalitarian community, the believers formed a surrogate family where people were included not by blood ties but on the basis of faith. The bonds among the members were the ties of brotherly and sisterly love.[13] As Elliott notes, seeing Jesus's intent as establishing a "community of equals" is not only incorrect but can also obscure its true original model as one of a household or family.[14]

When we understand the early Christian community as an inclusive one, we are also able to see the ramifications. This includes the radical nature of bonds within the new community, for example, as in the new relationship between Jew and gentile. Although Gal. 3:28 is often used as evidence of an egalitarian theology,[15] the passage does not speak of equality as much as unity, of being "one." Jew and Greek, slave and free, male and female, are not *isos*, "equal," but *heis*, "one." In other words, "universal integration into a new single community of Jesus followers is its point, not equalization of all members."[16] In this new community, distinctions are not eliminated as much as they have become irrelevant for determining who can be "in Christ" because now believers are children of God through faith rather than the law (Gal. 3:26). Similarly, when Paul says that "there is no distinction between Jew and Greek" (Rom. 10:12a), he is speaking of Jesus being Lord of "all who call on Him" (Rom. 10:12b). In terms of the reception of grace through Christ, there is no distinction among people.

It is critical to see the theological significance of the unity of groups such as Jew and gentile. Previously the gentiles had been "excluded from the commonwealth of Israel, and strangers to the covenants of promise, having no hope and without God in the world" (Eph. 2:12). Now, however, those who "formerly were far off have been brought near by the blood of Christ" (Eph. 2:13). As a result, the cross of Christ has worked to "reconcile" both Jew and gentile "in one body to God" (Eph. 2:16), and so Christ has made "the two into one new man" (Eph. 2:15). Now the gentiles are "fellow citizens" and members of "God's household" and members of the building that is growing into a "holy temple in the Lord" (Eph. 2:18–21). Thus, as R. J. McKelvey states, "This union is not simply the merging of the races but the creation

13. Elliott, "Jesus Was Not an Egalitarian," 89. For more on the church as a family and kinship in the "household of God," see deSilva, *Honor*, 199–239; Hellerman, *Ancient Church as Family*.

14. Elliott, "Jesus Was Not an Egalitarian," 89.

15. E.g., Jewett, *Man as Male and Female*, 142–47; Bilezikian, *Beyond Sex Roles*, 126–28.

16. Elliott, "Jesus Movement Was Not Egalitarian," 186.

of unity on a new and higher level."[17] Jew and gentile are now members of a new union in Christ, a union that is the holy temple of God.

However, the inclusion of disparate groups would have profound relational as well as soteriological implications. In the case of Jew and gentile, for example, unifying these two groups meant overcoming fundamental barriers that divided the two. The Jew/Greek separation was one of the basic divisions in the first century and had now been transcended in Christ.[18] He did this by breaking down the "dividing wall, by abolishing in His flesh the enmity" of the law (Eph. 2:14–15) that, while functioning to protect Israel from impurity through the gentiles, also alienated them from the gentiles and had become a source of hostility.[19] Laws such as those prohibiting eating with or marrying gentiles often led to Jewish contempt for gentiles, resulting in gentile hatred for and suspicion of the Jews.[20] Thus the two groups were characterized by a strong and mutual animosity.[21]

In place of this enmity, Paul speaks of establishing peace between Jew and gentile (Eph. 2:15). As Andrew Lincoln notes, this is a "relational concept" that presumes the need to overcome hostility between the two groups.[22] In Christ they could overcome the hostilities that existed in the world and instead love one another since they were now one in Christ and reconciled in "one body" (Eph. 2:16).

Richard Longenecker states in reference to Gal. 3:28, "The passage clearly suggests that on the basis of this new and objective reality a whole new set of attitudes and reactions are to be ours as Christians as we seek to express this reality in the Church and in society."[23] The new attitudes and reactions implied by the passage seem to point not to equality, at least in terms of sameness or fairness, as much as to a profound love for and acceptance of one another that binds the community together as one.

These relationships were to extend to all members of the community beyond Jew and Greek. The three pairings in Gal. 3:28, which also include male and female and slave and free, represented some of the leading ways people were separated from one another[24] and the sources of the most bitter hostility and

17. McKelvey, *New Temple*, 110.

18. Lincoln, *Ephesians*, 141.

19. R. Martin describes the law as being both a "protection" for Israel and also serving to "drive a wedge between Israel and her pagan neighbours" (*Reconciliation*, 185).

20. Hoehner, *Ephesians*, 370.

21. Lincoln, *Ephesians*, 142.

22. Ibid., 140.

23. Longenecker, *New Testament Social Ethics*, 31.

24. Fee, "Male and Female," 176.

animosities.[25] Now Paul uses them as examples of how the basic divisions that most hinder fellowship can be transcended in Christ so that believers can love one another and be one. Galatians 3:28 speaks of universal inclusion in salvation while also carrying radical implications for a relational oneness for believers.[26] The passage reflects the new unity of the believers in which groups that traditionally are separated from and hostile to one another can be unified and love one another in Christ.

Other passages give additional insight into the nature of this oneness among the different groups, in particular in their love for one another. Similar formulas in 1 Cor. 12:13 (which does not include the male/female pair) and Col. 3:11 (which adds "barbarian" and "Scythian") refer to their oneness as being in "one body" and are accompanied with an exhortation to love one another (1 Cor. 12:12–13; 13:1–13; Col. 3:11–15). In other passages as well, a description of oneness is accompanied by an admonition to love (Rom. 12:5, 9–10; Eph. 4:2–3, 4–6). Paul urges the believers to show "tolerance for one another in love, being diligent to preserve the unity of the Spirit in the bond of peace" (Eph. 4:2–3). Their unity should be so profound that they can share in one another's suffering and rejoice when others are honored (1 Cor. 12:26). Indeed, Col. 3:14 describes love as "the perfect bond of unity." While the believers were already "one" in the Spirit (1 Cor. 12:13), love created the deepest form of unity in the body (1 Cor. 13).[27] Thus what characterizes the community is the way in which the people of God love one another in their differences, not an overlooking or erasure of distinctions. Consequently, while other social implications such as equality could arise, these may be secondary to the larger concern for the loving unity of God's people in their differences. Love, not equality, leads to the true unity that Paul describes in which the members "may have the same care for one another" (1 Cor. 12:25). Equality speaks to one's

25. Jewett, *Man as Male and Female*, 143.

26. While complementarians have often emphasized the soteriological dimensions of the oneness of Gal. 3:28 (e.g., George, *Galatians*, 282–92), egalitarians have argued that the implications of the passage make such distinctions "irrelevant" in the church (e.g., Bilezikian, *Beyond Sex Roles*, 126–28). As we will see, Paul does see implications for such oneness in Christ as extending beyond equality of soteriological position, although he does not see a conflict of such equality with hierarchy and priority.

27. The role of love in creating unity was discussed among the Hellenistic philosophers as being vital to the harmony of bodies such as that of the city. For a larger discussion of the role of love in 1 Cor. 13 in forming deeper bonds of unity for the body of Christ, see Lee, *Paul*, 167–92. See also Mitchell (*Paul*, 165–71, 270–79) on love as the antidote to factionalism in its Greco-Roman context and in Paul.

personal privileges and rights, whereas love describes one's willingness to prioritize others.

Gordon Fee notes that Paul's driving concern is ecclesiology and who constitutes the people of God.[28] The people of God are "one" (Gal. 3:28) and are to love one another. In this way the formula in Gal. 3:28 stands in "contrast to commonly accepted patterns of privileged status and self-assertive prejudice in the ancient world."[29] It would be difficult to overestimate the radical nature of the relationships to which God has called the believers. As a result, the love between members of such disparate groups would be a powerful witness to the uniqueness of the Christian message.

It is vital to see the larger theological purpose of the unity of the community because Paul's overriding concern is not the rights of the individual but the glory of God as seen through the church. Paul does not deny the importance of rights but asserts that there is a more transcendent way. Thus he establishes his apostolic rights in 1 Cor. 9 only to relinquish them "for the sake of the gospel" (1 Cor. 9:22–23). He affirms that one may have the right to eat meat sacrificed to idols but should not act on this right if it causes another believer to stumble (1 Cor. 8:1–13). In this believers are to follow the example of Christ seen especially in Phil. 2:6–8, where Christ did not use his privileges as God and instead took the form of a slave, a person who has no rights.[30]

In all these examples, people are called to give up their privileges for the sake of the gospel and the unity of the church. The willingness to sacrifice for the good of another is the essence of love in the New Testament. Paul uses Christ's lowering and sacrifice as an example of the love the Philippians should strive to have among themselves (Phil. 2:2, 5–11). Giving up one's legitimate rights to prevent another believer from stumbling is a way in which love "builds up" (1 Cor. 8:1–13).

For Jesus, the command to "love your neighbor as yourself" is the greatest commandment after the one to love God, and he announces that the entire Law and the Prophets depend on these two commandments (Matt.

28. Fee, "Male and Female," 174.

29. George, *Galatians*, 285.

30. As M. Harris explains,

> In a fundamental sense slavery involves the absence of rights, especially the right to determine the course of one's life and the use of one's energies. What is denied the slave is freedom of action and freedom of movement; he cannot do what he wishes or go where he wishes. The faculty of free choice and the power of refusal are denied to him. . . . To be a slave was to be the property of another person, who could use or dispose of that "property" as if it were some inanimate chattel. (*Slave of Christ*, 107)

22:36–40). He gives a "new commandment" to the disciples to "love one another" as he loved them so that people will know they are his disciples (John 13:34–35). Jesus prays that the disciples may be "one" even as he and the Father are one so that the world may know that the Father has sent him (John 17:11, 22).

Similarly Paul states, "The whole Law is summed up in one word, in the statement, 'You shall love your neighbor as yourself'" (Gal. 5:14), citing Lev. 19:18, which in his day was considered a summary of the law's requirements for relationships.[31] Elsewhere he calls love the "fulfillment of the law" (Rom. 13:8–10) and says that the law of Christ is to "bear one another's burdens" (Gal. 6:2).[32] In this way their relationships with one another would be an essential arena in which the church fulfills the "law of Christ" (Gal. 6:2; 1 Cor. 9:21).[33] Consequently, Paul's ethic is one of building up one another (e.g., 1 Cor. 14:26; Eph. 4:12), which is accomplished through love, the willingness not to use one's rights for the sake of another (1 Cor. 8).

As mentioned earlier, the people of God were called to be a witness to the world. The eschatological body of Christ combined Jew and Greek, slave and free, barbarian and Scythian, and male and female into a unity in which all were called to love and serve the other. As fellow members of the body through the grace of God, they were to love one another irrespective of their current positions, whether a socially imposed position such as slave or free, one determined by a distinction based on creation such as male or female, or one related to an ethnic division with long-standing hostilities such as Jew or Greek.[34] While these distinctions were transcended in Christ, they were not irrelevant. Rather it was precisely *because* these distinctions existed that the believers' unity and

31. Thielman, *Paul & the Law*, 139.

32. Thielman observes that there is an eschatological aspect to Paul's understanding of obedience and the love command so that "to obey the law as it is summarized in the love command is to complete the requirement of the law in some ultimate and eschatological sense" (Thielman, *Paul & the Law*, 140).

33. Although the debate is certainly not yet settled over whether the "law of Christ" entails simply the command to love or additionally external principles from the example and teachings of Jesus, we can note here that the love command forms at least an essential component of the law of Christ. E.g., as Longenecker posits, the law may be "prescriptive principles stemming from the heart of the gospel (usually embodied in the example and teachings of Jesus), which are meant to be applied to specific situations by the direction and enablement of the Holy Spirit, being always motivated and conditioned by love" (*New Testament Social Ethics*, 15; *Galatians*, 275–76).

34. The New Testament describes how the early church acknowledged the continued Jew/gentile distinction. For example, the council of Jerusalem affirmed that gentiles did not need to become Jews in order to become part of the new movement. In 1 Cor. 7:18–19 Paul even "*prohibits* the erasure" of Jew/gentile distinction (Gundry-Volf, "Beyond Difference?," 21, italics original).

love would be so remarkable. The bonds between such socially disparate people were to be a hallmark of the Christian community as opposed to the divisions, competition, and antagonisms so prominently displayed in the world.

### *The Kingdom and Hierarchies*

The presence of hierarchies in the kingdom, and even more so their reversal, should also cause us to question the centrality of equality as a biblical theme. For example, while the family of God was redefined along religious and moral rather than biological lines, there remained hierarchy in the structure, even as there might be hierarchy in a traditional family.[35] Jesus called God "Father" (e.g., Matt. 12:50; Mark 14:36; Luke 11:2), and his followers were children of God (e.g., Mark 2:5) and brothers and sisters (e.g., Luke 8:21). Paul and the early church adopted a similar social structure in which God was "Father" and the believers were his adopted children (Rom. 8:14–23; Gal. 3:26–4:7), brothers and sisters (e.g., Rom. 1:13; 1 Cor. 1:10; 7:15; 1 Pet. 5:12; 2 John 13), and members of the "household of faith/God" (Gal. 6:10; Heb. 3:1–6; 1 Pet. 2:5; 4:17).[36] The members were to live according to the Father's will and honor him as the divine head of this family.[37] Hierarchy was also present among Jesus's followers, where status was determined by the length and degree of each person's association with Jesus. The Twelve had higher status than other disciples, with Peter, James, and John as the "inner core" of the Twelve having an even higher status.[38]

Other hierarchies are evident in the church itself, such as the appointment of elders, who are given charge over the church (1 Pet. 5:2), with the possibility of earning "double honor" (1 Tim. 5:17). Some inequalities result from God himself, as the Spirit sovereignly distributes gifts so that some are worthy of more honor or are "greater" (1 Cor. 12:22–24, 31). Numerous places in the Gospels speak of those who will be called "greater" or "least" in the kingdom (e.g., Matt. 11:11; Luke 7:28; 9:48).

However, as will be explored more in the next chapter, the point is not so much whether hierarchies are present as it is what they mean. In the kingdom, values of power and privilege are turned upside down, and they are upended according

35. "That all believers are 'brothers' eliminates the rabbi-student distinction, but says nothing about equality since brothers can be quite unequal in terms of position or privilege (as affected by age, birth mother, strength etc.)" (Elliott, "Jesus Was Not an Egalitarian," 82).

36. Elliott, "Jesus Movement Was Not Egalitarian," 177.

37. Elliott, "Jesus Was Not an Egalitarian," 87.

38. Ibid.

to the new values of the kingdom as seen in Christ himself. Christ's statements such as "the last shall be first, and the first last" (Matt. 20:16) and "whoever wishes to be first among you shall be slave of all" (Mark 10:44) are integral to our understanding of any "hierarchies" in the kingdom. As we will see, the reversal of hierarchies is a prominent way in which the power of God is displayed in the kingdom as well as a vital means to promote unity in the community.

Furthermore, these reversals must be seen in the context of their larger function in the kingdom. Again the case of Jew and gentile provides a helpful example. While the gospel is offered to all, it comes to the Jew first and then to the Greek (Rom. 1:16). In Rom. 2:9–10 we learn that Jews have priority over Greeks when it comes to honor or tribulation given for those who respectively do good or evil. Most of all, Rom. 9–11 teaches that the gentiles remain "secondary grafts" onto Israel.[39] Although all people can be "in Christ," there remains this distinction between Jew and Greek as the church is founded on the promises given to Israel. Paul later talks about the eschatological role of the Jews in bringing about the final blessings (e.g., Rom. 11:12–16). Thus, while Jew and gentile are "equal" in the sense of being "one" in Christ, and there is "neither Jew nor Greek" (Gal. 3:28; 1 Cor. 12:13; Eph. 2:13–18), at the same time the Jew has a special role in regard to the gospel.

As a result this greater narrative of Scripture must be considered in evaluating the significance of passages such as Gal. 3:28, since to say that Jews and gentiles are now "equal" obscures these larger and more significant points. Jew and gentile may indeed be equal, but that is not the most important and guiding point of the text. Rather, gentiles are now included along with Jews in the gospel, which then means that these natural enemies are to model the unity of the body of Christ by their deep love for one another. Thus the Jew/gentile relationship is an example of how relationships in the kingdom cannot be so easily conceived in terms of "equality" or "inequality" but are better understood in the context of inclusion into the one body of Christ through the grace of God.

## Women in the New Testament: Examples of Equality or Inclusion?

Two topics often seen as indicating egalitarianism are the acceptance of women as disciples[40] and the pouring out of the Spirit on both women and men at

39. Elliott, "Jesus Movement Was Not Egalitarian," 183.

40. E.g., see Spencer, who laments, "Why are some churches not following the example of Jesus? Sometimes today the church and academia are not instructing women as disciples, not

Pentecost.[41] Regardless of whether one concludes that "equality" is implied in these instances, our examination will show that both actions illustrate larger and more fundamental kingdom goals related to gender and the unity of the new inclusive community.

### *Women as Disciples*

To be a disciple of Jesus is to be a follower. The Greek term for disciple is *mathētēs*, which means "learner" or "student."[42] In the New Testament, disciples were those who responded to Jesus's command to follow him. Michael Wilkins notes two essential prerequisites for disciples: "paying the cost and committing themselves to the cause."[43] The teacher-disciple relationship required both learning the content and living out the teaching, in other words, a "total personal demand."[44] Thus, while the crowds might have physically followed him and been amazed at Jesus's teaching (e.g., Matt. 7:28) and come to him for miracles (e.g., Matt. 15:29–31), only those who obeyed his call to follow and serve him as Lord were disciples.[45]

The most famous disciples, of course, were the twelve apostles. Luke records that Jesus picked them from a larger group of disciples (Luke 6:13, 17). Matthew also refers to other disciples outside this core group (Matt. 8:21; 27:57; also 10:24–25, 42).

Women were part of this larger group that followed Jesus. One of the most remarkable features of the Gospels is the way in which women are portrayed as disciples. It would have been unusual in antiquity for women to be disciples of a great master, and the reaction by Jesus's own male disciples to the Samaritan woman reflected this attitude.[46] However, women appear significantly in this role. Mary Magdalene, Susanna, and Joanna the wife of Chuza (Herod's steward) along with "many others" accompanied Jesus and

---

listening to their spiritual discernment and not treating them equally as colaborers" ("Jesus' Treatment of Women," 141).

41. E.g., Bilezikian, *Beyond Sex Roles*, 122–25.

42. Kvalbein, "'Go Therefore, and Make Disciples,'" 49.

43. Wilkins, "Disciples," 177.

44. Meye, *Jesus and the Twelve*, 97.

45. Wilkins, "Disciples," 177.

46. Wilkins, *Following the Master*, 128–29. As Osborne recounts, "The basic scene [in Luke 8:1–3] is antithetical to Jewish mores; women never accompanied a rabbi and his band of disciples" ("Women in Jesus' Ministry," 280). Witherington notes that a woman could not be a disciple of a rabbi unless that person was her husband or master who was willing to teach her (*Women in the Ministry*, 117).

the Twelve on a preaching tour of Galilee, contributing to their support out of their own resources (Luke 8:1–3).[47]

Luke's use of "with him" terminology (*syn autō*) for the women is used in his Gospel to indicate discipleship (Luke 8:38; 9:18; 22:56).[48] Luke describes the women as being "with him," using what may be a technical phrase for discipleship (Luke 8:38; 9:18; 22:56).[49] Also his casual use of the feminine form of the word for disciple (*mathētria*) in reference to Tabitha in Acts 9:36 reflects a common understanding that the women believers were thought of as "disciples."[50] Mark's description of the women as "following" (*akoloutheō*) him also implies discipleship.[51]

Mary, the sister of Martha and Lazarus, is probably the most prominent example of a female disciple. In Luke 10:38–42 Jesus visits the home of Martha and Mary. Martha busies herself with preparations for a meal and asks Jesus to tell her sister Mary to help her. Jesus responds that "only one thing is necessary" and that Mary, who had been seated at Jesus's feet, "listening to His word," has chosen "the good part." Ben Witherington III notes that "to sit at the feet of" in some contexts means "to be a disciple of."[52] Luke similarly describes Paul as a disciple "at the feet of Gamaliel" (Acts 22:3).[53] In choosing to listen to Jesus, Mary demonstrates the proper action of a disciple: response to God's word.[54] In contrast Martha is one who is concerned with the "worries and riches and pleasures of this life" (Luke 8:14).[55]

Jesus's actions and words are a significant statement about the acceptance of women in the kingdom of God. Women were not traditionally disciples of a rabbi, and it would be unheard of for a rabbi to come into a woman's house

47. Some (e.g., Witherington, *Women in the Ministry*, 117) say that Jesus shows his high regard for women and his willingness to break social barriers in having the women accompany him, since it could have been scandalous to have female traveling companions. However, others (e.g., Wilkins, "Women in the Teaching," 103) have also noted that the Gospels give no indication of any criticism that accompanied these women who traveled with the group, perhaps reflecting a greater freedom in the Judaism of the day for women to travel with and join men in religious activities than is sometimes thought.

48. Wilkins, "Disciples," 178.

49. Brown, *Apostasy and Perseverance*, 83; Wilkins, *Following the Master*, 128.

50. Wilkins, "Disciples," 178.

51. C. Evans, *Mark 8:27–16:20*, 511.

52. Witherington, *Women in the Ministry*, 101.

53. Osborne, "Women in Jesus' Ministry," 281.

54. Bock, *Luke*, 1:1042.

55. Nolland, *Luke*, 2:606.

and teach her specifically.[56] Jesus also makes Mary the subject of his statement that such discipleship is the only "necessary" thing, taking precedence even over traditional roles.[57] Luke is telling his audience that Mary is a disciple and that her example is to be imitated.[58]

However, there are some critical elements that indicate another dimension of the portrayal of female disciples. Not only were women accepted and presented as exemplary disciples, but in a surprising reversal, they are even portrayed as being *more* faithful than the Twelve. All of the Twelve, with the exception of the beloved disciple, abandon Jesus at the critical final events of his earthly life. When Jesus is arrested, the disciples flee (Matt. 26:56; Mark 14:50). After the crucifixion they are in hiding because of "fear of the Jews" (John 20:19). Unexpectedly it is the women disciples who are portrayed positively. All four Gospels mention the presence of women at the crucifixion, including his mother and the women who had followed him from Galilee (Matt. 27:55–56; Mark 15:40; Luke 23:49; John 19:25–27). The Synoptic Gospels further record that some of the women were present when Joseph of Arimathea buried Jesus (Matt. 27:57–61; Mark 15:45–47; Luke 23:50–55), and they are the first to visit the tomb (Matt. 28:1; Mark 16:1; Luke 24:1; John 20:1).

In being the first disciples to return to the tomb, they become the first witnesses of the resurrection, as mentioned above.[59] Some have observed that women were not considered reliable witnesses.[60] According to rabbinic tradition, women were flighty and inferior,[61] and Josephus says that women's testimony should not be admitted "because of the levity and temerity of their

56. Witherington, *Women in the Ministry*, 101; Jewett, *Man as Male and Female*, 99.

57. Witherington also comments that Jesus is neither attacking these traditional roles nor devaluing Martha's hospitality but saying rather that if one's primary task is to be a disciple, other roles must be seen in this larger context (*Women in the Ministry*, 101). Kvalbein notes that Martha is corrected not for "worldly worries" but for "neglecting the instruction of Jesus as rabbi" ("Go Therefore, and Make Disciples," 50).

58. Witherington, *Women in the Ministry*, 101.

59. At the end the women too "fail" in their discipleship. Osborne notes that their failure to tell the disciples of Jesus's resurrection in Mark 16:8 parallels Peter's denial of Jesus in Mark 14 ("Women in Jesus' Ministry," 270). Malbon comments that since they look on "from a distance" in Mark 15:40, they are portrayed as "fallible." Nonetheless, overall they are still seen more favorably than the male disciples, who desert Jesus. Malbon summarizes, "Minimal emphasis is placed on their fallibility as followers in comparison with the crowd and especially the disciples" ("Fallible Followers," 43–46).

60. E.g., Jeremias, *Jerusalem*, 374–75; Borland, "Women in the Life," 119.

61. Witherington, *Women in the Ministry*, 117.

sex."[62] However, this view has been challenged lately, with some arguing that on many occasions such testimony would be accepted.[63]

The revelation to the women may exemplify the reversal of the old order not so much in terms of the validity of the women's testimony as in the implications of their social status. The presence of women at the crucifixion and then the empty tomb demonstrates a reversal of expectations because of women's lower status.[64] The structure of Jewish society was strongly masculine,[65] and that society held a low view of women.[66] As Elizabeth Malbon observes, the presence of the women at the crucifixion, along with the centurion, illustrates the reversal of insiders and outsiders and thus how the "first will be last, and the last, first" (Mark 10:31). "From the first-century Jewish and Jewish-Christian point of view, one could hardly be more of an outsider to the central dramas of religious faith and practice than a Roman centurion—or a woman!"[67]

Furthermore, the women's unique role as initial recipients of cherished testimony was an additional challenge to the old, male-oriented order. Richard Bauckham explains:

> It may be not so much their supposed unreliability as witnesses or their susceptibility to delusion in religious matters, but something even dearer to patriarchal religious assumptions: the priority of men in God's dealings with the world. In these stories, women are given priority by God as recipients of revelation and thereby the role of mediators of that revelation to men. Is this not part of the eschatological reversal of status, in which God makes the last first and the first last, so that no one might boast before God?[68]

In this way God challenges the world's assumptions to show his sovereignty. As a result, to focus on arguing about the implications of women's equality as disciples is to miss these other, and perhaps more significant, aspects of the portrayal of women in Jesus's ministry, which testifies to the inclusive

62. Josephus, *Ant.* 4.219.

63. E.g., Ilan, *Jewish Women*, 165–66. Witherington notes that among the rabbis there was mixed opinion regarding a woman's word of witness, vow, or oath. If a woman was not under the authority of her father or husband, her vows were considered as valid as a man's. He concludes, "A woman's vow or oath generally was accepted, and . . . her word carried more weight than that of Gentiles or slaves in some cases" (*Women in the Ministry*, 9).

64. Malbon, "Fallible Followers," 43.

65. Stendahl, *Bible and the Role of Women*, 27.

66. Witherington, *Women in the Ministry*, 10.

67. Malbon, "Fallible Followers," 42.

68. Bauckham, *Gospel Women*, 269.

community and the reversal of worldly evaluations in God's kingdom. The implications of the kingdom must first be understood according to the larger scheme of what God is doing in the world and how this relates to his purposes for people to understand their true position and so to glorify and worship him.

In sum, women can be disciples, and thus like men are called to learn and to follow their teacher. The principal distinction in regard to discipleship is not male versus female but responding to the gospel versus rejecting the gospel and being concerned with the affairs of the present life. As a result, there is a certain "equality" in that gender is not the primary qualification for discipleship.

At the same time, the inclusion of women as disciples taught additional and perhaps more foundational values of the kingdom. The theme of the inclusion of the outsider and the application of God's reversals challenge traditional categories. The significance of women disciples goes even beyond "equality" and points to the nature of the kingdom built on God's power and supernatural ways.

### *Women, Ministry, and Acts 2*

In Acts 2 the Holy Spirit comes upon the disciples in fulfillment of Jesus's promise (Acts 1:5; Luke 24:49) and Joel's prophecy (Joel 2:28–32). This event is notable in numerous ways, not the least of which is the universality of the pouring out of the Spirit on all, eclipsing issues of age, gender, and social status (Acts 2:17–18, 39).

Although it has been argued that the reception of the prophetic call by both women and men indicates that the "highest levels of ministry" are now open to women,[69] it is doubtful that this is the explicit purpose of the passage. Prophets certainly exhibited leadership as those who spoke for God as recipients and proclaimers of revelation. But it was still left to the church authorities, such as the elders, to confirm the message and then take action, as seen in Acts 15:28 and 21:10–14.[70] First John 4:1–3 shows that prophecies must be in line with the accepted tradition, so their words are to be tested because of the danger of false prophets. David Aune summarizes:

> Prophets were regarded as leaders only insofar as their messages were accepted as divinely inspired and authoritative articulations of the will of God. Individual prophets were not valued for their natural skills and abilities (like Christian

69. Bilezikian, *Beyond Sex Roles*, 124.
70. Aune, *Prophecy in Early Christianity*, 204–5.

> teachers), or for their age, wisdom and moral leadership (like bishops, presbyters, and deacons), but solely for their prophetic gifts.[71]

While prophets could claim a definite type of authority, their contribution still had to be validated by those who were given responsibility for the overall well-being of the congregation.

Furthermore, the prophesying of both daughters and sons does not reflect a new openness to women in a ministry that was previously closed to them, since Old Testament women such as Huldah and Deborah prophesied. Peter's main point is not that a gender barrier has been broken, because no such barrier in this regard seems to have existed in the first place. If there is a new functional equality in the New Testament, it cannot be proven from this passage. However, it is still a significant statement on the work of God in the new era in regard to gender.

In the Old Testament the Spirit of the Lord came upon people for specific tasks (e.g., Exod. 31:2–5; Num. 11:25–26; Judg. 6:34; 1 Sam. 10:10). Joel and then Peter affirm that in the last days, which are now here because of Christ, the Spirit will come upon all people as opposed to a chosen few. In addition, the Spirit will indwell God's people, rather than representing a temporary empowering for a particular work.

The coming of the Spirit, therefore, makes an important statement about the ministry of women in the larger context of the universality of ministry for all believers. The Holy Spirit will come upon all, and women are included along with men, as well as the young and the old and even slaves.[72] As Witherington summarizes, "In general the point of the Joel passage is that not just some but all of God's people from the least to the greatest will have the Spirit and be equipped for witness or service with various gifts in the eschatological age ushered in by Jesus."[73] In evaluating the significance of the gifting of prophecy in Acts 2, we must consider the greater context of God's eschatological purposes.

This work of the Spirit in Acts 2 is intimately connected with the inauguration of the new age. Joel's prophecy referred to the Day of the Lord, or the day of judgment. By virtue of his death and resurrection, Christ is Lord, and his lordship includes his role as Judge at the consummation of the age.[74]

71. Ibid., 211.

72. Keener (*Acts*, 1:882) notes that Joel's prophecy further reflects the way in which Luke "balances" men and women in this gift in his Gospel (e.g., Luke 2:25–27, 36; Acts 21:9).

73. Witherington and Hyatt, *Paul's Letter to the Romans*, 141.

74. Dodd, *Apostolic Preaching*, 13.

As a result, Joel's announcement highlights the redemption of God's people. The signs in heaven and on earth show the decisiveness of the times and the coming judgment (Isa. 13:6, 9; Ezek. 30:3; Zeph. 1:14–15), and Joel's prophecy gives hope that those who call on the name of the Lord will be saved (Acts 2:21; Joel 2:32).[75]

This eschatology is further seen in Peter's substitution of "in the last days" (Acts 2:17) for Joel's "afterward." Pentecost marks the beginning of the last days and starts the age of the Spirit.[76] As Richard Patterson and Andrew Hill note, as one of the three major Jewish feasts, Pentecost was prophetic of the Messianic redemption. Pentecost symbolized Israel's thankfulness both for the firstfruits of the grain harvest and the anticipation of its culmination in the fall. Consequently, it also marked the beginning of the church and "the inauguration of an era during which the souls of all people will be gathered in with great fullness through the gospel proclamation (cf. Rom. 11:13–24; 1 Cor. 15:20–23)."[77]

The work of the Spirit at Pentecost begins the fulfillment of a specific eschatological goal—the ingathering of God's people into the kingdom. Joel prophesied of the day when God would pour out his Spirit, and the world would hear the gospel.[78] Pentecost indicates the start of the last days, which would be a time of intense missionary activity.[79] As the proclamation moves from Jerusalem to the ends of the earth, the empowerment of the Spirit enables the disciples to testify to all the nations (Acts 1:8).

As the Old Testament prophets witnessed to God's word, so also are the believers enabled by the Spirit to testify to the knowledge of God in Christ.[80] The fulfillment of Joel's oracle focuses on prophecy, since "visions" and "dreams"

75. Larkin, *Acts*, 54.

76. Patterson and Hill, *Minor Prophets*, 135.

77. Passover was a reminder of Israel's liberation and looked to the Messiah's redemption, accomplished in Christ's death and resurrection. The Festival of Shelters at the end of the year marked Israel's rest in God, who had supplied the nation's needs, and so looked to the final rest in the messianic age (Patterson and Hill, *Minor Prophets*, 135–36).

78. C. Evans, "Prophetic Setting," 224.

79. Patterson and Hill, *Minor Prophets*, 134:

> It is no wonder, then, that the apostle Peter would be led to this text in his address on Pentecost (Acts 2), the occasion of the historical outworking of the promise of the outpoured Holy Spirit. Peter and the apostles saw in this event, which initiated the New Testament church, the beginning of those last days that would witness God's Holy Spirit at work, not only among the Jewish remnant but among all who would believe. It would be a time of increased missionary activity. For whoever calls upon the Lord in believing faith will be saved (Rom. 10:13).

80. Larkin, *Acts*, 54.

(Acts 2:17) were considered prophetic activities in the Old Testament.[81] Peter emphasizes the importance of this type of activity by adding "and they shall prophesy" (Acts 2:18), which was not part of Joel's original message. In this way the fulfillment of Joel's prophecy testifies to the empowerment of all of God's people for the purpose of the proclamation of the gospel.

The work of the Spirit also goes beyond proclamation. As David Peterson points out, dreams and visions are rare in the New Testament, and only a few people in Acts are specifically described as prophets (e.g., 11:27; 13:1; 15:32; 21:10). Therefore, Joel's prophecy may also be fulfilled in a more general way among believers. Peterson concludes that it is a way of describing "Spirit-directed ministry" and includes the creation of new communities that are "enabled to enjoy the messianic salvation and minister its benefits, both inside and outside their fellowship (cf. 2:41–47; 4:31–37; 8:14–17; 10:44–48; 11:14–18; 15:8; 19:1–7)."[82] We see this enablement in Paul's letters. For example, by the Spirit the believers are able to put "to death the deeds of the body" (Rom. 8:13) and produce "the fruit of the Spirit" (Gal. 5:22–23).

Thus Acts 2 speaks of Jesus's promised giving of the Spirit to his followers. Women are "equally" included in the outpouring of the gift of prophecy and the reception of the empowering Spirit. However, whether this carries further implications for equality is not the point of the passage. Instead, "inclusion" better captures the implications of Pentecost since it reflects the focus on participation of all in the blessings and mission of the kingdom rather than a distribution of rights or privileges.

## Conclusion

Complementarians hold that men and women are spiritually equal and are equally created in God's image, but with some functional differences.[83] In contrast, egalitarians believe that their equal standing before God results in equal opportunity for church ministry and shared authority in marriage.[84] However, we have tried to argue that, rather than attempting to determine what kind of equality is present, a more fruitful approach may be trying to see how the church is characterized by a larger concern that may then impact how we view equality.

81. Peterson, *Acts of the Apostles*, 141. Peterson notes that they are presented as "subsets" of prophesying.

82. Ibid., 142.

83. E.g., Saucy and TenElshof, "Conclusion," 340; Ortlund, "Male-Female Equality," 95, 99.

84. E.g., Groothuis, *Good News for Women*, 19.

The church is inclusive and in this way manifests the kingdom through the love and acceptance of all its members, despite any natural hostility they would otherwise have toward one another. Inclusion does not preclude rights, but as an orienting perspective it draws attention to participation in the kingdom and the redefinition of relationships within the community. It demonstrates kingdom values in the way the church manifests its holiness in love and unity. Whereas "equality" and "rights" focus on the individual benefit of the members, "inclusion" speaks of God's act of taking groups separated by natural hostility and suspicion toward one another and uniting them as one body and one holy temple whose members love one another as empowered by the Spirit. In this context it is not the obtaining of rights but rather the giving up of rights that provides a critical component for promoting cohesion and intimacy among the members. Furthermore, in the inclusive community there may still be hierarchies, although they are understood according to kingdom paradoxes. In the next chapter, we will see how the concept of "reversal" furthers our understanding of love and unity in the kingdom as it provides the transforming perspective on the "hierarchies" related to authority and leadership.

# 6

# Ministry, Part 2

## *Rethinking Authority and Leadership in the Body of Christ*

A primary aspect of the complementarian position is that men have a special role in the church and home generally defined according to "authority" and "leadership." However, since the New Testament turns ideas of power and identity upside down, we should consider carefully the impact of kingdom ideas such as unity, love, and reversal.

Many complementarians have noted that Jesus challenged conventional notions of power and have made "servant leadership" one of their main tenets. Even so, leadership and often authority are generally seen as the predominant ideas, and servanthood is then the attitude or manner in which this leadership is carried out—that is, leadership that is done in the manner of a servant. For example, in discussing the concept of authority, one scholar correctly points out that Jesus's words in Mark 10:42–45 do not mean that "servant leadership" should be set in opposition to or that it negates authority since Jesus had both. The subsequent point is that leaders (e.g., elders) "should use authority with a servant heart."[1] Thus both authority and servanthood are

1. Grudem, *Countering the Claims*, 97.

affirmed, but the actual outworking suggests that authority is the foundation and servant is the modifier.

Whether this type of primary emphasis on authority is warranted is worth examining. The objection is not with authority itself. Rather the problem lies in the prominence of authority as a critical defining point for the complementarian position as it places an undue focus on an aspect that has been critiqued and redefined in the New Testament. We must ask whether kingdom values have been properly integrated into the complementarian position and whether more transcendent values can be taken more fully into account. As a result, we will also demonstrate that "servant leadership" as it is commonly understood by complementarians does not sufficiently capture the New Testament understanding of leadership, and then we will present some possible ways of expanding the discussion.

## Considering Authority and Leadership

Both sides agree that "authority" is a legitimate concept in the New Testament.[2] The New Testament makes numerous references to Jesus's authority (e.g., Matt. 7:29; 9:6, 8). Authority is also seen in reference to governments (e.g., Rom. 13:1), individuals (e.g., 1 Cor. 7:4), and congregations (e.g., Titus 2:15).[3] Paul boldly speaks of and uses his apostolic authority (e.g., 1 Cor. 4:21; 2 Cor. 13:10; Gal. 1:1).

Within the congregations themselves, elders were the main locus of authority on a daily basis. First Peter 5:1–5 exhorts the elders to "shepherd the flock of God among you, exercising oversight [*episkopountes*]" over those "allotted to your charge," who are likely the members of a house church.[4] As Jobes notes, such oversight was necessary for the nurture and protection of a church undergoing persecution. She says, "By encouraging the elders to shepherd and the others to submit to that leadership, Peter underscores the importance of responsible church structure for seeing the Christian community

2. E.g., for an egalitarian view, see Liefeld, "Nature of Authority."

3. Regardless of whether one interprets 1 Tim. 2:12 and 1 Cor. 11:10 as supporting a complementarian or an egalitarian view, the underlying assumption of both passages is the validity of authority in a community setting, since the passages raise questions of what kind of authority is appropriate and necessary, not whether authority itself is a legitimate concept.

4. Davids, *First Epistle of Peter*, 180. The shepherd metaphor appears in the Old Testament (Isa. 56:11; Jer. 23:4; 50:6; Nah. 3:18; Zech. 10:3; Ezek. 34), and Jesus presents himself as the "Good Shepherd" (John 10:2–16). See Ferguson, *Church of Christ*, 321. Jobes notes the connection between shepherding and overseeing in Ezek. 34:11–13 in the Septuagint and concludes that Peter may be deliberately alluding to Ezekiel here in his use of similar language in 1 Pet. 5:2 (*1 Peter*, 199).

safely through the fiery ordeal of testing."[5] The churches are to "obey" those who "keep watch" over their souls (Heb. 13:17).

For the complementarian position, the distinction between the genders is often defined primarily according to male authority and leadership and female submission. For example, in one book the section "God's Order in Creation" contains three chapters to describe this order: (1) "The Created Order," (2) "Born Cursed," and (3) "Authority and Submission."[6] Others argue that "the New Testament shows that the basic relationships of life fit together in terms of authority and compliance."[7] These forms and applications may vary as, for instance, parents can require obedience from their children, governments can make regulatory laws, the church follows its servant-leaders, and wives are to submit to the sacrificial headship of their husbands.[8] According to one definition of masculinity, "AT THE HEART OF MATURE MASCULINITY IS A SENSE OF BENEVOLENT RESPONSIBILITY TO LEAD, PROVIDE FOR AND PROTECT WOMEN IN WAYS APPROPRIATE TO A MAN'S DIFFERING RELATIONSHIPS."[9] In the authors' more extended description of the meaning "to lead," they refer to "sacrifice for the good of women" and refer to Paul's admonition in Eph. 5:23 for husbands to love their wives, but again, it is descriptive and takes a more secondary place in defining "biblical manhood."[10]

We must ask whether these concepts necessitate such a dominant position in defining the *nature* of the debate and the respective positions and whether others might merit more prominent consideration. To this end we will examine the impact of bringing the notion of "servant" into the discussion of leadership and explore implications in terms of additional kingdom concepts.

## Leadership in the New Testament

The concept of leadership provides a broader way to understand the unique male role in the complementarian position, so the question then is what

5. Jobes, *1 Peter*, 299. Goppelt describes the general need for such leadership: "The high demands placed on the local congregation created the necessity . . . of a type of service that attended to the individual and restored those beset by inner conflict and those who had gone astray" (*Commentary on I Peter*, 344).

6. Kassian, *Women, Creation and the Fall.*

7. Piper and Grudem, *Fifty Crucial Questions*, 42.

8. Ibid., 42–43.

9. Piper and Grudem, "Vision of Biblical Complementarity," 35, emphasis original.

10. Ibid., 38.

leadership entails. The New Testament often depicts leadership, including its relationship to authority, in a way that runs counter to traditional understandings. Thus we will need to investigate how this "reversal" fits in with the nature and purpose of kingdom leadership.

Since the common term for Christian leadership is currently "servant leadership," we will consider what it meant to be a servant in the New Testament world. In addition, we will examine the use of "slave" language as it is also used in reference to leadership and is closely related to the idea of servanthood. Being a "servant" does more than modify or explain the type of "leadership" or "authority." The low status of a servant would be paradoxical when considered as the status of a leader. It would be a nonsensical concept according to views of hierarchy and order in antiquity and the associated expectations of honor.

We will show how the paradoxical combination of servant/slave and leader is intimately tied into the larger New Testament ideas of sacrifice, unity, and love. Consequently, these larger kingdom goals are more foundational for understanding New Testament leadership than authority. This does not preclude the possibility of a unique male "authority" but rather means that any understanding of authority and leadership must be integrated within these more fundamental kingdom concepts.

### *Rethinking Servant Leadership*

Being a servant does not negate leadership, as complementarians rightly note, but their correct relationship to each other is critical. Is there a "biblical balance" between the two[11] or some other way to conceive of their connection? The Gospels contain Jesus's well-known pronouncement about leaders. As noted earlier, in Matt. 20:20–28 Jesus tells the disciples that, in contrast to the rulers of the gentiles who "lord it over" others and "exercise authority over them," those who wish to be "great" should instead be a "servant" (*diakonos*), just as Jesus came to serve and to give his life for many.

The concept of authority is set in direct contrast to serving. Again this does not mean that Jesus was against the notion of authority. As Wilkins notes, to pursue positions of power and rule as a means of acquiring significance would be natural in the disciples' environment under Roman occupation. However, Jesus reverses conceptions of status by declaring that service is precisely what leads to being great in his community.[12]

11. Piper and Grudem, *Fifty Crucial Questions*, 21.
12. Wilkins, *Matthew*, 669.

In this context, "servant" would seem to do more than qualify "leadership." Instead it provides an essential component so that one must be a servant *before* one can be a leader. In other words Christ indicates that servanthood is a prerequisite for being a leader. Thus, rather than considering how servanthood modifies a type of leadership, it may be better to ask how servanthood forms a necessary basis for leadership, even authority, and how a kingdom perspective of reversal explains this paradoxical notion.

### *Leaders as Servants*

It will be helpful to begin by asking, Why should leaders be servants? While the answer may seem obvious ("because Christ was a servant"), there may be additional answers that will aid us in understanding the importance of being a servant in the kingdom. Christ's servanthood illustrates a critical way in which the kingdom of God confronts the so-called wisdom of the world, by a reversal in which God works through weakness rather than worldly strength. It is also the means by which the community becomes united, a key goal in the New Testament. In this way servanthood needs to be understood according to larger kingdom themes, including ones related to the corporate body.

First Corinthians provides a valuable look into Paul's concept of leadership as servanthood. One of the situations prompting the letter appears to be a quarrel among the Corinthians over their alignment with different leaders (1 Cor. 1:10–17). In response, Paul seeks to correct their perspective about the leaders themselves and how the Corinthians should view them. In the Corinthians' social situation, it would have been common to align themselves with a particular leader in order to benefit from that person's reputation.[13] However, Paul seeks to correct their notion of the importance of leaders by teaching the Corinthians how to assess leaders according to the cross in the eschatological age. Thus he tells them, "What then is Apollos? And what is Paul? Servants [*diakonoi*] through whom you believed, even as the Lord gave opportunity to each one" (1 Cor. 3:5) and then, "Let a man regard us in this manner, as servants [*hypēretai*] of Christ and stewards [*oikonomoi*] of the mysteries of God" (1 Cor. 4:1). The focus is not on themselves as leaders but on the one on whose behalf they serve and proclaim the gospel.

In 1 Cor. 1:12 Paul exhorts them not to be divided by attaching themselves to different leaders as patrons. As Andrew Clarke explains, it was common

13. Clarke describes the common practice of a young man establishing his reputation by attaching himself to someone of acknowledged reputation (*Secular and Christian Leadership*, 93).

in Greco-Roman society for the socially inferior person to be dependent on someone of higher status, and the socially superior man sought to enhance his status by having a large following of such adherents.[14] However, Paul inverts the status implications of the apostles. He utilizes menial images to describe himself and Apollos.[15] Paul lowers their status by saying they are merely fieldworkers performing manual labor (1 Cor. 3:6–8).[16] He also refers to manual labor in his use of the building metaphor, in which he is the one who lays the foundation of Jesus Christ while someone else builds upon it (1 Cor. 3:10–13). When Paul calls them *diakonoi*, he directly confronts the Corinthians' ideas that they are high-status patron figures.[17] He also says that rather than the Corinthians being attached to the apostles as leaders, the apostles are actually the ones who, as servants, belong to them (1 Cor. 3:21–23).

Furthermore, he makes clear that the emphasis is not on Paul and Apollos but on God, the source of growth (1 Cor. 3:6) and the one whom they serve. In 1 Cor. 3:5 he uses *ti* instead of the more personal *tis*. He asks, "What is Paul?" or "What then is Apollos?" rather than "Who is Paul?" and "Who is Apollos?" thus drawing attention to the role and task of the servants rather than the servants themselves.[18]

The terms Paul uses to describe himself and Apollos are relevant as well. John N. Collins argues that the root idea behind *diakonos* does not signify humility as much as service done for someone else.[19] In 1 Cor. 4:1–2, Paul calls them *hypēretai* of Christ and *oikonomoi* of the mysteries of God. The former term refers to those who take orders from someone else and whose significance is in connection with his or her master.[20] In the context of the household, an *oikonomos* was a slave who was responsible for overseeing the household, including other slaves.[21] As such, *oikonomoi* had to follow the master's instructions and were continually aware of their dependence and need to give an accounting.[22] In various ways Paul sends the message that the attention should be given not to the apostles but to the one who appointed them and the task for which they have been commissioned.

14. Ibid., 112.
15. Ibid., 119.
16. Garland, *1 Corinthians*, 111.
17. Clarke, *Secular and Christian Leadership*, 119–20.
18. Ibid., 119.
19. J. Collins, *Diakonia*, 194.
20. Garland, *1 Corinthians*, 125.
21. R. Collins, *First Corinthians*, 168.
22. Garland, *1 Corinthians*, 125–26.

Thus, in contrast to the Corinthians' emphasis on the status of the apostles and their desire to associate themselves with someone as their patron, Paul reverses the situation by lowering the apostles' status and saying that leaders actually belong to them and that the Corinthians should look to God, the ultimate source, rather than the apostles. Indeed, instead of being regarded as those with high status, the apostles are a "spectacle to the world," "the scum of the world," and the "dregs of all things" (1 Cor. 4:9–13). Rather than enjoying the privileges of a superior position, they are "without honor," "hungry and thirsty," "poorly clothed," "roughly treated," "homeless," "reviled," and "persecuted" (1 Cor. 4:10–12). Like Christ, they are "fools" and "weak" in the eyes of the world (v. 10), but according to God they are workers who help to build and care for his holy temple (1 Cor. 3:9–17).

Paul is not simply saying that they are leaders who have the attitude of a servant. He asserts that as servants they are the opposite of what the world esteems in status, privilege, and other worldly considerations when it considers those in their position. They are also merely those who have been tasked by a master, to whom they are responsible. As a result, their worth and identity come not from their own abilities but solely from God. The Corinthians should therefore esteem God rather than Paul and Apollos, who are merely the help God uses to accomplish his purposes. The apostles may be leaders with authority, but they are at the same time examples of the confounding ways in which God works through humility and weakness.

### *Leaders as Slaves*

Jesus also speaks of slavery when discussing authority and leadership, saying, "Whoever wishes to be first among you shall be your slave [*doulos*]" (Matt. 20:27–28; also Mark 10:44–45). *Diakonos* and *doulos* are closely associated, although *diakonos* is the broader term. A *doulos* is automatically a *diakonos*, but not every *diakonos* is a *doulos*.[23] Thus it is important to examine the specific contribution that slavery makes to our understanding of leadership.

The significance of Jesus's washing of the disciples' feet lay in that it was a task generally reserved for slaves, especially gentile slaves.[24] His act is an example of extreme humility,[25] but what also makes it striking is the way in

23. M. Harris, *Slave of Christ*, 179.

24. Combes, *Metaphor of Slavery*, 132.

25. As Morris notes, Jesus performs the task as an example to the disciples to be willing to perform the "lowliest service" for one another (*Gospel according to John*, 551).

which he reverses the expected roles since it is the disciples' "Teacher and Lord" (John 13:13–14) who washes their feet. As D. A. Carson explains, the disciples' shock is "their response to finding their sense of the fitness of things shattered" in Jesus's reversal of traditional roles.[26]

Paul calls himself a slave of Christ (e.g., Rom. 1:1; Gal. 1:10), but he is also a slave to all people in order to win them to the gospel (1 Cor. 9:19). Even more he describes his apostolic role to the Corinthians as being their *doulos* (2 Cor. 4:5).

Understanding leadership as slavery becomes especially relevant in light of the intense stratification of the New Testament world, where the evaluation of social relations revolved around status and honor. Peter Garnsey and Richard Saller describe the two and their relationship: "A Roman's status was based on the social estimation of his honour, the perception of those around him as to his prestige."[27] Consequently, honor was the most valued social commodity in the Roman world.[28] As Dio Chrysostom declares, "You will find that there is nothing else (besides honor), at least in the case of the great majority, that incites every man to despise danger, to endure toils, and to scorn the life of pleasure and ease" (*Or*. 31.17).[29]

The New Testament world was divided into various status groups, with each occupying a specific place along "the Roman hierarchy of honor."[30] Joseph Hellerman displays the hierarchy of status groups as follows:[31]

*Elites*
Senators
Equestrians
Decurions

*Non-elites*
Freeborn
Freedmen
Slaves

26. Carson, *Gospel according to John*, 462.
27. Garnsey and Saller, *Roman Empire*, 118.
28. Hellerman, *Embracing Shared Ministry*, 56.
29. And similarly, "However, this much is clear, that neither you nor any others, whether Greeks or barbarians, who are thought to have become great, advanced to glory and power for any other reason than because fortune gave to each in succession men who were jealous of honor and regarded their fame in after times as more precious than life" (*Or*. 31.20).
30. Hellerman, *Embracing Shared Ministry*, 26.
31. Ibid., 26–27.

The Romans had a highly stratified society, and their relations were characterized by a conspicuous social inequality. As a result, people were extremely conscious of their place in the order.[32] This high degree of social stratification meant that certain individuals had greater privileges with respect to power and status.[33] In this order, slaves were at the very bottom.[34]

Slavery also naturally connotes powerlessness and lack of freedom. Paul directly contrasts slavery with freedom in places such as 1 Cor. 9:19 and Rom. 6:20–22.[35] S. Scott Bartchy explains:

> As a slave, a human being was bodily and totally subjected to the practically unlimited power of an owner and the owner's heirs. As such, this slavery should be distinguished from other forms of exploitation of human labor or from dependence of any kind, financial or otherwise (e.g., day laborers, free gladiators, wagon drivers, contract workers, those paying off loans, and the like).[36]

Or as Carolyn Osiek states, "The power relationship is absolute: not only of one person over the production of the other, but over the other's self."[37] Slavery speaks of the opposite of personal power in one's relationship with others.

32. Ibid., 26.

33. Ibid., 52. As Clarke notes, "At all levels of community life people recognized and elevated the *status quo* whereby those of greater rank and social standing received due deference and honor" (Clarke, *Serve the Community*, 146–47).

34. Scholars have debated the social status of slaves. Bartchy, e.g., argues that slaves did not constitute a social class, so their individual honor and social status were dependent on their owner's status ("Slavery [Greco-Roman]," 6:66). However, as Hellerman notes, the ancients themselves, at least among the elites, had a more uniform assessment of slavery, especially when they considered legal status instead of the specific social location of an individual slave. In this regard, the Roman elite used this criterion to assign all slaves, regardless of wealth or relative power, to a single class situated unambiguously below all free persons (*Reconstructing Honor*, 138). Not even manumission could alleviate the dishonor associated with being a slave (Stegemann and Stegemann, *Jesus Movement*, 60).

35. "For though I am free from all men, I have made myself a slave to all, so that I may win more" (1 Cor. 9:19); "For when you were slaves of sin, you were free in regard to righteousness. . . . But now having been freed from sin and enslaved to God, you derive your benefit, resulting in sanctification, and the outcome, eternal life" (Rom. 6:20–22).

36. Bartchy, "Slaves and Slavery," 170.

37. Osiek, "Slavery," 174. This does not mean that individual slaves could not have authority or power in other contexts. They could be managers of large farms, households, or businesses, even sea captains and municipal officials. Since they were tied to their owner's status, they could even have power over freeborn people who had lower status than their owners (Bartchy, "Slaves and Slavery," 173–74). Their individual abilities, training, or position could give them influence and privileges that exceeded their legally defined status as slaves (Stegemann and Stegemann, *Jesus Movement*, 60, 88). However, they were still ultimately under the control of those who owned them.

To describe leaders as "slaves" had very important social connotations in terms of personal status and freedom. Dio Chrysostom proclaims, "Men desire above all things to be free and say that freedom is the greatest of blessings, while slavery is the most shameful and wretched of states" (*Or.* 14.1). Since the Roman hierarchy was closely aligned with the social value of honor,[38] it was expected that there would be a correspondence between the honor of an office and the social status of the officeholder.[39] Those at the top of the order were vigilant about guarding their social privileges.[40]

In this context, it is especially notable that Hellerman argues for seeing Christ's example in Phil. 2:6–11 as a reversal and subversion of the Roman *cursus* ideology. The *cursus honorum* was a sequence of offices or ladder of political advancement for the Roman senatorial class.[41] The goal was to ascend in status, and its ideology was replicated in various settings throughout the empire, such as the army and various religious cults.[42] However, Paul presents Christ not as following a prescribed course of ascending in status and offices but rather as descending in status by moving from his position and status with God to taking the form of a slave—who had the most dishonorable public status—to suffering an utterly shameful death on the cross, a punishment considered especially fitting for slaves[43] and regarded as "the most dishonorable experience imaginable."[44]

Although Christ could have rightfully used his status to dominate others and enjoy his privileges as God, he chose the opposite course and willingly endured extreme humiliation and served instead. Hellerman states, "In stark contrast to the values of the dominant culture, moreover, Paul's Christ surrenders his status willingly, and, most astoundingly, he ultimately receives the highest of honors at the hands of God himself, who thereby legitimates Christ's decidedly anti-Roman approach to power and status (vv. 9–11)."[45] Christ received these highest honors as he was vindicated by God, but they were preceded by earthly suffering and service. Paul presents Christ's example

38. Dio Chrysostom describes it as a "hierarchy of honors" (Hellerman, *Reconstructing Honor*, 53).

39. Ibid., 55.

40. Hellerman, *Embracing Shared Ministry*, 26.

41. Hellerman describes it as "the formalized sequence of public offices that marked out the prescribed social pilgrimage for aspiring senatorial aristocrats in Rome" (*Reconstructing Honor*, 1).

42. Ibid., 1, 56–62.

43. Hengel, *Cross*, 154.

44. Hellerman, *Reconstructing Honor*, 144–48.

45. Ibid., 2.

in a way that contradicts the basic model on which society was based. The redefinition of leadership as servanthood and slavery would have been viewed as directly challenging the present order, not simply modifying it.

Furthermore, for someone to act in contradiction to the expectations of their status was to introduce instability into the social order. As Dale Martin explains, "Everyone is much better off, according to benevolent patriarchal ideology, if people remain in their rightful places. Inferiors are happiest when they respect and follow those who are their natural superiors."[46] The order of the social body was a critical component of ancient life. However, the irony is that Paul views these actions as paradoxically leading to unity instead and the role of leaders in this way as critical for the body of Christ.

What we see, then, is a radical reversal in the way that status, power, and identity are to be perceived in the Christian community based on Christ's own sacrifice. Christ demonstrates not only service but also the way in which those with status are especially called upon to renounce their worldly privileges and rights and reverse the expectations of personal gain from their position. The end result of such actions is not the expected disorder and chaos but love and unity as Paul calls all believers, and leaders most of all, to imitate Christ in this way.

## The Role of Leaders and the Unity of the Body: The Power of Imitation

A significant contribution of leaders as servants/slaves lies in the example they set for others. When Peter objects to Jesus's washing his feet in John 13, Jesus answers that he has set an example for them. If he as their "Teacher and Lord" can do this for them, then they ought to do it for one another. Paul also regards setting an example as a critical component of his leadership. In 1 Corinthians he explicitly says that the Corinthians are to imitate his own example of being a servant, which is in turn an imitation of Christ's example (1 Cor. 4:16; 11:1). He presents Timothy as someone who has faithfully imitated Paul and will be able to remind them of his ways in Christ (1 Cor. 4:17).

Paul also appeals to his own example in Philippians. Hellerman argues that Paul applies and inverts his own *cursus honorum*, just as he does with Christ. In Phil. 3:5–6 he presents a list of Jewish honors (e.g., "circumcised [on] the eighth day, of the nation of Israel, of the tribe of Benjamin, a Hebrew born of Hebrews"), only to follow with a declaration that he considers all of these

46. D. Martin, *Slavery as Salvation*, 125. Elsewhere Martin notes, "Like the private body, the public body is a hierarchy," and "the body is hierarchically constituted and . . . illness or social disruption occurs when that hierarchy is disrupted" (*Corinthian Body*, 39–40).

things "as loss because of Christ" and strives instead to "gain Christ, and . . . be found in Him, not having a righteousness of [his] own derived from the Law, but that which is through faith in Christ" (Phil. 3:7–9).[47] Paul presents himself as an example to be followed, with Christ in Phil. 2 being the prior model.[48]

This then leads us to ask, Why should the congregation follow their leaders' example in this way? and Why is this such an important component of church leadership? In both Philippians and 1 Corinthians the reason for imitating Christ, and so Paul, is that their examples lead to unity, which we demonstrated earlier is a critical kingdom theme.

The context in which Paul presents the example of Christ's humility in Phil. 2:6–11 is a call for the Philippians to do the same for the sake of unity. Paul exhorts the Philippians to be "standing firm in one spirit, with one mind striving together for the faith of the gospel" (Phil. 1:27), and to be "of the same mind, maintaining the same love, united in spirit, intent on one purpose" (Phil. 2:1–2). They are to "regard one another as more important than [themselves]" (Phil. 2:3). Consequently, Paul calls them to have the mind of Christ (2:5) as exemplified in his lowering and sacrifice.

In 1 Cor. 1–4, Christ's example and Paul's apostolic servanthood are the basis for his argument against factionalism. Throughout the letter Paul points to his own example of not seeking the privileges of his position but rather demonstrating the willingness to suffer loss and to give up one's rights for the sake of another (e.g., 1 Cor. 8:13; 9:1–23). Love causes someone to focus on the benefit of others (1 Cor. 13). As a result, as mentioned previously, someone will seek the gift that edifies the entire church rather than oneself only (1 Cor. 14) or decide not to use his or her right for the sake of helping another believer (1 Cor. 8:13).

The irony is that this reversal of traditional expectations leads to unity. Rather than stability obtained by each part living according to its worldly status, unity is achieved by the self-sacrificial behavior of the entire body, and especially the high-status members. This then leads to a critical component of leadership for Paul. As the apostles follow the model of Christ, their lowering, self-sacrifice, suffering, and other-oriented concern and behavior set the example for others for the unity of the community. Their example is particularly powerful because, as leaders, they would be least expected to do so, just as the nature of Jesus's humility was shocking because of his ultimate status as God.

47. Hellerman, *Embracing Shared Ministry*, 76–77.
48. Oakes, *Philippians*, 103–4.

Leaders in the local church community are to do the same thing. Paul saw himself as an example for the leaders of local churches.[49] Peter says that the elders are to be examples of Christ's suffering on their behalf (1 Pet. 2:21) and humility (1 Pet. 5:5), rather than "lording it over those allotted to [their] charge" (1 Pet. 5:3).[50] As Peter identifies himself as the apostolic role model to the elders in 1 Pet. 5:1, the elders are to be examples to their flocks so that they might be like Christ to one another.[51]

This, of course, is not the only role of leaders, but it is a particularly vital one, especially if we are considering what it means for a leader to be a "servant." We should also note the result of viewing leaders as servants in this way. Leaders are not set apart from the community but rather are integrated into the community so that their example becomes replicated throughout the entire body. As Robert Saucy and Judith TenElshof describe, leadership takes place "*among* the people ('You are all brothers')" rather than being "hierarchical authority *over* them."[52] Subsequently, any notions of authority and leadership in the church must be understood in the larger context of this role and purpose of leaders.

Finally, we should note another aspect of kingdom reversal that is relevant to the discussion of authority and servant leadership, the idea that Christ's power is "perfected in weakness" (2 Cor. 12:8–10). As we have noted earlier, God's reversals make clear how accomplishments are the result of divine, not human, working. This concept becomes particularly apt when considering

49. Garland describes how Paul saw himself as an example for local leaders in 1 Corinthians: "The gist of Paul's argument is this: if they are to regard ministers such as Paul, Apollos, and Cephas as menial underlings who belong to them and as God's household managers whose chief duty is faithfulness, then they also need to regard their local leaders in the same way" (*1 Corinthians*, 126).

50. Michaels summarizes, "Here the contrast with 'lording it over your respective congregations' places the emphasis not on exemplary moral behavior in general but specifically on setting an example of humility and servanthood. . . . The elders are to be good leaders of their congregations precisely by being good servants, so that the members of the congregation will in turn become servants to each other" (*1 Peter*, 286).

51. In discussing the translation of *martys* in 1 Pet. 5:1 as "witness" rather than "eyewitness," Jobes describes the relationship between Christ, Peter, and the elders and their congregations:

> The apostle willingly embraces apostolic leadership of the church, making himself vulnerable to the same hostile forces that killed Jesus. Those who follow in the footsteps of Jesus (2:21) witness to the truth of his message as they share in the suffering of rejection he experienced. This construal of *martys* coheres well with the major theme of 1 Peter: all believers are called to suffer as necessary for their faithfulness to Christ. Here Peter is the apostolic role model for his fellow elders, who are being called upon in turn to be role models (5:3) for all in the Christian community. (*1 Peter*, 302)

52. Saucy and TenElshof, "Complementary Model," 323.

the role of leaders, since in Paul's day they were presumably the ones who exhibited personal superiority.[53]

In addition to the passages from 1 Corinthians, Paul in 2 Corinthians associates his servanthood as taking place "in much endurance, in afflictions, in hardships, in distresses, in beating, in imprisonments, in tumults, in labors, in sleeplessness, in hunger" (2 Cor. 6:4–5). He later validates his status as an exemplary servant of Christ by enumerating the following qualifications:

> In far more labors, in far more imprisonments, [I was] beaten times without number, often in danger of death. Five times I received from the Jews thirty-nine lashes. Three times I was beaten with rods, once I was stoned, three times I was shipwrecked, a night and a day I have spent in the deep. I have been on frequent journeys, in dangers from rivers, dangers from robbers, dangers from my countrymen, dangers from the Gentiles, dangers in the city, dangers in the wilderness, dangers on the sea, dangers among false brethren; I have been in labor and hardship, through many sleepless nights, in hunger and thirst, often without food, in cold and exposure. (2 Cor. 11:23–27)

However, God strengthens Paul and his coworkers in their hardships so that they are "afflicted in every way, but not crushed; perplexed, but not despairing." The purpose of their suffering and endurance is to carry about "in the body the dying of Jesus, so that the life of Jesus also may be manifested in [their] body" (2 Cor. 4:8–10). The passage contrasts their vulnerability with God's sustaining power.[54]

For Paul the new age is based on the cross, which means that a believer lives like Christ, that is, sacrificially and with a willingness to suffer and serve. In the believer's so acknowledging and living according to human weakness, the power of God is made evident. Paul answers those who criticized his human "weaknesses," including his afflictions, by proclaiming that God has given "this treasure in earthen vessels, so that the surpassing greatness of the power will be of God and not from ourselves" (2 Cor. 4:7). However, he did not consider suffering as an end in itself. His higher purpose was to manifest the resurrection life of Jesus in his own life, which entailed a power that represented the overcoming of the old order.[55]

53. Clarke describes the qualities ascribed to leaders as including status, patronage and friendship, and oratory. For more, see *Secular and Christian Leadership*, 23–29.

54. Kruse, *2 Corinthians,* 107.

55. Savage, *Power through Weakness*, 175–77.

Leaders teach and demonstrate the new way in Christ, a way that depends on power through weakness (reversal) and results in the loving unity of God's people. The relationship of leadership to servanthood must consider these concerns of how Christ's example is essential for understanding God's ways in the new age. As such, "servanthood" does not simply describe a manner but demonstrates God's ways in that it is not the leader but God who gives the growth. The result should be a community that is subsequently marked by similar self-giving love by all as they imitate the pattern set by the leaders.

Christ's example of leadership as servanthood illustrates how God worked *through* the cross, not just in the humility that led Jesus *to* the cross. Through

### Robert Greenleaf on Servant Leadership

The thoughts of the founder of the servant leadership movement offer some help on how to consider this concept. The term "servant leadership" originated with Robert Greenleaf, a Quaker, who applied his ideas primarily in the business management field. Greenleaf insists that the "servant-leader" is servant first, not leader first, and articulates the critical differences between the two types in his seminal essay:

> The servant-leader *is* servant first. . . . It begins with the natural feeling that one wants to serve, to serve *first.* Then conscious choice brings one to aspire to lead. That person is sharply different from one who is *leader* first, perhaps because of the need to assuage an unusual power drive or to acquire material possessions. For such it will be a later choice to serve—after leadership is established. The leader-first and the servant-first are two extreme types. (*Servant as Leader*, 7, italics original)

Greenleaf also describes what he sees as the different dynamics that occur with one who is a servant first as opposed to a leader first:

> The natural servant, the person who is *servant first*, is more likely to persevere and refine a particular hypothesis on what serves another's highest priority needs than is the person who is *leader first* and who later serves out of promptings of conscience or in conformity with normative expectations. (Ibid., 8)

When one begins by considering oneself to be a servant, the end result is noticeably different from when one begins by thinking of oneself as a leader. In the former, making other's needs primary is a natural occurrence, whereas in the latter, serving is a later, and secondary addition. Greenleaf causes us to ask the question, Is the point to be a leader who serves or a servant who leads?

servanthood, then, leaders exemplify the way in which the new age is based on the cross and weakness and create a community whose members relate to one another in this way.

## Conclusion

This chapter has not attempted to make a judgment on whether a special male leadership role is a biblical concept but rather to reexamine our understanding of leadership and the centrality of authority in the complementarian position. The New Testament certainly affirms the validity of both. At the same time it identifies as a vital component setting an example of being like Christ that believers can follow in their relationships with one another, which then leads to the unity of the church, God's holy temple. This is not the only aspect of authority and leadership for the Christian community, but a fundamental one, and one that should profoundly impact our overall view of the nature, goals, and purposes.

The New Testament's statements about authority and leadership in the church, whether male or female, show that servanthood is a fundamental concept that goes deeper than an attitude. As a result, complementarians (as well as egalitarians and anyone who applies servant leadership to the community) need to ask whether their definitions view suffering, humility, weakness, and a lowering of status as integral to a kingdom understanding. When "servant" only modifies an understanding of leadership and authority, it cannot challenge or change the nature of either in the way that the New Testament seems to do.[56]

For example, if servant leadership is "sacrificial," it would be good to ask what is being sacrificed. Being a servant or slave in the ancient context meant a deep loss of status and honor, which were essential components of a person's identity and key measures of a person's worth. For a person to become a servant or slave meant giving up these critical markers of identity. In today's terminology, we might say that this person became a "nobody." It also meant the loss of the right to self-determination and self-assertion. But for Paul, this is precisely what freed him to consider others before himself. Thus

56. John Hutchison describes the essential challenge regarding Jesus's concept of authority here in the context of James and John's request in Mark 10:38–39: "But their request for personal positions of eminence also revealed a limited perspective of self-centeredness and a failure to grasp something crucial about the road ahead. Glory and positions of authority would come only through the road of suffering, sacrifice, and servanthood" ("Servanthood," 62).

Paul in Phil. 3:3–6 declares that he puts confidence not in human markers of identity but rather in Christ. Whether or not a unique leadership role is given to men in the New Testament, it is critical to examine the assumptions and values behind our models and the priority given to the various elements that constitute our position. We would do well to ask whether our conceptions of leadership and authority recognize the equivalent of this paradoxical kind of social lowering and abasement and, consequently, the vital component leading to a Christ-focused and other-oriented perspective in the church that produces unity. Furthermore, we must ask whether our structures give the glory to God, who gives the growth, or the people occupying the positions.

# 7

# Marriage, Part 1

## *Adam and Eve in Genesis 2–3*

> Eve usurped Adam's headship and led the way into sin. And Adam . . . allowing the deception to progress without decisive intervention . . . abandoned his post as head. Eve was deceived; Adam forsook his responsibility.[1]

> Conspicuously absent in Genesis 1–2 is any reference to the divine prescription for man to exercise authority over woman. . . . The total absence of such a commission indicates that it was not part of God's intent. . . . Any teaching that inserts an authority structure between Adam and Eve in God's creation design is to be firmly rejected since it is not founded on the biblical text.[2]

Did God give Adam special authority and leadership responsibilities that exemplify biblical manhood? Does the creation account instead depict only mutuality and equality between the man and the woman? For complementarians God ordained a structure for male-female relationships from the beginning. For example, one view is that although Adam and Eve are spiritual equals, Adam was to be the "head" of Eve, and he sinned in forsaking his leadership responsibilities and allowing her to lead when she ate from the

1. Ortlund, "Male-Female Equality," 107.
2. Bilezikian, *Beyond Sex Roles*, 41.

tree.[3] Egalitarians point to the mutual relationship between the two. Both were to reign over God's creation, and neither had a particular leadership role or authority over the other.[4]

As with other passages in the debate, the main questions about Gen. 1–3 revolve around the possible authority and leadership of the man and the equality of the man and the woman. However, we will demonstrate that there are other, and perhaps more fruitful, ways to approach the passage and determine its contribution to our understanding of gender. In the next two chapters we will turn our attention to marriage, examining Gen. 1–3 and Eph. 5:21–33 to illustrate in more detail how the themes discussed may underlie central passages in the debate. Additionally, we will demonstrate how these two passages are integrally linked to provide an overarching kingdom perspective on marriage based on unity and a "reversal" that demonstrates God's superiority.

In the current chapter, we will use a literary approach to determine the main emphases of the passage in regard to the relationship between Adam and Eve and how these might impact our perspective on gender. Whether or not Genesis speaks of male authority and leadership, one cannot deny that after Gen. 1, Adam and Eve are not described in an identical fashion. At the same time, they were created for a relationship characterized by unity. The larger question then revolves around the significance of these differences and their intended union.

In utilizing a literary approach to examine the particular roles of Adam and Eve in the story, I will present the evidence from the text itself for indicators of the emphases of the passage and what these contribute to our understanding of gender. In the end I hope to show that reading the text in this way can yield insights that go beyond the categories of "authority" and "equality," and that these can be understood in light of larger concerns such as holiness and unity.

## Understanding Adam and Eve from a Literary Perspective

In recent years interpreters have increasingly paid attention to the literary quality of many biblical passages and the need to interpret them accordingly.

3. E.g., Ortlund says that the passage presents men and women as being "spiritually equal" in terms of bearing God's image and being "vice-rulers" but that the man also "*bears the primary responsibility to lead the partnership in a God-glorifying direction*" ("Male-Female Equality," 99, 108, italics original).

4. E.g., Hess, "Equality."

Authors such as Robert Alter have played a key role in this interpretive shift, and various scholars in the gender debate have adopted their methods.[5] However, there is still more work that can be done. A more overarching literary analysis of Gen. 1–3 can produce valuable insights by providing a different perspective on the way in which the story presents its main themes and defines the main characters.

In narrative the purpose is not to give theological pronouncements as much as to tell a story. While the story may include such pronouncements, meaning is more often conveyed through more subtle means. We learn by paying careful attention to the *how* as well as the *what*. The author presents a story from a particular perspective and guides our understanding of and response to the person or situation.[6] It is in this shaping and guiding that we learn the significance of a situation or person and how we are to make a proper evaluation. The role of the interpreter is to discern the way in which the author is trying to guide these perspectives and responses. For example, scholars accept that the Gospel writers were not impartial reporters of facts about the life and death of Jesus, but rather each used his sources in his own way to present a portrait of Jesus that differed in themes and emphases from those of the other Gospel writers. As Tremper Longman explains, "The point is that we do not have so-called objective, neutral, or unshaped reporting of events. (As many have pointed out, there is no such thing as a brute fact; an uninterpreted historical report is inconceivable.)"[7]

In a similar way, Gen. 1–3 is told from a particular perspective. The author's values and purpose shape the presentation of the story. A literary approach will

5. E.g., see the remarks by Schreiner, "Another Complementarian Perspective," 290. Longman states that a literary approach is justified, even necessary, because the biblical texts "are obviously self-conscious about form" (*Literary Approaches*, 9). Ryken states bluntly, "The Bible demands a literary approach because its writing is literary in nature" (*How to Read the Bible*, 30). A major obstacle is that we do not have the primary sources for understanding ancient narrative technique as we have, e.g., in ancient rhetoric, with handbooks written by authors such as Aristotle and Cicero. As Alter states, "One of the chief difficulties we encounter as modern readers in perceiving the artistry of biblical narrative is precisely that we have lost most of the keys to the conventions out of which it was shaped" (*Art of Biblical Narrative*, 47). However, Alter still thinks "we may be able to recuperate some essential elements of ancient convention and thus to understand biblical narrative more precisely" (ibid., 49).

6. In modern literary studies, "author" generally refers to the "man or woman who actually composes the text." The "narrator" is viewed as a rhetorical device referring to the "one who tells the story." The text may also involve an "implied reader," or "*the author as he or she would be constructed, based on inference from the text*" (Longman, *Literary Approaches*, 84–85, italics original). Sternberg notes that in biblical texts the implied author and narrator "practically merge into each other" (*Poetics of Biblical Narrative*, 75).

7. Longman, *Literary Approaches*, 57.

help us to understand the message the author was trying to convey through the presentation of events and characters, including any ideas regarding the respective roles of Adam and Eve.[8]

## Interpreting the Narrative Genre

Identifying the genre is a key step in "prompting a reading strategy and ruling out false expectations and standards of judgment of a text."[9] By identifying a passage as narrative, interpreters can bring proper assumptions and expectations to the interpretive task. Because narrative describes and illustrates more than states, we do not often find explicit pronouncements on issues. Because of this, the interpretive process is different from that of other genres. As writing teachers through the years have exhorted their students, good narrative will *show* rather than *tell*. "It enacts rather than states. Instead of giving us abstract propositions about virtue or vice, for example, literature presents stories of good or evil characters in action. The tendency of literature is to embody human experience, not to formulate ideas in intellectual propositions."[10] As a result, interpreters need to approach the text differently than they do for writing that is more expository.[11] Because narrative tends to express truth indirectly instead of propositionally, the need to infer meaning from a story is an inherent aspect of interpreting the genre.[12]

Leland Ryken uses the example of Ps. 23 to demonstrate the impact of a literary approach. The psalmist never makes a direct reference to God's providence or defines it, even though it is clearly the major theme. Instead the idea of God's providence is conveyed through a metaphor of God as a shepherd caring for his sheep and through concrete images, such as the green pastures, water, and the rod and staff.

8. Applying a literary approach to Scripture is not to say that a biblical account is fiction. Rather it recognizes that the Bible displays literary characteristics and that applying the tools of literary analysis can help bring out the meaning of the passage (Longman, "Literary Approach," 386). As Longman summarizes, "A literary approach explores and makes explicit the conventions of biblical literature in order to understand the message it intends to convey" (*Literary Approaches*, 60).

9. Longman, *Literary Approaches*, 83.

10. Ryken, *How to Read the Bible*, 17–18.

11. Ibid., 11.

12. "There is an obvious indirection about the storyteller's approach to truth. Instead of stating ideas propositionally, the storyteller presents living examples of one principle or another, one aspect of reality or another, leaving the reader to infer from those themes" (ibid., 59).

> The LORD is my shepherd,
> I shall not want.
> He makes me lie down in green pastures;
> He leads me beside quiet waters.
> He restores my soul;
> He guides me in the paths of righteousness
> For His name's sake.
>
> Even though I walk through the valley of the shadow of death,
> I fear no evil, for You are with me;
> Your rod and Your staff, they comfort me.
>
> (Ps. 23:1–4)

In comparison, Ryken notes the specific reference to God's providence and the use of abstract theological language in the Westminster Confession: "God the Creator of all things doth uphold, direct, dispose, and govern all creatures, actions, and things, from the greatest even to the least, by His most wise and holy providence."[13] In interpreting narrative, then, we should not always expect to find direct statements of truth. These may occur, but more often we will find truth *shown* to us. This includes Gen. 1–3, which "almost totally avoids stating the truth about God and creation abstractly. It embodies everything in the concrete form of characters performing actions and saying things that we overhear."[14]

Ironically, the evangelical community's very quest for truth may unintentionally hinder its exegesis of narrative passages pertaining to the gender issue. Because the Bible is the source of ultimate truth, interpreters tend to concentrate their analyses on answering vital theological questions. However, these questions are not necessarily the principal ones the text was intended to address. The focus on abstract ideas can obscure the importance of stories in the biblical author's worldview.[15]

While conceptual and doctrinal questions are essential, Alter warns against "the tendency of scholars to ask questions about the biblical view of man, the biblical notion of the soul, the biblical vision of eschatology, while for the most part neglecting phenomena like character, motive, and narrative design as unbefitting for the study of an essentially religious document."[16] An overly narrow emphasis on finding propositional truth may cause an interpreter to

13. As quoted in ibid., 16–17.
14. Ibid., 19.
15. Ibid., 22.
16. Alter, *Art of Biblical Narrative*, 22.

neglect the more subtle clues about the portrayal of characters and events that routinely occur in narrative. In this way a literary analysis may ask different questions and so yield types of insights that differ from those resulting from an approach that concentrates on doctrine, and these insights can ultimately help in producing doctrine.

The desire to answer pressing contemporary questions such as "Does the husband have authority over the wife?" or "Who makes the final decision in a marriage?" means that interpreters often come to the text with preset questions that require specific types of answers and thus leave little room for an alternative. A literary approach can help overcome this tendency to ask and answer predefined questions. It begins not by asking "Does God give Adam a special authority?" or "Are Adam and Eve equals?" but rather by asking questions such as "What does the author intend to convey about Adam and Eve?" and "What does the passage tell us about God and his relationship with and purposes for Adam and Eve?" Although the latter questions may lead to an answer that addresses authority and/or equality, they are not limited to or automatically centered on these concerns.

## Genesis 1–3 in Literary Perspective

### *The Purpose and Relationship of Adam and Eve*

A literary analysis attempts to highlight features of the text that might be overlooked in a traditional exegesis.[17] As described above, interpreters should expect to learn from a narrative's indirect statements. Narrative prompts the reader to consider the surface structure of the story and the way events and characters are portrayed. For example, the interpreter may examine what events or details are selected, omitted, or emphasized. Discerning the arrangement of the story may provide key indicators for identifying its theme. One may also study the development of a character or the contribution of literary devices such as metaphor and irony.

Since biblical narratives "consist mainly of dramatized scenes and a minimum of explanatory comment," recognizing the subtle clues in the text becomes that much more relevant.[18] In our text, Gen. 1–3, we will specifically

17. As Longman states, it "is a partial analysis. It is best taken as an aspect of the historical-grammatical approach to the text. . . . A literary analysis will both highlight aspects of the passage that were previously unnoticed and also throw new light on the text as it is viewed from this different perspective" (*Literary Approaches*, 75).

18. Ryken, *Words of Delight*, 45.

consider the role that repetition plays in outlining the main theme and the importance of dialogue and actions in defining the main characters. Furthermore, we will analyze the roles of Adam and Eve within the progression of the entire plot.

### *The Relationship of Genesis 1 to Genesis 2–3*

Most interpreters see a shift beginning in chapter 2 (or more precisely 2:4), and many see chapters 2–3 (or 2:4–3:24) as forming a distinct unit. Gordon Wenham notes that the clause "This is the history (account) of X" demarcates a cycle of narratives. Here the phrase sets apart the unit 2:4–4:26, which itself contains three distinct narratives, one of which is the story of the garden of Eden in 2:4–3:24.[19] John Skinner describes Gen. 2–3 as a "complete and closely articulated narrative."[20]

Genesis 1 provides a general account of creation, with the more specific account beginning in chapter 2. Aída Besançon Spencer describes Gen. 1 as providing an "overview" of creation with chapter 2 looking back and focusing on the end of one day, day six.[21] John Walton sees many of the functions related to Gen. 1:28–29 as "elaborated" in Gen. 2.[22] Genesis 2–3 expands on Gen. 1 in numerous ways. For example, where 1:27 simply records that "male and female He created them," Gen. 2 describes the initial creation of the man from the earth followed by the creation of the woman from the man. Likewise they, out of all of God's creation, are told to "rule" in Gen. 1, but Gen. 2 provides more detail on what the rule will entail as the narrative concentrates more intensely and in more detail on the man and the woman.[23] The way in

19. The other two are the story of Cain and Abel in 4:1–16 and the account of Cain's family in 4:17–26. See Wenham, *Genesis 1–15*, 49. Similarly, Walton sees Gen. 1 as describing the "initial period" of God's creation, and then beginning in Gen. 2, there is a series of separate accounts that connect this period to the time of the patriarchs (*Genesis*, 57, 163).

20. Skinner, *Commentary on Genesis*, 51.

21. Spencer, *Beyond the Curse*, 23. Likewise, Speiser says that 2:4–3:24 "deals with the origin of life on earth, as contrasted with the preceding statement about the origin of the universe as a whole" (*Genesis*, 18).

22. Walton, *Genesis*, 187. Or as McKeown states, chap. 1 provides the "majestic overview," while chap. 2 "selects certain aspects of creation and deals with them in more detail" (*Genesis*, 30).

23. While both are told to "subdue" the earth and to "rule," this does not necessarily mean that they share equally in these tasks. E.g., if I cannot be in class and leave the duties to my teaching assistants, telling the class, "My teaching assistants will be in charge while I am gone," this does not automatically mean that they share equally in their responsibilities, since I may give them different tasks. It is merely a statement that I have generally designated who will lead the class in my absence. The specific duties are left ambiguous at that point in order to make the main point that the teaching assistants are in charge as opposed to someone else or

which Gen. 2–3 provides more specificity to the overview of Gen. 1 impels us to take a closer look at these chapters to see whether they will shed light on God's intentions for Adam and Eve.

### *Adam's Charge to Keep the Command as the Central Conflict*

Although intimately tied to Gen. 1, Gen. 2–3 can be analyzed as a discrete unit because it has a self-contained plot.[24] In Gen. 2–3 the plot revolves around the creation and fall of Adam and Eve. God creates Adam and charges him to cultivate the garden and keep the command not to eat from the tree of the knowledge of good and evil. He then creates Eve, after which both Adam and Eve disobey and are judged.

As in other narratives, the central conflict organizes the story.[25] Longman notes the importance of conflict in moving the plot of a narrative forward: "The conflict generates interest in its resolution. The beginning of a story, with its introduction of conflict, thus pushes us through the middle toward the end, when conflict is resolved."[26] As we will see, in Gen. 2–3 the conflict revolves around whether Adam and Eve will obey God.[27] When God gives the command to Adam not to eat of the tree of the knowledge of good and evil, it is the only place in Genesis where the divine command is introduced with the formula, "The Lord God commanded" (2:16).[28] In numerous ways the narrative highlights the critical perspective of obedience, as we also see that God's command is now followed with a penalty for transgression: death (2:17).

---

no one. These duties may then be clarified later. Thus, even though Gen. 1 does not indicate a difference in responsibility or duties, it does not mean that the author cannot go into more detail in this area later. As part of the account of the days of creation, Gen. 1:28 simply indicates that humans are given rule over the earth as opposed to the animals and other creatures, which were created on the other days. This is the primary context with which to interpret the significance of the statement.

24. Aristotle (*Poetics* 7.26–29) described plot as containing a beginning, a middle, and an end. Thus a plot can be seen as a "*whole* or complete action" (Ryken, *How to Read the Bible*, 40, italics original). While a story may be part of a larger plot, it also forms a self-contained unit. E.g., the sacrifice of Isaac forms its own plot at the same time that it is part of the larger plot concerning the story of Abraham. By analyzing chaps. 2–3 as a separate unit, we can discern its unique contribution to the whole.

25. "The essence of plot is a central conflict or set of conflicts moving toward a resolution. One of the very first things to pay attention to when reading a story is the conflicts that organize the story from the very beginning" (Ryken, *How to Read the Bible*, 40).

26. Longman, *Literary Approaches*, 93.

27. For a similar view, see Mettinger, *Eden Narrative*, 29: "The plot is centered on the radical choice of the first human couple: to obey or not to obey the divine commandment."

28. K. Matthews, *Genesis 1:1—11:26*, 210.

As a story of origins, the passage traces the creation and fall of the first man and woman. However, the story's structure draws special attention to Adam's reception of, transgression of, and then finally judgment for breaking the command not to eat from the tree of the knowledge of good and evil. While Eve is also responsible for keeping the command, her role is not identical. Instead the narrative stresses her role as Adam's helper and the way in which she helps or hinders his ability to fulfill this commission.

The command structures the story and provides the key for interpreting the passage. Its essential place in the narrative is seen in the way it is repeated throughout the story. James Resseguie notes that repetition can identify the structure and design of the narrative.[29] Even more, it highlights the most significant parts of the narrative.[30] "The most reliable guide to what a story is about is the principle of repetition. What keeps getting repeated in a story invariably becomes the central focus—the thing toward which everything points."[31]

In Gen. 2–3 God's command not to eat of the tree of the knowledge of good and evil is stated five times. It is stated directly to Adam three times: in the beginning when God gives him the command and twice at the end of the narrative when God confronts Adam and then pronounces judgment. In the middle of the narrative, both the serpent and Eve repeat the command, although with some striking variations. However, it is not simply the number of occurrences that is striking but also the way in which the command is related to the characters.

In the first occurrence God gives the initial command to Adam not to eat from the tree.

> Then the Lord God took the man and put him into the garden of Eden to cultivate it and keep it. The Lord God commanded the man, saying, "From any tree of the garden you may eat freely; but from the tree of the knowledge of good and evil you shall not eat, for in the day that you eat from it you will surely die." (Gen. 2:15–17)

29. Resseguie, *Narrative Criticism*, 42.

30. Tannehill notes that repetition provides the key to interpreting the text because it allows the text itself to disclose its emphasis (*Sword of His Mouth*, 43). Anderson identifies the following potential functions for repetition: (1) to highlight or draw attention; (2) to establish or fix in the mind of the implied reader; (3) to emphasize the importance of something; (4) to create expectations, increasing predictability and assent; (5) to cause review and reassessment; (6) to unify disparate elements, sometimes creating a background pattern against which other elements can be understood; (7) to build patterns of association or draw contrasts (*Matthew's Narrative Web*, 44–45).

31. Ryken, *How to Read the Bible*, 59.

This is the first time God speaks directly in the passage. Robert Tannehill notes the importance of dialogue in narrative:

> The use of dialogue in a dramatic scene involves the expansion of the amount of space in a writing given to a segment of time in the story, compared to the alternative possibility of presenting an event or series of events in a brief summary. Thus dialogue in a dramatic scene emphasizes, while summary narration of events gives them a subordinate position.[32]

Only the command not to eat of the tree, and not the command to cultivate the garden, is presented as a spoken command. The centrality of this particular command in the progression of the story is furthermore demonstrated in that throughout the rest of the story, the narrative continually presents it as direct speech either by God himself or as repeated by the other characters.

There has been much argument concerning the significance of the prohibition being given to the man and not the woman. Complementarians often argue that this reflects God's intention for male leadership,[33] while egalitarians counter that God gave it to Adam first simply because Eve was not yet created.[34] It is best to view this event within the overall narrative. As we will see, the story uniquely relates the command to Adam throughout the passage. God speaks the command three times altogether, and each time it is directed to Adam alone. These three occurrences present a complete picture: God gives Adam the command (Gen. 2:16–17), confronts him about breaking the command (Gen. 3:11), and then judges him for the transgression (Gen. 3:17–19).

The second and third statements of the command occur in the pivotal scene with the serpent. The serpent and Eve have an exchange that centers on the command.

> And [the serpent] said to the woman, "Indeed, has God said, 'You shall not eat from any tree of the garden'?" The woman said to the serpent, "From the fruit of the trees of the garden we may eat; but from the fruit of the tree which is in the middle of the garden, God has said, 'You shall not eat from it or touch it, or you will die.'" (Gen. 3:1b–3)

32. Tannehill, "Disciples in Mark," 391.

33. Schreiner notes, "God likely commissioned Adam to instruct Eve about this command, signaling Adam's responsibility for leadership and teaching in the relationship" ("Another Complementarian Perspective," 291).

34. Hess, "Equality," 83.

This is the moment when Adam and Eve must decide whether they will obey God. The "test motif" is often the key to a story, such as when Abraham must decide whether to sacrifice Isaac.[35] Ryken notes, "Many a biblical protagonist achieves full heroic stature in the moment of choice. The choice, indeed, is what the story is finally about."[36] Tragically they fail, as Eve eats first and then gives the fruit to Adam, who also eats.

For the fourth occurrence, God directly asks Adam alone whether he has kept the command: "Have you eaten from the tree of which I commanded you not to eat?" (Gen. 3:11b). If the main point were simply the transgression, we would expect God to confront both of them in this way. But God speaks only with Adam in this regard and asks Eve the more generic question, "What is this you have done?" (Gen. 3:13). Only Adam is confronted specifically in reference to the command, just as he is the only one to whom it is explicitly given. Since repetition is an indication of the focus, this consistency is noteworthy. The continual relating of the command to Adam is reinforced when we come to the third time God states the command, the fifth occurrence in the overall passage. God directly relates Adam's punishment to breaking the command, something that, again, he does not do to Eve. "Then to Adam He said, 'Because you have listened to the voice of your wife, and have eaten from the tree about which I commanded you, saying, "You shall not eat from it" . . .'" (Gen. 3:17).

Thus there is a striking and important pattern here: God gives the command directly to Adam, asks only Adam whether he broke the command, and specifically relates Adam's punishment to the command. It is not that Eve is exempt from obeying and suffering the consequences of her sin since she is punished as well. Rather, we can note that from a literary perspective, the narrative is crafted in such a way as to draw special attention to Adam's special relationship to and responsibility for keeping the command.

### *Adam's Role as the One Who Was Disobedient*

The special attention paid to Adam and the command highlights Adam's disobedience. It does not seem to matter *why* he broke the command, as much as *that* he broke it. In addition to the repetition of the command to

35. Ryken, *How to Read the Bible*, 50–51. Mettinger has also identified the "test motif" in the passage and calls it "an important but surprisingly neglected feature of the text," although he does not distinguish any differing responsibilities between Adam and Eve regarding the test (*Eden Narrative*, 23).

36. Ryken, *How to Read the Bible*, 51.

Adam, there are other ways in which the narrative concentrates on his act of disobedience. Unlike with Eve, there is a distinct lack of explanation for Adam's transgression. In Gen. 3:6 we learn that Eve sees that the tree was "good for food, and that it was a delight to the eyes, and that the tree was desirable to make one wise." For Adam, however, we learn only that he ate. The text gives only the barest description of what happened. Eve gives the fruit to Adam, and he eats (Gen. 3:6; cf. Gen. 3:12). There is no mention of desire or intention on his part.

When God confronts Eve about her sin, she says that the serpent deceived her (Gen. 3:13). However, when God confronts Adam, he replies, "The woman whom You gave to be with me, she gave me from the tree, and I ate" (Gen. 3:11–12). On the one hand, we learn that Adam has a tendency to blame, since he blames Eve and God—Eve because she gave him the fruit, and God because he gave him Eve.[37] On the other hand, there is still no mention of Adam's motive. We gain insight into this aspect of his character, but we still do not know why he did it. He does not say he was deceived, coerced, and so on. All we know is that Eve gave the fruit to him and he ate.

Adam's portrayal is also unique in that all the other characters repeat, at least to some degree, some version of the command. Variation within repetition can help clarify the significance of events and characters. As David Gunn and Danna Fewell note, "Repetition and variation can equate and contrast events or characters . . . inviting the reader to consider the significance of similarities and dissimilarities."[38]

God, of course, gives the command. The serpent manipulates the command to entice Eve, asking her whether God has forbidden her from eating of "any" tree of the garden. Eve adds a prohibition, saying she is not to "touch" as well as eat from the tree, and she also describes the tree as the one "which is in the middle of the garden" (Gen. 3:3) instead of the tree of the knowledge of good and evil.[39] Adam is the only one who does not state the command at all, whether accurately or inaccurately, yet his relationship to the command provides a main point for the narrative. God gives him the command, confronts him about the command, and judges him for breaking the command. While much of the dialogue revolves around the command, indicating its importance in the overall narrative, for Adam the spotlight is on his choice to obey God or not.

37. E.g., Bar-Efrat, *Narrative Art*, 75.

38. Gunn and Fewell, *Narrative in the Hebrew Bible*, 148.

39. While various interpretations have been given for each character's motivation behind these changes, it is not a key issue for our immediate purpose, which is to demonstrate the overall centrality of the command for the narrative.

The significance of Adam's failure can be seen in his punishment. Adam's disobedience, as opposed to Eve's, has a consequence directly related to breaking the command. God forewarned that death would be the result of disobedience, and in the end death is the judgment pronounced on Adam for his transgression. As God gave the command to Adam alone, he now pronounces death as a result of Adam's sin.

> By the sweat of your face
> You will eat bread,
> Till you return to the ground,
> Because from it you were taken;
> For you are dust,
> And to dust you shall return.
> (Gen. 3:19)

God does not ascribe death as a direct consequence of Eve's disobedience as he does for Adam. Furthermore, if it were simply a matter of sin leading to death, then the punishment should be given to Eve, who sinned first. Instead death is attributed to Adam, whom God specifically warned that this would be the result of disobedience. The warning and fulfillment theme that frames the narrative is tied to Adam's sin alone.

In narrative, actions are essential to understanding a character. As Shimon Bar-Efrat explains:

> A person's nature is revealed by deeds; action is the implementation of character, and individuals are disclosed through their deeds no less than through their words. . . . In biblical narrative deeds do in fact serve as the foremost means of characterization, and we know biblical characters primarily through the way they act in various situations.[40]

Even though some have proposed that Adam's failure was that he did not take the "lead" in resisting Satan's temptation and instead stood by passively while Eve fell into sin,[41] the text itself points to the primary aspect of his failure as his disobedience instead.[42] The importance of Adam's disobedience should

40. Bar-Efrat, *Narrative Art*, 77. Ryken similarly asserts that in the Bible, characters are known primarily through their actions (*How to Read the Bible*, 38).

41. Ortlund, "Male-Female Equality," 107.

42. Furthermore, Genesis explicitly identifies Adam's sin as "listening to the voice of your wife" in Gen. 3:17. As Wenham notes, "listen to the voice of" is an idiom for "obey." Other examples include Gen. 16:2; Exod. 18:24; and 2 Kings 10:6 (*Genesis 1–15*, 82). Rather than

not be underestimated, especially since Paul affirms this understanding in Rom. 5. Paul does not describe Adam as someone who abandoned his headship but rather as someone whose disobedience led to death. "Therefore, just as through one man sin entered into the world, and death through sin, and so death spread to all men, because all sinned" (Rom. 5:12; see also 5:17–19). As in Gen. 2–3 Paul also assigns the responsibility for sin and death entering the world to Adam and not Eve, even though she ate first. As God warned Adam that death would be the result of his transgression, so does Paul view death as coming through Adam.

Paul furthermore contrasts Adam with another man who is ultimately faithful to God's commands and brings life instead.

> For if by the transgression of the one, death reigned through the one, much more those who receive the abundance of grace and of the gift of righteousness will reign in life through the One, Jesus Christ. So then as through one transgression there resulted condemnation to all men, even so through one act of righteousness there resulted justification of life to all men. For as through the one man's disobedience the many were made sinners, even so through the obedience of the One the many will be made righteous. (Rom. 5:17–19)

If death came through the disobedience of one man, Adam, then in a similar manner, life comes through the obedience of another man, Jesus Christ. In sum Paul describes both Adam and Christ in terms of their "single decisive deeds,"[43] and both Rom. 5 and Gen. 3 portray Adam's deed as his disobedience.

We noted earlier that obedience was critical for understanding the importance of holiness, including corporate holiness as God's people were instructed to live in proper relationship with one another. Obedience in general is a central theme throughout the Old Testament, where God's relationship to his people is intimately connected with obedience to his commands.[44] In Genesis Adam's

---

stating that Adam abandoned his headship to Eve, the passage conveys that Adam disobeyed God in obeying Eve instead, which is consistent with the rest of our interpretation that focuses on Adam's disobedience as the key to understanding his role in the story. Mettinger sees this as an explicit point of connection with Deuteronomistic theology: "Instead of listening to what God commanded, the man listened to the voice of his wife" (*Eden Narrative*, 51).

43. Seifrid, "Romans," 628.

44. As Wenham (*Genesis 1–15*, 90) explains,

> As a paradigm of sin this model would be equally at home in any of the great theological traditions of the Old Testament. The covenant theology expressed most clearly in Deuteronomy insists that disobedience to God's commands brings the curse and ultimately death (e.g., Deut. 30:15–19). The prophets similarly harp on this issue (e.g., Isa. 24:4–6;

disobedience led to death, expulsion from the garden, and separation from God. The Old Testament patriarch Abraham was extolled for his faith, but it was a faith manifested in his obedience, especially his willingness to sacrifice Isaac in response to God's command. God demanded Israel's obedience to his laws so that the nation could be holy.

The obedience or disobedience of God's people to his commands is a central and recurring theme in Scripture. Abraham obeyed. Israel did not obey. Christ obeyed. The church is called to obey (e.g., Rom. 1:5; 6:16–17; 16:26; 2 Cor. 9:13; 2 John 6). Adam was the first in a line of God's people to be given a command, and as such was a prototype of those whose obedience or disobedience would reflect their relationship with and faith in God.

### *Eve's Role as the Helper Who Is Deceived*

The question then becomes, what is Eve's role? This is particularly acute since both she and Adam transgressed God's command, but the forewarned punishment of death is attributed only to Adam. Genesis 1 states that both Adam and Eve are created in God's image and told to rule over the creatures of the earth. As the first humans they are told to "be fruitful and multiply" (Gen. 1:28) and subdue the earth. Beginning in Gen. 2, however, we learn of some important distinctions between the two.

Genesis 2:18 says that God creates Eve because it is "not good" for man to be alone, and so Eve is to be his "helper." She is to be Adam's companion and to assist him. The major motifs related to Eve are: (1) She is "like" Adam and so is the only one who is a suitable companion for him. Because she is "like" Adam in that she is another human being, his female counterpart made in God's image, she is in a sense his equal. However, more fitting terms to describe her relationship with Adam would be "sameness" and "unity" rather than "equality." The goal of their relationship, to become "one flesh," also reflects the importance of her likeness to Adam. (2) She is created for a specific purpose as Adam's "helper." Understanding the significance of her role as "helper" lies not as much in a determination of relative authority or equality as in a careful examination of the way that the narrative portrays the type of help she is to give and what actually happens.

---

Jer. 21:8). It is just as central in the wisdom tradition too: "There is a way which seems right to a man, but its end is the way to death" (Prov. 14:12; 16:25).

As noted above, Mettinger likewise sees the theme of obedience to the divine command leading to life as reflecting Deuteronomistic theology (*Eden Narrative*, 49–55).

### *Eve as the One Who Is "Like" Adam*

In Gen. 2–3 Adam is called to unity with Eve, the one who is different from Adam but also is "like" him.

Adam's speech after her creation is particularly revealing.

> This is now bone of my bones,
> and flesh of my flesh;
> She shall be called Woman,
> Because she was taken out of Man.
> (Gen. 2:23)

Anne Lapidus Lerner notes that Adam's speech, the first human speech in Genesis, emphasizes Eve's sameness with Adam and not her uniqueness.[45] She is a suitable partner because, unlike the other creatures of the earth, she is "like" him. Furthermore, the creation of Eve is also for the purpose of human completeness, since it is "not good" that man is alone.[46]

Wenham observes that "flesh and bone" was a Hebraic way of referring to one's relatives. Consequently, "just as blood relations are one's flesh and bone . . . so marriage creates a similar kinship relation between man and wife."[47] Adam's speech affirms that Eve is a more fitting companion for him than the animals because she shares his humanity. The intimate unity between the two is revealed further as the text goes on to state that the goal is for the man to be "joined to his wife" and "become one flesh" (Gen. 2:24). As Eve was taken from Adam's flesh, so will they be rejoined as one. In this way, "marriage achieves a reunion of what God divided in the creation of the woman."[48]

However, the sameness of the man and the woman and their intimate unity do not automatically mean that they are "equal." In addition to Adam's representative function, their sequential creation needs to be considered. It will be helpful to compare the Genesis account with another ancient creation account in order to highlight by contrast this significance.

In Atrahasis, the Babylonian story of the flood, the gods create man and woman simultaneously. The purpose is to create humans to work for them.[49]

45. Lerner, *Eternally Eve*, 42.
46. Belleville, "Egalitarian Perspective," 30.
47. Wenham, *Genesis 1–15*, 70–71.
48. Hess, "Equality," 88.
49. "Let man carry the toil of the gods" (line 197 of tablet I, from Lambert and Millard, *Atra-Ḫasīs*, 57).

To accomplish this, Mami, the "Mistress-of-All-the-Gods,"[50] proceeds to form humans out of clay. She takes fourteen pieces, divides them into two groups of seven, and places a brick between the two groups. From the pieces of clay, she forms seven males and seven females, who are completed in "pairs" by the birth-goddesses.[51]

[Prince] Ea spoke

> . . . ] . he was prompting her
> . . . she] recited the incantation
> After she had recited her incantation
> [She] put [her hand out] to her clay,
> Seven she put on the right,
> [Seven] she put on the left,
> Between them she placed the brick.
> [. . .] . . . hair (?), she . . . the cutter of the umbilical cord.
> The wise and learned
> Twice seven birth-goddesses had assembled,
> Seven produced males,
> [Seven] produced females.
> The birth-goddess, creatress of destiny—
> They completed them in pairs,
> They completed them in pairs in her presence,
> Since Mami conceived the regulations for the human race.

The contrast between the simultaneous creation of men and women in Atrahasis and the sequential account in Genesis makes the story of Adam and Eve more striking. If the intent was to convey equality between male and female, then a two-stage creation would seem to hinder more than help the point. As Thomas Schreiner notes, "If the only point of the story were the equality of men and women, then creation at the same point in time would be most fitting."[52] However, Adam is created first, and further, Eve is created *from* Adam. At the very least, the two-stage creation raises the question of whether the biblical account was intended to portray their equality.

50. Line 247 of tablet I (ibid., 61).

51. Lines 1–14 of tablet I (ibid., 61–62). See also lines 256–59 of tablet I, from "The Atrahasis Story," in Matthews and Benjamin, *Old Testament Parallels*, 20; and lines 249–60 of tablet I, from Lambert and Millard, *Atra-Ḫasīs*, 61.

52. Schreiner, "Another Complementarian Perspective," 290.

However, the opposite issue is whether the two-stage creation then supports the authority and leadership of the man over the woman. Complementarians have pointed to the role of primogeniture, or the privileges of the firstborn, as indicating Adam's headship.[53] Egalitarians have countered that there is no logical connection between the rights of the firstborn and creation order in terms of authority,[54] and also the law of primogeniture was not ironclad, since it was often overturned in Scripture.[55]

For our purposes we can note that from a literary standpoint, the text itself indicates the significance of being first. Whether or not primogeniture comes into play, there are consequences to Adam's being created first. Eve is created for Adam, and not the other way around.[56] As we have seen, it is Adam who is originally given the command, an event that happens before Eve is created. This is not accidental but rather is an integral part of the narrative, since he is ultimately held accountable for his obedience to it in a way that Eve is not. Thus the passage as a whole portrays Adam, *as* the first created if not *because* he was the first created, as carrying a different significance and holding a different accountability than Eve. As a result, as we have discussed Adam's responsibility, it may be fruitful to examine Eve's unique role in relation to the command and obedience to it.

### *Eve as "Helper"*

The significance of Eve's role as Adam's helper has been a major issue. Egalitarians note that since God is called Israel's helper, the term cannot

53. E.g., Hurley, *Man and Woman*, 207–8; Grudem, *Evangelical Feminism*, 67–68.

54. Hess, "Equality," 84.

55. E.g., Groothuis, *Good News for Women*, 221; Keener, "Women in Ministry," 240. Keener also notes that primogeniture generally applies to inheritance rights. Groothuis further argues that the purpose of the sequential creation was for man and woman to learn of their need for each other.

> The two-stage creation of humanity highlights the lesson God was trying to teach, namely, that "it is not good for the man [i.e., the human] to be alone" (2:18). God illustrated the point by having the man be alone for a time, and by showing the man that it was "not good." . . . God's method of creating man and woman demonstrated their interdependence, their oneness, their need for one another, and the basis for their capacity to love one another as partners for a lifetime. (*Good News for Women*, 137)

However, only the man learns of his need for the woman, not the converse. Because "it is not good for man to be alone," woman is created for the man. There is no corresponding statement regarding the woman's need for man. Again, Paul supports this understanding of the creation account when he says, "man was not created for the woman's sake, but woman for the man's sake" (1 Cor. 11:9).

56. Adam's "centrality" in this way is also noted by Paul in 1 Cor. 11:8–10. See Finley, "Relationship of Woman and Man," 56.

automatically imply subordination.[57] Scholars on both sides rightly point out that context is the key to determining the significance of Eve's help.[58]

From a literary perspective, if the command plays a critical structural and framing role in the narrative and so in the characterization of Adam, we may ask whether the same applies to Eve. It should be noted that the command provides the most immediate context, since her description as Adam's helper occurs immediately after God instructs Adam (Gen. 2:16–18). Thus at least a part of her "help" to Adam may include helping him to keep the command as well as cultivating the earth.

While Eve, like Adam, disobeys God, the text highlights a different type of relationship to the command. Although it is implicit that Eve also is to obey, God never speaks directly to her concerning the command, as he does repeatedly with Adam. The text's explicit depiction of her interaction with God's word takes place in a very different setting.

The pivotal event in the entire story is Eve's temptation. This event is important, not only because it leads to Eve's sin, but perhaps even more so because it leads to Adam's downfall as well, since "she gave also to her husband with her, and he ate" (Gen. 3:6). Although Eve was to help Adam obey God, she not only failed in helping Adam keep the command but ironically was also a principal player in his disobedience.

Furthermore, the passage develops Eve's failure as helper by paying special attention to the way in which Eve failed because she was deceived. The story provides a detailed account of her deception by the serpent (3:1–7). He questions her ("Indeed, has God said, 'You shall not eat from any tree of the garden'?"), and she responds ("From the fruit of the tree which is in the middle of the garden, God has said, 'You shall not eat from it or touch it, or you will die.'").

The serpent's words cause her to see the fruit as desirable, so she disregards God's command and eats. This more extended portrayal provides a stark

57. E.g., M. Evans, *Woman in the Bible*, 16–17.

58. Eve's role as helper may include helping to fulfill the mandate to "be fruitful and multiply, and fill the earth" in Gen. 1:28. See, e.g., Clines, *What Does Eve Do?*, 33–37; Schreiner, "Another Complementarian Perspective," 292–94. However, Finley cautions that Eve's role in reproduction does not exclude her from also having dominion over the earth ("Relationship of Woman and Man," 54–55). Walton argues that reproduction would be one of Eve's functions as Adam's partner but that function is not the same as purpose. E.g., one function of the garden would be to provide food, but food is not necessarily the purpose of the garden (*Genesis*, 187–88). Other proposals include offering Adam "*strong partnership*" (Belleville, "Egalitarian Perspective," 27, italics original) and rescuing Adam in his inadequacy as God rescues his people (Bilezikian, *Beyond Sex Roles*, 28).

contrast to the very sparse description of Adam's transgression, in which the text says only that Eve gave the fruit to Adam and he ate. Additional attention on Eve's deception comes later, when God confronts her and she says, "The serpent deceived me" (Gen. 3:13). The identification of this literary focus on Eve also finds a correspondence in Paul's understanding of Eve. Both times that Paul speaks of her are in reference to her deception (2 Cor. 11:3; 1 Tim. 2:13).

Although interpreters today generally do not take the event to mean that Eve, and so women in general, are more easily deceived, complementarians commonly argue that it reflects an inversion of God's order, whereby the serpent attacks Eve rather than Adam as the appointed leader or Eve usurps Adam's headship.[59] However, since God does not confront any of the parties—Adam, Eve, or the serpent—about such an inversion, there is more likely a different explanation, at least as a primary point of the story.

Deception is an important theme throughout Scripture. God warns his people not to be deceived by false prophets (Jer. 29:8). The psalmist speaks of David as one who is not deceived by his enemies (Ps. 89:22). The king of Assyria warns Judah that Hezekiah is deceiving them when he assures them that God will deliver them and exhorts them to surrender (2 Kings 18:29). In the New Testament this theme appears primarily when the text speaks about deception leading God's people away from him and into sin or preventing the world from seeing the truth about God. Second John 7 warns about the "deceivers" who "do not acknowledge Jesus Christ as coming in the flesh." Titus 1:10–11 says that the "deceivers . . . must be silenced" because of the damage caused by their false teaching. In 2 Cor. 11:3 Paul mentions Eve in order to warn the church—both men and women—from similarly being deceived and so led astray from Christ. Eve's deception serves as a negative example for all members of the church to be on guard against falling away.

However, our passage does not imply that Eve is naturally more prone to deception but rather makes clear that deception is the work of Satan. Genesis 3

59. E.g., as Ortlund argues,

> [Eve's] calling was to help Adam as second-in-command in world rulership. If the roles had been reversed, if Eve had been created first and then Adam as her helper, the Serpent would doubtless have approached Adam. So Eve was not morally weaker than Adam. But Satan struck at Adam's headship. His words had the effect of inviting Eve to assume primary responsibility at the moment of temptation. . . . Presumably, she believed that she could manage the partnership to both Adam's and her own advantage, if she would only assert herself. ("Male-Female Equality," 108)

highlights the serpent's role since it describes the serpent as "more crafty than any of the wild animals the LORD God had made" (Gen. 3:1 NIV). Bar-Efrat notes that direct characterization is rare in biblical narrative, and when it does occur, "the trait noted by the narrator is always extremely important in the development of the plot."[60] Thus the story emphasizes the serpent's craftiness as the explanation for Eve's deception. There is no corresponding description of Eve, especially in terms of her gullibility.

Eve's deception has tragic consequences. Like Adam she suffers the immediate effects of eating from the tree—feeling the shame of her nakedness and the need to hide from God—and later, judgment from God. However, a literary analysis also highlights the critical role that her deception plays in leading to Adam's transgression and thus what it contributes to the overall plot. Eve's actions play a major role in providing "causal coherence" to the story.[61] Cause-effect connections are key to unifying a plot.[62] If the plot of Gen. 2–3 revolves around Adam's ability to keep the command, Eve's role can be understood in relation to Adam's commissioning. She comes to the fore here because even though she was created as Adam's helper in carrying out the commission, her actions instead lead to his downfall since she is the one who gives him the fruit, as a result of which he disobeys God and eats.

Eve's deception begins a chain of events that ultimately leads to the consequences for which Adam is responsible: death and the cursing of the ground. That she is the critical link in this tragic turn of events is particularly ironic because she was created to be his helper. If Adam is the prototype of those who will disobey God, Eve is the first in a line of those who turn from God and the truth because they are deceived, with disastrous results.

### *The Significance of the Theme of Unity*

The story of Adam and Eve presents vital principles about obedience that will be carried into the rest of Scripture. Also, because of their failure to obey God, their intended unity is shattered. Their calling to be "one flesh" in Gen. 2:24 is a call to reunite what was separated in creation, but they do not achieve this. The importance of the motif of unity between the first man and the first woman should not be underestimated, especially since it reappears in Eph. 5,

60. Bar-Efrat, *Narrative Art*, 53.

61. Ryken, *How to Read the Bible*, 48.

62. "A unified plot is not a mere succession or accumulation of events but a sequence of events that are linked by a chain of cause and effect" (ibid., 36). Bar-Efrat notes that a plot consists of "a meaningful chain of interconnected events" (*Narrative Art*, 93).

not only in relation to Christian husbands and wives but also as part of the "mystery" of Christ and the church.

The story gives very little explicit information about Adam and Eve's relationship. After Eve's creation, the narrative jumps immediately to the temptation, fall, and judgment. Although we noted the significance of dialogue above, Adam and Eve never speak directly to each other during the entire narrative, but speak only to God when he confronts them.

However, there are other ways that we learn about their relationship, and in this Adam plays a critical role. He is the only one who speaks directly of the other, and the content of his words is revealing since in both occurrences it reflects their unity or disunity. When Eve is created, he declares that she is "like" him in being "bone of my bones and flesh of my flesh" (Gen. 2:23), but there is no corresponding response from Eve. After this comment about their "sameness," his next comment reflects their separation. Adam distances himself from Eve by blaming her, the person with whom he was supposed to be united, whereas Eve blames a third party, the serpent. Although earlier he considered Eve a suitable companion because she is like him, he now describes her as "the woman whom you gave to be with me" (Gen. 3:12). Instead of using kinship language to describe her relationship to him, he now speaks of her impersonally as "the woman" and as one who was given to him by a third party. His words no longer reflect an intimacy with Eve. As Alan Jon Hauser remarks, "She has become an object, not a companion."[63]

Adam's objectification of Eve is even more striking because only Adam receives any explicit instruction about their unity. The man is the one who is to leave his father and mother and cleave to his wife so that they may become one flesh, a union that involves numerous aspects beyond the sexual to include spiritual, emotional, and kinship relations.[64] Adam is supposed to achieve the reunification of the two, but he fails profoundly. This is a critical, but mostly overlooked, aspect of Adam's failure.

In contrast to Adam, Eve is never given any instruction for the relationship, and her words also do not provide any commentary on their relationship in any way. This is not to say that Eve was never given any commands or did not have any thoughts on the matter. The point is that this is what the author has decided to use for portraying their relationship in this passage. Adam is the one who is instructed to achieve marital unity, but he actually does the opposite.

63. Hauser, "Genesis 2–3," 394.
64. Wenham, *Genesis 1–15*, 71.

Recognizing the significance of unity, including unity as the responsibility of the husband, may provide a helpful perspective for our contemporary questions. If God commissioned Adam to promote the unity of the marriage, then it is difficult to imagine that "authority" would be a main characteristic of his responsibility since power relationships tend to separate rather than create intimacy. At the same time, because Adam has a particular role in regard to the unity with Eve and the need for obedience to God's direct command, it is also difficult to see their relationship as primarily one of functional "equality."

## Conclusion

This chapter has attempted to examine the portrayal of Adam and Eve in a manner that goes beyond the categories of "authority" and "equality." Genesis 1:28 describes their shared mandate to "subdue" and "rule," while Gen. 2–3 explores the relational dimension of Adam and Eve with each other and with God, their obedience to God, and their unity with each other.

Within this portrayal there are noteworthy differences between the two. In many ways Adam has the principal focusing role of the narrative. The consequences for disobedience center on Adam. It is only after he, not Eve, eats that their eyes are opened. The stated warning for disobedience to God's command—death—depends on Adam's, and not Eve's, obedience. Thus, at least in this area, they are not "equal." Adam's transgression introduces death into the entire world, and Paul shares this assessment of Adam's representative function. He describes in Rom. 5:12–21 that the disobedience of one man, Adam, brought sin, death, and condemnation in contrast to the obedience of another man, Christ, that brought grace, life, and justification.

Genesis 2–3 consistently and strikingly portrays Adam and Eve's relationship in an asymmetrical way. Adam provides the source for Eve's creation, and he is the only one told to bring unity to the relationship. He is the one who discovers that he needs Eve, not the other way around.

Adam's act of naming Eve falls in line with this trend. There has been much discussion over whether Adam's naming of Eve represents his authority over her.[65] But at the very least we can say that it is part of a pattern of representing Adam as the one from whom the relationship consistently begins, at least

65. For the different arguments and counterarguments, see, e.g., Schreiner, "Another Complementarian Perspective," 294–97; Finley, "Relationship of Woman and Man," 55; Ortlund, "Male-Female Equality," 102–3; M. Evans, *Woman in the Bible*, 16; Groothuis, *Good News for Women*, 127–29; and Hess, "Equality," 82.

from a narrative standpoint. Eve does not name Adam, nor do they name each other; rather, Adam names Eve. She is his helper, and not the other way around. Paul also characterized their relationship as one in which Eve was created from Adam and for him (1 Cor. 11:8–9).

The only action in which Eve is the source or initiator is when she eats the fruit and gives it to Adam, which points to the centrality of this event in her characterization. This does not mean that these are the only such actions that occurred, but they are the ones the author has chosen to present and through which we are to understand the story.

Consequently, while Adam and Eve's relationship revolves around unity and love, it is also characterized by more than equality. At the same time, it lacks any explicit commands for Adam to exercise authority *over* Eve but does emphasize the obedience of both Adam and Eve to God. Whatever the nature of any authority Adam might have, it is not presented in a dominant fashion. Furthermore, it is difficult to see how authority would be a primary characteristic of Adam's role if one of his main duties is to create unity between the two.

Instead, it is important to consider seriously the only direct instruction Adam is given in regard to his relationship with Eve, that is, his responsibility in Gen. 2:24 for their unity—to "cleave" so that they may be one flesh. In the next chapter, we will see how Paul reiterates the goal of unity as the husband's primary duty in Eph. 5:21–33. We will examine the way in which Eph. 5 speaks of the expectations for husband and wife in relation to Genesis, especially in how the relationship that was broken in the garden is to be restored in the kingdom and the coming of Christ. Thus, as Adam and Eve violated God's holiness in their disobedience to the command not to eat, so did they not achieve holiness in their personal union.[66] Now the responsibility of the man manifests itself in giving himself for his wife rather than abandoning or blaming her, and thus imitating the last Adam rather than the first.

In conclusion, if either "equality" or "authority" is present in this passage in some way, it must be understood in the context of these larger and more dominant concerns of unity, holiness, and obedience. The significance of Adam's relationship to God's command and the unity of Adam and Eve are critical overarching perspectives on the passage. Adam is to keep God's

66. Some scholars have argued that the garden of Eden is to be understood as a temple, with Adam as the guardian. See, e.g., Beale, *Temple and the Church's Mission*, 66–70; Kline, *Images of the Spirit*, 35–42; Barker, *Gate of Heaven*, 68–103; Wenham, "Sanctuary Symbolism." Walton sees indications that Genesis portrays the garden as sacred space, so Adam's tasks are of a priestly nature (*Genesis*, 173).

command and create unity with Eve. Eve is charged with helping Adam, and both are called to obey God. Sadly, both fail, with disastrous consequences. But the story does not end there, as Paul sees the solution in the coming of Christ. His obedience overcomes the effects of Adam's disobedience, and in Christ, husbands will no longer be the cause of separation with their wives but will instead bring about the unity that God intended from the beginning.

# 8

# Marriage, Part 2

## *Husbands and Wives in Ephesians 5*

The importance of unity in the account of Adam and Eve compels us to ask how this impacts the depiction of marriage in the New Testament, especially since Paul specifically refers to Gen. 2:24 in Eph. 5:21–33, a passage that is at the center of the evangelical gender debate.[1] In this section we will pay special attention to this pivotal passage, both because of its relationship to Genesis and also because it provides a substantial theological and cultural window into understanding the significance of "headship."

The discussion has generally revolved around two areas: (1) the meaning of "head," or *kephalē*, and whether it carries connotations of authority and (2) the impact of the cultural context and whether recognizing the patriarchal culture in which the passage was written leads to the conclusion that Paul's instructions are not timeless and transcultural but culturally bound. However, we will argue that there is a need to revisit the passage with additional considerations as related to the critical kingdom themes already outlined. First, the presence of a "reversal" will show that the significance of *kephalē* lies both in

1. An earlier version of this chapter appeared in Lee-Barnewall, "Turning Κεφαλή on Its Head."

what it means or implies in its cultural context and also how Paul transforms its significance in comparison with what was accepted in that time, as might be expected from a gospel that opposes the values of the world. Furthermore, the theme of unity needs to be given proper priority in analyzing the passage because of Paul's use of Gen. 2:24, especially considering its critical role in Genesis as a description of Adam and Eve's relationship.

Therefore, as we consider the significance of Eph. 5, we will pay special attention to the way in which it represents a kingdom version of marriage that sees the essential goal as the fulfillment of the one flesh union that happens as the husband follows the example of Christ as the self-sacrificial head. As a result, the issue is not a clear-cut one of whether the husband has "authority" over his wife as the head as opposed to the wife's being an "equal" partner in the marriage. Rather the passage is shaped by ideas that are more immediately relevant to kingdom priorities, such as reversal, sacrifice, love, and unity. We will also examine the implications of Paul's principles of marriage for understanding the church's corporate relationship to Christ as his bride in light of these greater themes for what they may contribute to our understanding of gender.

## The Meaning of *Kephalē*

Much of the discussion of Eph. 5:21–33 has revolved around the meaning of *kephalē*. The most prominent proposals have included "authority" and "leadership" for complementarians and "source (of being)" and more recently "preeminence" (without connotations of hierarchy or authority) for egalitarians. These definitions reflect the issue of whether Eph. 5 speaks of male authority and leadership in the husband-wife relationship. Thus, even though some argue that the proposal by some egalitarians for *kephalē* to mean "preeminence" is an admission of hierarchy[2] and even though complementarians have softened their stance by talking of "servant leadership," the dividing line continues to be the question of whether there are connotations of authority in the passage. We will see that while *kephalē* can have connotations of "authority," the main significance of its use is the way in which Paul reverses the cultural expectations of the "head" according to the radical new values of the Christian community.

2. Or as Grudem states, it could imply a "wrongful kind of male superiority" with connotations that "deny our equality in the image of God" (*Evangelical Feminism*, 211).

### *The Interpretative Context*

Perhaps the most commonly cited study in understanding *kephalē* as "authority" is Wayne Grudem's essay.[3] Grudem surveys 2,336 examples in the literature most relevant to the New Testament period and argues that there is demonstrable evidence that it could be used metaphorically to mean "authority over."[4] As a result, "authority over" can be seen as a "legitimate sense" of *kephalē*,[5] and he concludes that this is the best sense in Eph. 5. However, while Grudem is correct in asserting that *kephalē* can carry connotations of authority, he provides less evidence to support that this is specifically Paul's intent in Eph. 5.

A related definition is *kephalē* as meaning "leadership." Clinton Arnold's survey of the medical literature in regard to the relationship of the head to the body reveals that the more nuanced understandings of "leadership" and "source of provision" may be more fitting.[6] Connotations of authority may be present but do not necessarily form Paul's primary concern in his use of the metaphor.[7]

Egalitarians have proposed other ways of understanding *kephalē*. Catherine Clark Kroeger argues that the term should instead be translated as "source" and cites a passage from Cyril of Alexandria in which he identifies *kephalē* with *archē* four times.[8] Several decades earlier Stephen Bedale similarly proposed that by biblical times, the two terms had become closely associated.[9] But as Gregory Dawes points out, while it may be possible that "source" is present in terms of the *sense* of the metaphor, this is not the same as saying that one can *translate* the metaphor as "source":

> To *translate* the word as "source" is to prejudge an important issue: it is to imply that in this context the word is functioning as a dead metaphor. It implies

3. Grudem, "Survey of 2,336 Examples"; Grudem, "Meaning of *Kephalē*." Also Fitzmyer, "Another Look at Κεφαλή."

4. Grudem cites forty-nine occurrences, or 2.1 percent of the total instances and 16.2 percent of total metaphorical uses ("Survey of 2,336 Examples," 51).

5. Ibid., 59.

6. Arnold, "Jesus Christ." See also Dawes, *Body in Question*, 129–33, who suggests the meanings "authority" and "source of life and growth."

7. Dawes's survey of the Greek medical writers on the literal relationship of the head to the body leads him to conclude that both "authority" and "source" are possible senses of the metaphor, although in its context in Eph. 5 the metaphor indicates authority (*Body in Question*, 129–37).

8. Kroeger, "Classical Concept," 268.

9. Bedale, "Meaning of Κεφαλή," 213. Bedale also concluded that *kephalē* "unquestionably carries with it the idea of 'authority,'" although the authority "derives from a relative priority (causal rather than merely temporal) in the order of being" (ibid., 215).

> that a contemporary reader would have understood the word in the same way as he or she would have understood ἀρχή, that is, independently, without any reference to that which the science of anatomy would describe as a "head."[10]

As will be discussed in more detail below, understanding the significance of "head" entails examining how it would have been seen in its relationship to the physical body.

A third option is presented by Richard Cervin, who argues that *kephalē* indicates "preeminence."[11] Rather than meaning "authority over," Paul is "merely employing a head-body metaphor" in which the head is the topmost and most conspicuous member of the body.[12] However, it is very difficult to imagine a situation in antiquity where a person could be recognized as having a sense of prominence that is devoid of any substantive privilege or power.[13] On closer examination of the ancient sources, we will see that the precise reason why the head has the favored position is that there is a fundamental and necessary connection between position and function.

### Kephalē *in Antiquity*

The rise of rhetorical criticism in the study of biblical texts has revealed the importance of understanding the author's argumentative strategy and the intended effect on the audience. Since rhetoric depended not only on the meaning of words but also on the way in which those words were used in arguments,[14] we need to examine carefully the use of the head-body metaphor in antiquity to determine its specific use in this passage. The use of common rhetorical conventions shows a continuation with a tradition. The key element was the way in which someone applied the conventions to make a particular point.

10. Dawes, *Body in Question*, 126, italics original.

11. Cervin, "Rebuttal," 85–112.

12. Ibid., 110–12. Similarly, Liefeld suggests, "*prominent*," "*eminent*," and "*representative*" ("Women, Submission and Ministry," 139–40, italics original).

13. Or as Blomberg states, "It is unclear if an entity can be most or even more prominent without implying at least some kind of functional superiority in the context at hand" ("Complementarian Perspective," 156).

14. The beginning of the present interest in the rhetoric of biblical texts is often traced to James Muilenburg's presidential address to the Society of Biblical Literature in 1968. Muilenburg focused mostly on rhetoric as style, and Mack notes that "his understanding of rhetorical criticism could not encompass a raft of questions already on the horizon about the role of literature within a culture and about the effective difference a piece of writing might make within a given social history" (*Rhetoric and the New Testament*, 13). For a history of the early development of rhetorical criticism in biblical studies, see ibid., 9–24.

By examining prominent uses of the image of the body in antiquity, we will discover that Paul refers to the head in relationship to the body in a traditional way but also radicalizes it according to the gospel. In other words, he "turns it on its head" to make a point about how God has transformed marriage relationships in the eschatological age. To this end we will examine the common uses and assumptions of the body metaphor as they relate to the position and privileges of the head. As Grudem states, it is necessary "to ask exactly which characteristics of a physical head were recognized in the ancient world and were evident in those contexts where people were metaphorically called 'head.'"[15] We will then see how Paul's use in many ways follows the standard application and yet at crucial points diverges from the common application. These divergences, which represent a startling reversal of societal expectations, are ultimately what define his concept of headship and so the relationship between husbands and wives in the kingdom.

### The Basic Use of the Head-Body Metaphor

The body metaphor was diverse and flexible and could be used to illustrate a number of situations. A common theme was the unity and diversity of the body. For example, the body was a common *topos* in antiquity in political speeches arguing for unity in the form of *homonoia*, or "concord" speeches.[16] According to this use, the group, which was not limited to formal political associations, was like a body in that it was composed of various parts that needed to cooperate in order to survive or for the "common good."[17]

Sometimes the metaphor highlighted a single part. In the famous Menenius Agrippa fable, the body learned the importance of the belly. In his attempt to quell the rebellion against the senate, Agrippa told a story about the body's revolt against the belly. In the fable the other body parts objected that they had to provide for the belly, while the belly merely enjoyed the food that was brought to it. However, when they tried to starve it into submission by refusing to feed it, they ended up weakening the entire body. Thus the body learned that the belly's distributive function was necessary for the survival of the whole. Agrippa argued that although the belly did not initially seem to serve any useful function, it served a very necessary function, and in a

15. Grudem, "Meaning of *Kephalē*," 460.

16. E.g., D. Martin, *Corinthian Body*, 38–47; Mitchell, *Paul*, 157–64. Some famous examples of these speeches would include Antiphon's *On Concord* and Isocrates's *Panegyricus*.

17. Philo, *Decal.* 150; Dio Chrysostom, *Or.* 34.20. For a more extensive description of the various uses of the body metaphor, see Lee, *Paul*, 29–58; and Mitchell, *Paul*.

similar manner, the senate performed a critical role in administrating the labor of others.[18]

In addition to the stomach, other parts such as hands[19] and feet[20] were used, as was the head. What often characterized the use of the head in the metaphor was how it commonly depicted the superior and leading part of the body, the one most important for the overall health of the body.

For the medical writers such as Hippocrates and Galen, the head or brain was seen as the leading member of the body since it coordinated all the activities of the other members.[21] For example, Hippocrates states, "Neither [the heart or the diaphragm] has any share of intelligence, but it is the brain [*enkephalos*] which is the cause of all the things I have mentioned" (*Morb. sacr.* 20.27–29).[22] This common physiological understanding is then reflected in various places, such as in Plato[23] and Philo.[24]

When the concept of headship was applied politically, there was often an emphasis on the power and authority of the head. Plutarch relates, "But after Vindex had openly declared war, he wrote to Galba inviting him to assume the imperial power, and thus to serve what was a vigorous body in need of a head [*kephalēn*], meaning the Gallic provinces" (*Galb.* 4.3). We see this in Seneca, who sees Nero as the head of Rome, his body (*Clem.* 1.4.3). He discusses how the whole body (*corpus*) is the servant of the mind. Thus "the hands, the feet, and the eyes are in its employ; the outer skin is its defence; at its bidding we lie idle, or restlessly run to and fro; when it commands, if it is a grasping tyrant, we search the sea for gain" (*Clem.* 1.3.5). The body's loyalty to the head as its sovereign is so great that it will even "thrust a right hand into the flame" or plunge "willingly into a chasm" if necessary (ibid.).

18. Livy, *History of Rome* 2.32.12–2.33.1; Dionysius of Halicarnassus, *Ant. rom.* 6.86.1–5; Plutarch, *Cor.* 6.2–3.

19. Plutarch, *Praec. ger. rei publ.*, 812B–E, *Frat. amor.*, 478C–E; Aristotle, *Eth. nic.* 1.7.11–12; Xenophon, *Mem.* 2.3.17–19.

20. Xenophon, *Mem.* 2.3.17–19; Plutarch, *Frat. amor.* 478C–E; Aristotle, *Eth. nic.* 1.7.11–12.

21. Arnold, "Jesus Christ"; Dawes, *Body in Question*, 129–33.

22. As cited in Arnold, "Jesus Christ," 352. Galen speaks of the head's sovereignty over the body when he states, "To most people the head seems to have been formed on account of the encephalon and for that reason to contain all the senses, like the servants and guards of a great king" (*De usu partium* 1.445.14–17, as cited in Arnold, "Jesus Christ," 354).

23. "The divine revolutions, which are two, they bound within a sphere-shaped body, in imitation of the spherical form of the All, which body we now call the 'head,' it being the most divine part and reigning over all the parts within us. To it the gods delivered over the whole body they had assembled to be its servant" (*Tim.* 44d, as cited in Arnold, "Jesus Christ," 352).

24. Philo calls humans "a kind of ruling head" (*archikē tis kephalē*) of all living creatures (*QG* 2.9).

The body will do this because it knows the critical role of the head. Seneca describes the head's role when he says that the people are "guided by his reason, and would crush and cripple itself with its own power if it were not upheld by wisdom" (ibid.).

The head's literal position as the topmost member in the body plays a large role in this characterization as the leading part because its high stature represents or makes it worthy of greater power and privilege. For example, Philo says the head is sovereign because it is the highest part of the body: "Nature conferred the sovereignty of the body on the head [*kephalē*] when she granted it also possession of the citadel as the most suitable position for its kingly rank, conducted it thither to take command and established it on high with the whole framework from neck to foot set below it, like the pedestal under the statue" (*Spec.* 3.184).[25] For Philo the head's position on top of the body cannot be separated from its subsequent duties. Because the city's acropolis is the highest point, it is also the most fitting place for the city's center and fortress.

In the following passage, Philo adds protection to the head's/citadel's duties: "And where in the body has the mind made its lair? . . . Some have regarded the head, our body's citadel, as its hallowed shrine, since it is about the head that the senses have their station, and it seems natural to them that they should be posed there, like bodyguards to some mighty monarch" (*Somn.* 1.32).[26] Elsewhere, in discussing Ptolemy's superior accomplishments as measured against other kings, Philo uses the metaphor to illustrate that "as the head takes the highest place in the living body, so he [Ptolemy] may be said to head the kings" (*Mos.* 2.30).

The head's position is a reflection of the substance of its position as the most accomplished member of the body. Headship could represent other types of superiority beyond military leadership. Philo states, "So then one such [wise] man in a city, if such be found, will be superior to the city, one such city to the country around, one such nation will stand above other nations, as the head [*kephalē*] above the body to be conspicuous on every side" (*Praem.* 113–14).

Thus the position itself was defined by ability and function. Headship served as more than an honorary title, although the substance of the head's prominence could vary. Overall the head was considered preeminent because its highest position indicated its superior role.[27]

25. Similarly he says in *Somn.* 2.207, "'Head' [*kephalēn*] we interpret allegorically to mean the ruling part of the soul, the mind on which all things lie."

26. Philo also cites the importance of the head in *QG* 2.5: "The head, like the citadel of a king, has as its occupant the sovereign mind."

27. In another passage, Philo calls the virtuous person the "head" of the human race, the one from whom all other people draw their life force, just as the head is the first and best part of the

However, if "head" signifies prominence because of its leading role in the body, this does not imply that we can simply transfer meanings of leadership and authority wholesale into Ephesians. As emphasized earlier, in rhetoric it was not the appearance of a common metaphor but its specific use that was significant. It becomes critical at this point to examine more closely the *way* in which Paul uses the image, and it should not surprise us to see that Paul makes a radical transformation. Our next step will be to take a closer look at the expectations regarding love and leadership in ancient uses of the head-body metaphor.

### Expectations regarding the Head-Body Metaphor

Because of the head's prominent status and role, a common theme emerges in treatments of headship in antiquity of the head as the most important member of the body. Thus Plutarch relates how Antigonus described his position as head or general as "the one who saves everything else" (*Pel.* 2.1–2).[28] Seneca calls Nero the "head" of Rome, which is his body, and describes his importance in this way, "It is not strange that kings and princes and guardians of the public order . . . are held more dear even than those bound to us by private ties; for if men of sense put public interests above private, it follows that he too is dearer upon whom the whole state centres. . . . For while a Caesar needs power, the state also needs a head [*capite*]" (*Clem.* 1.4.3).[29]

The passage from Seneca reflects the idea that the underlying concern in regard to the health of the body was the well-being of the whole—that is, the "common good." One was compelled to do what was most necessary for the survival of the entire body, and some parts had greater priority and

animal (*Praem.* 125). While there was debate over whether the head or the heart was the guiding member, the passage does reflect a tradition of ascribing the most important role to the head.

28. Polyaenus (*Stratagems of War* 3.9.22) relates how Iphicrates describes an army using the figure of the body: "The phalanx he called the breast, the light armed troops the hands, the cavalry the feet, and the general the head. If any of the inferior parts were wanting, the army was defective; but if it wanted a general it wanted every thing" (translation from D. Martin, *Corinthian Body*, 93–94).

29. Seneca explains the emperor's importance for Rome:

> For he is the bond by which the commonwealth is united, the breath of life which these many thousands draw, who in their own strength would be only a burden to themselves and the prey of others if the great mind of the empire should be withdrawn. . . . Just so long will this people be free from [destruction] as it shall know how to submit to the rein; but if ever it shall tear away the rein, or shall not suffer it to be replaced if shaken loose by some mishap, then this unity and this fabric of mightiest empire will fly into many parts, and the end of this city's rule will be one with the end of her obedience. (*Clem.* 1.4.1, 2–3)

status because the survival of the entire body depended more on them than on others. The head played perhaps the most critical role in the survival of the body. As a result, a vital concern was to protect the head at all costs. Seneca describes how the people are willing to give their very lives in order to protect Nero as their head:

> [The king or prince] alone has firm and well-founded greatness whom all men know to be as much their friend as he is their superior; whose concern they daily find to be vigilant for the safety of each and all. . . . In his defence they are ready on the instant to throw themselves before the swords of assassins, and to lay their bodies beneath his feet if his path to safety must be paved with slaughtered men; his sleep they guard by nightly vigils, his person they defend with an encircling barrier, against assailing danger they make themselves a rampart. (*Clem.* 1.3.3)

> Not without reason do cities and peoples show this accord in giving such protection and love to their kings, and in flinging themselves and all they have into the breach whenever the safety of their ruler craves it. Nor is it self-depreciation or madness when many thousands meet the steel for the sake of one man, and with many deaths ransom a single life, it may be, of a feeble dotard. (*Clem.* 1.3.4)

The people are willing to make this sacrifice for him because they know that the safety of the whole depends on his well-being. Seneca quotes Virgil and then summarizes, "'If safe their king, one mind to all; Bereft of him, they troth recall.' Such a calamity would be the destruction of the Roman peace, such a calamity will force the fortune of a mighty people to its downfall" (*Clem.* 1.4.1–2).

Furthermore, not only does the body seek to protect the head, but the head's duty is to ensure its own preservation, as Plutarch observes: "For if, as Iphicrates analyzed the matter, the light-armed troops are like the hands, the cavalry like the feet, the line of men-at-arms itself like chest and breastplate, and the general like the head, then he, in taking undue risks and being over bold, would seem to neglect not himself, but all, inasmuch as their safety depends on him, and their destruction too" (*Pel.* 2.1). Since the "common good" demands that the most important part be preserved in order to ensure the survival of the whole, for the head to endanger itself is seen not as a noble action but rather as a misguided one.[30] Instead, it was the duty of the leader to

30. "Therefore, Callicratidas, although otherwise he was a great man, did not make a good answer to the seer who begged him to be careful, since the sacrificial omens foretold his death; 'Sparta,' said he, 'does not depend upon one man.' For when fighting, or sailing, or marching under orders, Callicratidas was 'one man'; but as general, he comprised in himself the strength

see to his own safety so that he could ensure the safety of all. Thus Plutarch summarizes, "The worth of the commander is a great thing . . . and his first duty is to save the one who saves everything else" (*Pel.* 2.1–2).[31] Because of the need to save the whole, it naturally followed that the body should preserve the members with the primary roles in ensuring the survival of the whole. In many cases, this meant the head, the leader and guide of the body.

Finally, another aspect of the tradition was that the head, as ruler, was not called to be the one who loves but rather was more deserving of being loved. Thus Seneca specifically states that the people's actions in sacrificing themselves for Nero are their demonstration of "love" for their head,[32] in response to which Nero is to show not love but mercy (*Clem.* 1.5.1–2).

Aristotle also states the expectations in terms of love for the superior by the one over whom he stands when he states: "For it would be ludicrous if one were to accuse God because he does not return love in the same way as he is loved, or for a subject to make this accusation against a ruler; for it is the part of a ruler to be loved, not to love or else to love in another way" (*Eth. eud.* 7.3.4). The difference was a reflection of the asymmetrical relationship between the head and the body for the good of the whole, an understanding that resulted in a set of expectations conforming to the nature of each part's position.

In conclusion, the metaphor was a graphic representation of the roles of the head and the body. The superior physical placement of the head was symbolic of its leading role in the body and resulted in specific behavioral expectations for both parties.

## The Husband as "Head" in Ephesians 5:21–33

The normal expectation for the metaphor is that the head is the leader and provider of the body. Consequently, it is the head's responsibility to ensure

and power of all, so that he was not 'one man,' when such numbers perished with him" (Plutarch, *Pel.* 2.1).

31. Cervin casts doubt on the relevance of this passage because Plutarch is "merely employing a simile" as opposed to a metaphor ("Rebuttal," 101). Grudem says that the example is still useful although it should be placed in a "different category" ("Meaning of *Kephalē*," 439). However, simile and metaphor were not considered fundamentally different by the rhetoricians. Thus Aristotle (*Rhet.* 3.4.1–2) states, "A simile is also a metaphor; for there is little difference. . . . [Similes] should be brought in like metaphors, for they *are* metaphors, differing in the form of expression" (translation from Kennedy, *Aristotle*, italics original).

32. As cited earlier, "Not without reason do cities and peoples show this accord in giving such protection and love [*protegendi amandique*] to their kings, and in flinging themselves and all they have into the breach whenever the safety of their ruler craves it" (*Clem.* 1.3.4).

its own safety, and the body's responsibility to sacrifice itself for the sake of the head. As a result, we would expect Paul to instruct the wife, the body, to be willing to sacrifice for the sake of the husband, the head. Such instructions would be the most logical since, according to common reasoning, the body could not survive without the head. But that is not what we find; rather, Paul states the reverse. The husband as the head is called to give himself up for the wife as his body, just as Christ gave himself up for the church, which is his body.[33] Furthermore, where normal expectations would have the body being the one to love the head, Paul states that the husband as head is to love his wife as his body as Christ loved the church.

The fundamental nature of the reversal is critical. It would have struck Paul's audience not only as odd but even more so as being against nature. The sacrifice of the head would be suicidal for the entire body since the head provides guidance for the whole. The reversal in expectations in regard to love would also seem shocking in light of traditional honor conventions because Paul tells the most esteemed part, the head, to love the body.

Maintaining the natural order was key to preserving society, and one accepted aspect of this order was the husband as ruler over the wife,[34] due to his superior nature.[35] It was vital that all parties conform to the hierarchy, especially since the household order was seen as a microcosm of society. Keeping the household order was indispensable to guaranteeing order in society as a whole.[36] Since "the man is intended by nature to rule as husband, father, and master," deviating from this hierarchy was harmful to the state as well as the household.[37] When Paul asks husbands as heads to sacrifice themselves for

33. Thus the emphasis is on Christ's love for the church as a whole rather than as individuals. Some have noted that this is the only passage in the New Testament that explicitly refers to Christ's love for the church. See Hoehner, *Ephesians*, 749; Schlier, *Brief an die Epheser*, 255.

34. See Balch, *Let Wives Be Submissive*, 23–62. E.g., Aristotle states, "There are by nature various classes of rulers and ruled [*ta archonta kai archomena*]. For the free rules the slave, the male the female, the man the child in a different way" (*Pol.* 1.5.6).

35. "For the male is by nature better fitted to command than the female. . . . It is true that in most cases of republican government the ruler and the ruled interchange in turn . . . but the male stands in this relationship to the female continuously" (Aristotle, *Pol.* 1.5.2); "The male is by nature superior and the female inferior, the male ruler and the female subject" (Aristotle, *Pol.* 1.2.12); "The man has the rule of this house by nature. For the deliberative faculty in a woman is inferior. . . . Rational household management, which is the control of a house and of those things related to the house, is fitting for a man" (Areius Didymus, 149.5, as quoted in Balch, *Let Wives Be Submissive*, 42); "The woman, says the Law, is in all things inferior to the man. Let her accordingly be submissive, not for her humiliation, but that she may be directed; for the authority has been given by God to the man" (Josephus, *C. Ap.* 2.201).

36. Malherbe, *Social Aspects*, 51.

37. Lincoln, *Ephesians*, 358.

their wives, he asks them to do something that goes against this fundamental order of society, which would be considered disruptive and even dangerous.

It is also enlightening to examine the significance of Paul's reversal of status conventions. When Paul asks husbands, and not wives, to love and sacrifice, this reversal would be shocking in light of traditional status conventions because he tells the most honored part, the head, to perform the duties of the less honored member.

As described earlier, the quest for honor was central in the ancient Mediterranean culture. As Bartchy states, "Among all social classes, traditional male socialization programmed males to pursue a never-ending quest for greater honor and influence."[38] Since honor for men was gained through domination of others, the husband would have been expected to dominate and be served by his wife.[39] However, Paul states that he should instead do the opposite and exercise his headship through service and sacrifice.

In the ancient Mediterranean world, masculinity was closely connected to personal freedom and one's power over others, so to attack a man's authority was to attack his masculinity.[40] As the head of the wife, the husband would have been expected to exercise power over his wife, and not to do so would have been considered shameful. Timothy Gombis also observes that in other ancient household codes, the main attention was on the "comfort and happiness" of the husband.[41]

When Paul tells wives to submit to their husbands and to do so because he is the head (Eph. 5:22–24), he would seem to be agreeing with these values. But when he instructs husbands in the content of this headship, he presents a startling reversal. Contrary to common conceptions of what is fitting and thus honorable, husbands are to love their wives and give themselves up for them.

While this behavior would be shameful in the larger culture, it was considered honorable in God's economy. This is why it is imperative to note that Paul connects the husband's actions with Christ. He plays on the head-body metaphor in order to present a picture of the husband-wife relationship in which the husband as the head is called to fulfill his role paradoxically, by sacrificing himself and loving the body, rather than saving his own life and receiving love. As Christ did not use the rights of his headship for his own

38. Bartchy, "Who Should Be Called Father?," 136.
39. Ibid., 136.
40. Larson, "Paul's Masculinity."
41. Gombis, "Radically New Humanity," 325.

gain but instead sacrificed on behalf of the church, so too are husbands to sacrifice for, rather than dominate, their wives.

### Headship and Unity

Paul also says that the reversal seen in the love of the husband relates to the one flesh unity of Gen. 2:24. The use of Gen. 2:24 brings us back to our earlier discussion of Adam and Eve. In Genesis the one flesh unity was Adam's primary imperative in his relationship with Eve, and he was unable to fulfill it. Now under the new covenant, the husband's ability to love his wife as Christ loves the church enables him to "cleave" to his wife and be "one flesh" with her in all its fullness.

Furthermore, Paul says that Gen. 2:24 applies not only to the husband and wife but also to Christ and the church, as he uses the passage to support his statement regarding Christ in Eph. 5:30 that "we are members of His body."[42] Arnold argues that this "strongly suggests" that Paul sees a typological relationship between marriage and the relationship of Christ and the church so that it goes beyond analogy or comparison to indicate a "new reality."[43] While this does not mean that all parts of the passage can be interpreted typologically, Paul is saying that the unity of husband and wife as "one flesh" prefigures the intimate relationship of Christ and the church.[44] The surprising nature of this relationship is why it is called a "mystery," or something that could be known only through God's revelation.[45] The further description of it as a "great" mystery indicates that it is something important

42. Arnold (*Ephesians*, 395) further notes that Paul adds "for this reason" to the LXX version to connect the passage more closely to his argument that Gen. 2:24 supports the union of Christ and the church.

43. Ibid., 396. Other scholars dispute the presence of typology here, seeing the "mystery" as referring only to human marriage or only to the union of Christ and the church. For a discussion of these positions, see Hoehner, *Ephesians*, 776–78.

44. Arnold, *Ephesians*, 396. Thielman sees the primacy of the Christ-church reference for three main reasons: (1) Paul explicitly says that the Genesis quotation applies to Christ and the church (v. 32); (2) Paul opens the quotation with "because of this" (*anti toutou*), which most naturally refers to the preceding statements in vv. 29c–30 concerning Christ's care for the church; and (3) the use of "nevertheless" (*plēn*) in v. 33 brings the reader back to Paul's train of thought prior to beginning his digression in 5:29c. Thus the quotation and the explanation in 5:31–32 are all part of the digression concerning Christ and the church. Therefore, "as surprising as it may seem, Paul is saying in 5:31 that God has instituted marriage 'because' the church is Christ's body" (*Ephesians*, 389).

45. Thielman notes, "The application of Gen. 2:24 to the union of Christ with the church would be nonsensical apart from a special revelation from God that tells of this application" (*Ephesians*, 389).

or profound.[46] Thus Paul indicates in Eph. 5:32 that Gen. 2:24 is actually a statement about the church and Christ, so Christ's union with the church is the way in which to understand the husband-wife relationship.

For both the husband and Christ, the one flesh union is connected with sacrificial love, a critical component of Paul's understanding of headship. What is also striking about Paul's argument is that while it would be expected that in Christ both the husband and the wife are to love each other, in Eph. 5 Paul specifically discusses the love of the husband only. It is only his role, not hers, that is compared with Christ's love for the church. Therefore, we must ask why Paul specifically assigns this type of significance to the husband's love only, and not the wife's love for the husband.[47]

There is no doubt that the wife is to love her husband, as all members of the community would be called to love one another (e.g., John 13:34; 1 Cor. 13). We have also seen that love, the imitation of Christ's sacrificial example, creates greater unity within the church among the individual members. All may be members of the body of Christ in the Spirit (1 Cor. 12:13), but all are still called to love one another in order to become one in a deeper way, as love is the "perfect bond of unity" (Col. 3:14). In Phil. 2:1–11 Paul exhorts the Philippians to be unified by imitating Christ in the way he became a servant even though he could have exercised his privileges of being God. Significantly, Paul also describes this as "love" in Phil. 2:2. However, Eph. 5:25–32 adds another dimension when it focuses on the initiating love of the head for the body in relationship to the unity between Christ and the church and the husband and the wife. In other words, while all believers are to love one another like Christ for the purpose of unity within the body, there is something unique about the love of the head (Christ or the husband) that relates to the unity between the body (the church or the wife) and itself in regard to the "one flesh" union.

The relationship between a love that originates with the husband and an intimate marital relationship is also found in the Old Testament in relation to God and Israel. In Hosea God is portrayed as the one who continually seeks after Israel. Even though Israel has abandoned him for other lovers, God proclaims that he "will allure her, bring her into the wilderness and

46. Best, *One Body in Christ*, 179.

47. In Colossians, Paul similarly calls on all the believers to love one another as their obligation as members of one body (Col. 3:12–15) and goes on to enjoin husbands specifically to love their wives (Col. 3:19). He does not give a corresponding obligation for wives to love their husbands, thus indicating again that he is speaking of a specific duty of husbands to wives here.

speak kindly to her" (Hosea 2:14). Israel will respond, and the result will be the restoration of the relationship as when Yahweh first honeymooned with Israel in the wilderness (2:15).[48]

In Hosea, "husband" is a metaphor that signifies intimacy.[49] Hans Walter Wolff further notes that the expression "I will speak to her heart"[50] is from the language of courtship and seeks "to overcome sorrow and resentment . . . obstinacy and estrangement"[51]—in other words, to produce relational union rather than separation. The use of "my husband" may reflect the idea of belonging and a "deep personal relationship" with the wife in contrast to the legal position of the husband as "my lord," or "owner" of the wife.[52] The concept of intimacy is presented boldly in Hosea 2:20, which states that Israel will "know the Lord," using the term (*yāda'*) that connotes sexual intimacy and is used metaphorically for intimacy in a covenantal sense.[53] J. Andrew Dearman highlights the significance of knowing God in Exod. 6:2–7, when God tells Moses to deliver a message to Israel: "Say, therefore, to the sons of Israel . . . 'I will take you for My people, and I will be your God; and you shall know [*yāda'*] that I am the Lord your God, who brought you out from under the burdens of the Egyptians.'" In this passage God is saying not that he will reveal a previously unknown name but rather that the Israelites will recognize the significance of this name. Similarly, in Jer. 16:21 the message is, "I am going to make them know—This time I will make them know My power and My might; And they shall know that My name is the Lord." In Hosea the Israelites will "know," that is, relate to the Lord in a "new and significant way."[54] More than any other metaphor, including God as the Father or Shepherd of his people, the image of the husband highlights the love and trust that should exist between God and his people.[55]

Thus, in both the Old and the New Testaments, the marital metaphor brings connotations of intimacy and describes unity as related to the initiating

48. Although seen most profoundly in Hosea, this theme appears elsewhere in the Old Testament. For example, Isa. 61:10 also describes God's initiative as the bridegroom initiating this intimate relationship. See Beale, *Revelation*, 939.

49. Dearman, *Book of Hosea*, 124.

50. Or in the NASB, "speak kindly to her."

51. Wolff, *Hosea*, 42.

52. Ibid., 49. Some, such as Stienstra, argue that it is simply a reference to the idols that the Israelites worshiped and with whom they committed adultery (*YHWH Is the Husband*, 120). However, others, such as Hubbard, agree that it is also a "warmer, more intimate name" (*Hosea*, 85).

53. Stuart, *Hosea–Jonah*, 60.

54. Dearman, *Book of Hosea*, 129.

55. Stienstra, *YHWH Is the Husband*, 96.

actions of the husband/bridegroom. In the Old Testament Yahweh tenderly allures Israel. In the New Testament the "one flesh union" is associated with the sacrificial love of Christ and the husband with the church and the wife, respectively. Ephesians adds an additional dimension in that Paul says that such intimacy directly corresponds to the husband's fulfillment of his position as "head." But it is also accomplished through a reversal of the world's expectations of this duty, a reversal that is grounded in the significance of Christ's own saving actions and reflects the paradoxical values of the kingdom.

In the world the life of the body revolves around the head, and its role in the unity of the body is particularly important. For example, Seneca describes the head, Caesar, as "the bond by which the commonwealth is united" (*Clem.* 1.4.1). For Paul, the head is also the source of unity, but only as the head acts in a manner that is very unheadlike, by not exerting power or privilege but rather doing the opposite.

This is the crucial element of the "reversal." The point is that it is the head, not any other member of the body, that is acting in this way. The husband, like Christ, accomplishes his purpose by acting in a paradoxical kingdom way. Yet he must first be the head in order for his actions to be effective. Thus he leads and provides, but not as the one with privileges associated with the honored position, as would traditionally be the case. As with Christ, the head/husband sacrifices rather than expecting sacrifice from the other. As the head, he fulfills his duty through the application of kingdom values rather than exercising his worldly rights.

Consequently, the wife is to submit to a husband who loves her as his own body (Eph. 5:28–29). Whether or not verse 21 refers to a type of mutual submission,[56] we must note that Paul specifically calls on wives to submit and does not similarly address husbands. If Paul had intended only for believers to submit to one another in an equivalent way, there would be no need to give these specific instructions. As a result, we should consider the nature of the wife's submission.

56. Although the verb *hypotassō* does not appear in v. 22, it can be understood from the appearance of the verb in v. 21. As O'Brien explains, "[V. 21] is tightly linked with what immediately follows: there is no verb in verse 22, and so 'submitting' must be understood from verse 21 for its meaning and sense. The idea of 'submission' is unpacked in verse 22 without the verb being repeated" (*Letter to the Ephesians*, 403). Thielman cites three ways of interpreting "to one another": (1) the mutuality of v. 21 reveals his real thoughts, but he "allows an inconsistently authoritarian ethic from the tradition that he uses to slip through his editorial net"; (2) in v. 21 Paul introduces the topic of submission, and then in 5:22–6:9 he illustrates how this submission should work; and (3) Paul is saying that "there is a sense in which even those in authority 'submit' to their subordinates" (*Ephesians*, 372–73).

Frank Thielman notes that the two terms Paul uses, *ektrephei* and *thalpei*, were often used for the "physical nurture and emotional warmth that one person gives to another" and so express Paul's desire for husbands to provide for their wives physically and emotionally.[57] In the kingdom the image is not authoritarian but profoundly personal and relational.[58] As mentioned in our discussion of the early chapters of Genesis (chap. 7), it is difficult to imagine an emphasis on authority as leading to the intimate "one flesh" union.[59]

As with Israel in the Old Testament and the church in the New, the wife is the one who responds to the husband's loving actions that are intended to draw her to him.[60] In the fall Adam distanced himself from Eve by blaming her, rather than manifesting a true "one flesh" union. Instead of taking responsibility for his own transgression, he was essentially willing to sacrifice *her* by trying to place the blame on her in an attempt to save himself (Gen. 3:12), thus displaying the antithesis of the attitude expected of a husband in Christ. In Ephesians the husband/Christ creates intimacy by caring for the wife/church as much as he does for himself and so provides the nurture and care that is necessary for an intimate union. Whereas as a result of his sin Adam identified Eve impersonally as "the woman whom You gave to be with me," now the husband who is in Christ considers the woman as his very body

57. Thielman, *Ephesians*, 388.

58. Since Paul says that wives should submit "as to the Lord," this would also not reflect a harsh, controlling authority. As Arnold notes, "The way they respond to Christ should then inform the way they respond to their husbands" (*Ephesians*, 380).

59. Numerous commentators have pointed out the difference between Paul's use of "submission" (*hypotassō*) in Eph. 5:22//Col. 3:18 and the exhortation to obedience (*hypakouō*) given to children and slaves (Eph. 6:1, 5; Col. 3:20, 22). As Moo notes, "'Obedience' naturally fits a situation in which orders are being issued and in which the party obeying has little choice in the matter. Submission, on the other hand, suggests a voluntary willingness to recognize and put oneself under the leadership of another" (*Colossians and Philemon*, 301). O'Brien further observes that while it was commonly understood that wives had to obey their husbands, the actual use of *hypotassō* in reference to their obligations was not widespread (*Colossians, Philemon*, 221). He refers to Rengstorf ("Die neutestamentliche Mahnungen"), who found two examples (Plutarch, *Conj. praec.* 33; Ps-Callisthenes 1.22.4), which are then cited by other scholars. Lincoln argues that the two terms are "frequently synonymous" and "to subordinate oneself to another may well entail being willing to obey that person, and that such obedience would certainly have been seen as part of a wife's role in most parts of the ancient world" (*Ephesians*, 367–68). However, it may still be significant that Paul does not use a term with the more obvious connotations of obedience.

60. Dunn notes that the idea of a husband's loving care for his wife is not uniquely Christian and cites Musonius, *Orationes* 13A, as the "classic expression" (*Epistles*, 248). However, Musonius speaks of the "mutual love" of the husband and wife, with the result that "such a union is beautiful" (translation from Lutz, *Musonius Rufus*, 88–89). In contrast, Paul highlights the initiating love of the husband and the wife's submission leading to unity. As already described, the focus in antiquity was on the rule of the husband over the wife.

and is willing to give himself up for her rather than trying to save himself by blaming her.

In this passage the wife is called to submit not to a patriarchal authority but to her husband's headship, which creates a deeper unity because the one with the privileges and position of authority sacrifices himself instead on behalf of the body. Instead of being ruled by her husband because she is seen to be inferior, her relationship with her husband becomes a prime example of the kingdom ethic of reversal. The one who would normally be expected to serve becomes the object of sacrificial love.

## Conclusion

A debate revolving around whether Ephesians 5 speaks of male "authority" as opposed to gender "equality" cannot adequately do justice to the nuances of Paul's use of the head-body metaphor. Instead, it may actually be a misleading entry point from which to concentrate our exegesis of the text.

Because the goal of unity is tied so strongly to the actions of the head, the implications of the passage go beyond mutuality and equality. This centrality of the head's role must be considered carefully, especially because of the connections with the Genesis account. As in Genesis, there is a noteworthy asymmetry between the husband and the wife, since it is the husband who is directly connected with the "one flesh" command. Whether or not this reflects a "hierarchy" with connotations of "authority," the larger issue may be how these gender distinctions serve God's purposes in illustrating the ways of the kingdom as they involve Christ's humility and sacrificial example as the basis for intimate unity.

Thus an important part of understanding these distinctions rests on the significance of the comparison of the example of Christ and the duties of the husband. For many complementarians, this leads to seeing headship as traditional male leadership that is then softened or moderated because it is done in a *manner* that reflects Christ. According to this definition, love serves an adverbial and qualifying function, so that headship is "exercised in love"[61] as Christ loved the church.

But Christ's humility is a defining aspect, and not simply a qualifier. The uniqueness of eschatological headship lies not in modification but in reversal and paradox. Paul is not speaking of traditional patriarchy being carried out

61. Grudem, "Survey of 2,336 Examples," 57. Similarly Knight states, "[Love] is clearly how the apostle demands that the husband exercise his leadership in everything as the head over the wife" ("Husbands and Wives," 171).

in a sacrificial way; rather he refers to an essential aspect of the husband's role as "head," which results in unity.

It is important to see the role of Christian marriage in God's intended purposes for the church. It has been argued that Eph. 5 was designed to present a good witness for the Christian community in a society in which non-Christian husbands expected their wives to be subordinate. In this understanding, Paul appears to uphold the patriarchal order, but not for the purpose of proclaiming a universal ethic. Instead, he makes an accommodation to the dominant social structures so Christians could peacefully coexist with the rest of society and also to provide a cultural defense of the faith so it could gain a more receptive hearing in the Roman world.[62]

Paul's instructions for the believers to obey government (Rom. 13) and pray for their rulers so they can live a "tranquil and quiet life" (1 Tim. 2:2) certainly attest to his desire for Christians to live peacefully in the broader community. His language of headship and submission for husbands and wives in Ephesians may at first glance seem to reflect another attempt for Christians to live according to larger social expectations. But a closer look at the cultural context reveals that while Paul was aware of these expectations, he does not conform to them but rather subverts the traditional order by describing an ethic that asks the head to act in a socially shameful and dishonoring way, that is, the way of the cross (e.g., 1 Cor. 1:18–31).[63] Rather than being accommodating, Paul proposes a way that would be seen as causing great social disruption. The irony is that he says that in Christ it actually leads to the opposite, creating intimate unity and harmony between husband and wife.

As Gombis has noted, Ephesians is concerned not so much with apologetics to the outside world as with "the internal life of the new creation

62. In other words, Paul (or otherwise the author of Ephesians) did not necessarily intend his instructions to be timeless principles but rather reiterated societal expectations, because he was concerned that the Christian communities avoid accusations of subverting society by disrupting the status quo in regard to the household (see, e.g., Lincoln, *Ephesians*, 359–60; Keener, *Paul, Women, and Wives*, 139–56). Webb further notes that the submission of women to their husbands made practical sense in a society in which women had fewer rights and resources. He cites the following factors: "differences in spouses' ages (the female was often significantly younger), differences in amount of formal education, differences in opportunities to acquire and hold resources, lack of informational sources within the home, women's lack of social exposure." Since these features no longer apply today, the contemporary application would likewise change ("Redemptive-Movement Hermeneutic," 398).

63. In Col. 3:18–19 Paul similarly says that husbands are to love their wives and wives are to submit. However, instead of presenting the body metaphor here, he says that the wife's submission should be "as is fitting in the Lord."

communities."[64] Gombis draws on the *oikonomia* tradition, in which the household was "a chief basis, paradigm, and reference point for religious and moral as well as social, political, and economic organization, interaction, and theology."[65] As noted earlier, the household would be seen as a microcosm of the state,[66] and so would be a "concrete model" for how believers could live out their calling as the "household of God" (Eph. 2:19).[67] Rather than upholding the traditional model of the husband as ruler over the wife, Paul instead presents the kingdom model of the husband as head of the wife in the same manner that Christ is the self-sacrificing head of the church. In this way marriage demonstrates the relationship of Christ and the church in which the two are bound together deeply as a result of Christ's love.

The kingdom of God transforms headship in direct opposition to the way it would be expected in a society that supremely values power, honor, and status. According to Paul, headship manifests itself through sacrifice and love, rather than having the head preserve its own life and receive love in a self-focused and self-benefiting manner. Ironically, this reversal of expectations is precisely what leads to the fulfillment of the one flesh union of Genesis, for both the husband and the wife, and Christ and the church.

Headship, thus, is centered on, not just qualified by, the defining event of the crucifixion. As Christ brings greater unity to the body, Paul likewise calls the husband to fulfill the one flesh union through love and sacrifice.

64. Gombis, "Radically New Humanity," 318. This is not to say that there is no apologetic purpose in other instances that discuss the wife's submission. Titus 2:5 tells wives to be submissive to their husbands "so that the word of God will not be dishonored." In 1 Pet. 3:1–7, Peter states explicitly that the wife should be submissive so that the unbelieving husband may be won to the faith. Thus each statement must be understood in its own terms. As Achtemeier states in regard to 1 Peter, "The conduct of wives with non-Christian husbands is the chief concern of the author here" (*1 Peter*, 210). In Ephesians, Paul's focus is on the husband's headship for the unity and flourishing of marriages among believers.

65. Gombis, "Radically New Humanity," 320, citing Elliott, *Home for the Homeless*, 213.

66. Malherbe, *Social Aspects*, 51.

67. Gombis, "Radically New Humanity," 322.

# Final Thoughts

Many people may want answers to questions such as "So, what can women do?" However, I have purposely decided not to answer these questions because I believe that before we can move forward or explore another direction, we must spend some time rethinking foundational issues. Although some will understandably be disappointed that I do not present conclusions that are more concrete and practical, it is a premise of the book that we need to consider the larger theological foundations of the issue before moving on to specific formulations. A main point of the book has been to argue for the very need to reexamine these foundations and to suggest a possible direction for forward movement. If it can prompt this kind of discussion, it will have fulfilled its purpose.

### Reframing the Issue

We began this study by analyzing how dominant social trends have often impacted the gender debate by influencing the framework of the discussion, moving the overall trajectory in an increasingly individualistic direction based on self-fulfillment even as it dealt with issues of authority and equality. In light of this, we have tried to show the need to go back to Scripture to see whether there are other, more transcendent and corporate concerns with which to view gender than those presented by the two current positions.

The crucial component to reframing the debate is to consider God's purposes for his people and how these are accomplished in the new age. The eschatological pouring out of the Spirit on all genders, ages, and ethnicities for the prophetic and universal proclamation of God's redemption provides a valuable means for building up the church through the gifting of all believers. The Spirit is God's empowerment, and he is given to all believers.

This gifting may result in "equality," although in the context of God's purposes it is better understood as leading to "inclusion," since the dominant concern is not individual rights and benefits but God's grace to all his people, Jew and gentile, male and female. The focus is on what God gives, or perhaps better, the God who gives, and not what people receive. The point is not that God is or should be fair, but that he is merciful and sovereign to give salvation and new life in the Spirit to all who call on the name of the Lord (Rom. 10:13).

At the same time, whether or not Pentecost leads to egalitarianism, the coming of the Spirit marks a turning point in the outworking of ministry among God's people. Complementarians should be able to integrate this concept more fully into an overall theology of ministry for both men and women. They should be able to show how the ministry of leaders points toward God, not the leaders themselves, and highlights the power of the cross, not just personal areas of competence and responsibility. Furthermore, both positions should be able to show how their view promotes love and unity in the body.

This is why perspective matters. The framing of the issue reveals the type of information we want, but Scripture often challenges our perspective. As detailed in the introduction, Paul says in Rom. 5–6 that the correct way to consider sin is not to ask, "Does grace mean we can/should continue sinning?" but rather, "Now that we are in Christ, what is our new relationship to sin, and how does that then impact how we live?" The way we pose our questions profoundly impacts the kinds of answers we receive. For Paul sin looks very different from the standpoint of new life in Christ than when one is enslaved to sin (Rom. 6:16–20). Rather than focusing on whether one can continue to sin, Paul demonstrates that renewal in Christ means one no longer *has* to sin. One's very relationship to sin has changed because of grace, so the relevant questions change as well.

In regard to gender, we can similarly change our questions. The current situation often highlights practical concerns regarding what women can or cannot do or who makes decisions. Such questions ultimately need to be answered. However, the wisest course may not be to use them as a starting point. When they do form our starting point, the answers predictably revolve around the construction or absence of rules. While our practical questions are also based on deeper, underlying concerns such as "Who has authority?" or "Are men and women equal?" the point is not simply whether men have a special leadership role or what rights women have. Instead, gender in the Bible may relate more fundamentally to the holiness of God's people and the impact of grace on relationships in the family of God, so that the focus is on God and the good of the other rather than oneself. In this there is a corporate orientation as the church and Christian marriage demonstrate the superiority of the way of the cross. Keeping larger purposes such as these in mind may then provide a better context in which to answer the practical questions and other concerns.

Thus it seems better to investigate what Scripture has to say without being limited to preset categories so we can capture more and grander aspects of God's plan. More appropriate questions may include ones such as, "What are God's purposes for his people, and how is gender relevant to these purposes?" From this vantage point we can gain a larger perspective with which to view individuals, rather than focusing on the individuals themselves, thus lessening the possibility of an overly self-oriented focus. The focal point is not the believers but God, who is preparing a people for himself and to make himself known to the nations.

## Moving Forward

To help change our perspective on the debate, we have attempted to highlight underutilized categories, such as unity and reversal, which have led to further categories such as love, suffering/sacrifice, and holiness. There may also be additional avenues where more research can benefit the gender issue.

One of these areas, for example, may be the Adam/Christ comparison. We noted Adam's representative significance in Gen. 2–3 and the connections in Paul's Letter to the Romans. As explained earlier, the narrative describes Adam and Eve as being called to unity at the same time that Adam is held accountable for obedience to God's word in a way that Eve is not. Paul then makes a similar connection in Rom. 5:12–21, specifically citing Adam, not Eve, as being responsible for the introduction of sin and death into the world and then contrasting the consequences of Adam's transgression with the blessings of Christ's obedience. One scholar has described the comparison between the two in Phil. 2:6–8 as Christ's perfect expression of the image of God in his "self-negation" and "self-giving" in contrast to Adam's depreciation of the image in his "self-grasping" after his own gain.[1]

1. Savage, *Power through Weakness*, 150–51.

There has been little discussion of the implications of the Adam/Christ comparison from either an egalitarian or a complementarian viewpoint. Some egalitarians have applied the passage to show that Adam's culpability indicates Eve's deception and transgression should not result in her subordination.[2] This may be correct, but it is also important to consider the positive contribution of the passage, and not just what it does *not* support. The passage presents a remarkable differentiation that naturally leads to a need for further explication.

Complementarians have argued that it indicates Adam has a responsibility to lead in his relationship with Eve.[3] However, Paul sees implications that are more radical. The condemnation of all humanity as a result of Adam's disobedience and then Paul's identification of Christ as the "last Adam" (1 Cor. 15:45) and the "second man" (1 Cor. 15:47) points to a far greater importance to Adam than simply a leadership of Eve. I suspect that at least part of the explanation of the relationship of Adam and Eve lies in the themes of holiness and obedience to God's word, which are critical ideas suggested in our literary analysis of Gen. 2–3.[4] In the end, the example of the last Adam leads to unity both in the church and in marriage.

It would also seem important for evangelicals to consider carefully the terms used. For example, "patriarchy" is sometimes used to describe the complementarian position,[5] but as an emotionally charged term it should be applied with great care. Anthropologist Charlotte Seymour-Smith notes that there is no generally accepted definition, and there is also confusion concerning what domestic and political aspects must be present for a society to be deemed "patriarchal." Furthermore, elements of patriarchy may also be combined with those of matriarchy and equality. She argues that the term "patriarchal" may be best reserved "for those societies in which the expression of male dominance is particularly extreme and systematic, such as those in which the legal rights of women and children are totally subject to the authority

2. Some examples include Belleville, *Women Leaders*, 170–71; Fee, "Hermeneutics," 378.

3. Ortlund, "Male-Female Equality," 107–8; Schreiner, "Another Complementarian Perspective," 315.

4. Obedience to God remains central in the life of the church, as the Spirit empowers believers to become "obedient from the heart" (Rom. 6:17) and "slaves of righteousness, resulting in sanctification" (Rom. 6:19). Believers are to be obedient to the law of Christ and so are bound to God's word. As Deidun states, "The fact that the Law's rôle in God's plan is brought to an end with the coming of faith does not mean that the *demand* expressed in the Law is laid aside. On the contrary, it is only in the economy of faith that the Law as the expression of God's eternally valid demand is brought to fulfillment" (*New Covenant Morality*, 153, italics original).

5. E.g., Balswick and Balswick, who discuss "hard patriarchy," in which the husband has authority over the wife and makes final decisions in the marriage; and "soft patriarchy," characterized by "servant leadership" ("Marriage as a Partnership," 449).

of the male."[6] Because of the broad range of definitions and the possibility of misunderstanding, and especially as complementarians have moved toward servant leadership, it may not be a helpful term to describe the position.

On the other side, evangelicals can apply caution in their use of "feminism" to describe the egalitarian position. We have shown the connections with and history of the evangelical movements in relationship to secular feminism, but considering the negative connotations often associated with the term, we may be wise to use it only when the historical context is very evident. It can also be noted that although the term "feminism" is now applied to the nineteenth-century movement, or what is also known today as the "first wave" of feminism, it was first used in the early twentieth century.[7] Because of the possible pejorative use of these and other terms, they should be used judiciously and only when the context is clearly understood.

Another term that can cause confusion and misunderstanding, although without the same explosive potential, is "complementarity." Egalitarians correctly note that it does not automatically lead to assumptions of hierarchy.[8] They rightly observe that gender differences can coexist with equality. At the same time, they can do more to describe what they mean by "complementarity," since, as far as I am aware, there is not yet a robust explanation of what these gender differences might look like, as has been done by complementarians.

Other previously used terms have much potential for expanding the discussion. More work could be done on understanding what is meant by "mutuality." This concept is often seen as part of the egalitarian position.[9] But mutuality does not necessarily imply a corresponding equality and an absence of hierarchy. Rather mutuality can coexist with hierarchy, as it does in 1 Pet. 5:5, where those who are younger are told to "be subject to your elders," but all are told "clothe yourselves with humility toward one another."[10] Clarke notes that Paul's body metaphor has both mutuality and hierarchy. All parts are necessary, leading to mutual dependence, while at the same time there is

6. Charlotte Seymour-Smith, "Patriarchy," in *Macmillan Dictionary of Anthropology* (London: Macmillan, 1988), 217–18, cited in Elliott, "Jesus Was Not an Egalitarian," 80–81.

7. Braude, "Religions and Modern Feminism," 1:12.

8. Thus the subtitle of the book by Pierce and Groothuis defending the egalitarian position is *Complementarity without Hierarchy*, 15.

9. E.g., as Groothuis says, "The Bible, although adapting the form of its message to the form of patriarchal culture, does not make a clear advocacy of male supremacy but rather teaches principles of mutuality and equality which actually subvert cultural patriarchy" (*Women Caught in the Conflict*, 153).

10. Lincoln, *Ephesians*, 366.

a hierarchy in the ordering of the parts (1 Cor. 12:27–31).[11] Both notions are likewise present in the household.[12] Thus he asserts, "There is a danger that unity or mutuality be confused with or interpreted as equality."[13] Bengt Holmberg points out that in regard to the leaders of a church and the congregation, there can be a relationship of "mutual, but not symmetric, dependence on each other."[14]

Considering the role of mutuality can benefit both positions and thus the overall discussion since it relates strongly to unity. For example, Gal. 3:28, which we discussed in terms of "inclusion," has stronger implications for the diverse groups to be "one" in their love for one another than "grant[ing] equal status and privilege"[15] to these groups, as in an egalitarian interpretation. At the same time, the complementarian assertion that Gal. 3:28 refers to an equality in "spiritual standing" as God's "image-bearers"[16] but with differences in "role and function in the church"[17] focuses more on the separateness of the genders than on their intimate unity. Both positions, therefore, may miss the critical relational dimension of the passage, which speaks to the oneness of God's people who are reconciled in the new age.

The debate may benefit greatly from the infusion of new categories and a reexamination of old ones. In another example, Clarke suggests some parts of Paul's ministry might be better understood as "non-hierarchical" rather than "egalitarian." Major examples would be Paul's use of "brother" language, which would not have been understood as egalitarian in Paul's Greco-Roman context but rather would convey "mutual dependence, support and love" with the possibility of status differences among brothers (e.g., the inheritance rights of the firstborn). Likewise Paul's use of *syn-* language, such as in his references to fellow workers, or *syndouloi* (e.g., Rom. 16:3, 9, 21), reflects "common fellowship, shared circumstances, or shared goals."[18] Thus "'co-worker' does not necessarily imply equality but rather co-operation, that is, helping in a task where there is unity of purpose, rather than an equal worker with God."[19] This understanding of how Paul speaks of believers

11. Clarke, *Pauline Theology*, 133–37. He also says that Paul does argue for a form of equality in all members of the community being equipped by the Spirit for all of the community.

12. Ibid., 136n20.

13. Ibid., 91.

14. Holmberg, *Paul and Power*, 120.

15. Payne, *Man and Woman*, 85.

16. Knight, *Role Relationship*, 7–8.

17. House, *Role of Women*, 118.

18. Clarke, *Pauline Theology*, 93–94.

19. Ibid., 94.

and their work on behalf of Christ accords well with our contention that one of the New Testament's major underlying concerns is the unity of the people of God.

Furthermore, I suspect that exploring "servant leadership" can be enormously fruitful for the entire discussion. Egalitarians can reconsider the critical role of authority and leadership, as these have often been downplayed in promoting mutual submission.[20] Complementarians can reexamine what they mean by "servant leadership." We have shown how "servant" is more than a modifier of "leadership," because in the kingdom both are present yet in a paradoxical relationship. Since Jesus as well as Paul claim authority, even as they speak of being servants and slaves,[21] an additional area of study may be how these two aspects are reconciled or otherwise coexist.[22] The full impact of "reversal" must come into play, since the New Testament challenges hierarchy to show God's power, and the cross of Christ was the ultimate display of power working through weakness.[23] The theme of "reversal" is critical for understanding how God's value system impacts believers in their relationship with God and others and in their self-understanding.[24] In regard to leadership, servanthood does not simply qualify leadership but transforms it.[25]

20. E.g., Bilezikian ("Biblical Community," 8) states, "There is no mandate and no allowance in the New Testament for one adult believer to hold authority over another adult believer. It is simply not there. Instead, the overall rule calls for mutual submission among all believers out of reverence for Christ (Eph. 5:21)." However, Liefeld notes that "an understanding of authority in the New Testament is crucial to decisions regarding the ministry of women in the contemporary church" ("Nature of Authority," 255).

21. E.g., as Clarke notes in reference to Jesus's washing of the disciples' feet in John 13:13–17, the passage describes "Jesus taking the role of a servant in washing the feet of the disciples, yet simultaneously and rightfully being recognized as teacher, lord and master" (*Pauline Theology*, 98).

22. Or as Santos describes, they "can be held together in a healthy tension" (*Slave of All*, 272).

23. As Barnett observes, "The powerful salvation of God had been wrought in the powerless crucified One" (*Second Epistle to the Corinthians*, 572).

24. As York says regarding the Lukan depiction of reversal, "The theme of bi-polar reversal constantly reminds them that human action is to mirror the value system of God. God reverses the human understanding of the values of honor and shame. The proper human response is therefore to reverse those values in one's self-understanding and in the treatment of others" (*Last Shall Be First*, 162). He defines "bi-polar reversal" as "a statement that contains two parts. The first part presents an idea, and the second part, utilizing the same key terms, negates the first," as in Luke 9:24 (ibid., 36).

25. As Nelson describes, "Rather than prizing a greatness like that of kings and ruling benefactors who expect to receive public acclaim, and over-valuing the status of honoured leaders . . . , the apostles are to adopt the lowly way of service and devote themselves to meeting the needs of others in their communities. This reversal of norms, however, does not amount to the abdication of leadership, but its transformation in keeping with the exemplary yet unconventional precedent of Jesus the servant-leader" ("Flow of Thought in Luke 22:24–27," 122).

It is vital to keep in mind that God often works in paradox and mystery in accomplishing his goals, which are more often than not beyond our natural understanding. We must be careful not to impose our own standards of what is acceptable, desirable, and reasonable onto the biblical text, particularly since a dominant theme of Scripture is the undermining of human logic. God's perspective does not always accord with human ways, concerns, and categories, and the theme of reversal powerfully illustrates how he acts in opposition to human rationality. As a result, it becomes a compelling means and opportunity to confront the limitations of our contemporary understanding. As Norman Perrin notes, "The theme of eschatological reversal is one of the best attested themes of the message of Jesus. It proclaims the Kingdom as eschatological reversal of the present and so invites, indeed demands, judgment upon that present."[26] Understanding the function of the reversals in regard to gender has the potential to provide insight not only into the immediate issue but also into our general understanding of God's ways.

## Some Cautions

I have attempted to show that our current categories of understanding gender are insufficient and there may be other, more helpful ways of trying to comprehend the biblical message about men and women. As I have tried to emphasize throughout, this does not mean that these previous concerns are absent but rather that, if they are present, they may be transcended and transformed by other aspects of the gospel message.

Both authority and leadership now exist in a paradoxical relationship in which they may be fully present while at the same time be characterized by servanthood and what is associated with servanthood and even slavery. An oppressive, self-serving, or authoritarian leadership is not biblical leadership but the opposite. "Servant leadership" does more than soften our attitude toward leadership and instead includes the acceptance of suffering and loss by those who would be "great." The "servant leader" who follows Christ's example depends on God alone, not on a position of influence and power, for identity. Our notions of authority or leadership must be able to account for Paul's conception of power manifested through weakness as a means of displaying the power of God among his people.

26. N. Perrin, *Jesus*, 52.

But the New Testament ethic also transcends rights. Paul affirms their importance, but states that what matters more is one's willingness not to act on one's right if it will lead to a greater good. When Paul calls people to give up rights for the sake of others and the furtherance of the gospel, he exhorts them to place their trust in God, the one who ultimately justifies and rewards. In some cases, to see rights as foremost can actually harm another person and hinder the gospel (e.g., 1 Cor. 8:1–13; 9:1–23).

In both instances it is critical to note that the context for these transformations is the way in which they lead to oneness. The example of Christ's humility, the willing non-use of rights and privileges, is what Paul says the believers should follow in order to have the desired unity. The progress of the gospel takes precedence over Paul's personal rights (1 Cor. 9). Church leaders are not to grasp for power but are to be the first to set the example of sacrifice and suffering, to give up the rights of their position for the sake of the whole. The loving sacrifice of the husband in Eph. 5 stands in direct opposition to social expectations of the privileges and obligations of the head and yet leads to intimate union with the wife. All these behaviors assume that other persons are the objects of concern, so in this way believers are able to "with humility of mind regard one another as more important than [themselves]" and so "not merely look out for [their] own personal interests, but also for the interests of others" (Phil. 2:3–4).

Thus the New Testament speaks of the inability of either authority and leadership or equality and rights to produce unity in and of themselves. Promoting personal rights is intrinsically about what benefits or is fair to the individual rather than building relationships between individuals. Authority may provide order and efficiency but not intimacy. Again, this is not to say that either is "wrong" but rather that both are limited. I am not denying the possibility of these as categories for understanding gender, but I urge evangelicals to consider how these relate to a more corporate perspective. We can reframe the debate by asking additional questions such as "How could male leadership lead to unity and oneness?" and "How could equality promote sacrificial living on behalf of others?"

Our theological perspective also matters because both positions are subject to their own forms of corruption by sinful humanity. Authority and leadership can of course engender an abuse of power. They can also foster paternalism. Thus Paul says the purpose of his authority (*exousia*) is not for himself but for "building up" the congregation (2 Cor. 10:8; 13:10). For Paul, "authority" is not a personal possession but task-oriented. Paul spoke strongly against leadership that led to the increased status of the person, and we must honestly assess the results of our current conceptions of leadership.

A focus on rights and equality can easily lead to an individualistic pursuit of self-interest and result in a perspective that is preoccupied with autonomy and personal benefit over seeing the self in relationship with others. The insistence on rights can be harmful if it causes someone to overlook or make secondary concerns for the impact of one's actions on others. This self-focus contrasts Christ's overriding concern for others, and we must ask whether our striving for equality highlights individual gain rather than a willingness to suffer loss for someone else.

One striking aspect of this kingdom perspective is the way it challenges our modern perceptions of the importance of the individual. For the complementarian view, the reversal of hierarchy and the notion of the leader as slave or servant should speak to a dependence on God both for one's identity, which rests in God rather than personal status, and for personal gain, which ultimately comes when God vindicates those who have suffered and sacrificed for his sake in the present age. For egalitarians, we see that the goal is not the acquisition of appropriate rights as much as the ability to see how the higher way is a readiness to give them up for the sake of another.

The goal for both sides can be to make the more fundamental consideration not personal benefit or position but the imitation of Christ in the willingness to suffer loss for the benefit of others. This speaks to the larger goal of love and unity in the corporate body, as the church models the example of Christ for a watching world. Richard Hays summarizes the corporate perspective of the Bible:

> The biblical story focuses on God's design for forming a covenant *people*. Thus, the primary sphere of moral obedience is not the character of the individual but the corporate obedience of the church. . . . The community, in its corporate life, is called to embody an alternative order that stands as a sign of God's redemptive purposes in the world.[27]

Within this understanding, the body of Christ becomes a prime means for the manifestation of God's values, values centering not on self but on the other.

This certainly does not mean that the individual self is unimportant. However, Paul saw his own identity as being in Christ, which then enabled him to sacrifice worldly gain for the benefit of others. This is why Paul in Phil. 3 repudiates his earthly credentials for the sake of knowing Christ and exhorts the Philippians to follow his example in imitating the example of Christ as the basis for their unity and love.

27. Hays, *Moral Vision*, 196–97, italics original.

In light of our natural propensity to prioritize ourselves, we might do well to be self-critical of our own motivations and weaknesses. Does a focus on male authority lead to improper attention on and status for those in leadership instead of God, whose servants they are, or the members of the body of Christ, whom leaders are called to equip? Does an emphasis on rights feed an unhealthy desire to satisfy our own needs rather than seeking God first in humble dependence and obedience? Being aware of our tendencies can help to build bridges by demonstrating our sincerity to seek God's truth and what is beneficial for all involved. All positions are subject to corruption, and we should not be so defensive over our view that we cannot look honestly at unintended consequences and learn from our mistakes.

## Conclusion

If neither authority nor equality is sufficient for explaining gender in the Bible, a paradoxical "reversal" applied to both concepts can help point us to critical kingdom goals. What "authority," "leadership," "equality," and "rights" have in common is that they often highlight the individual over the community and God himself. What their reversals share is the potential to guide us to a greater acknowledgment of God's sovereignty and a recognition of God's ways in which the willing sacrifice for the other through the denial of self-interest results in unity and love.

Believers are joined in the Spirit, resulting in the need to maintain unity and build up the body. The community, which already exists as "one" in Christ and in the Spirit (e.g., 1 Cor. 12:13; Gal. 3:28), is called to even greater unity in love (e.g., John 13:34; Col. 3:14). The main point is not to have a community that is "fair" or properly organized. While these characteristics might well be part of the church, they must be subsumed under overriding kingdom priorities related to the inclusive, loving community that lives in dependence on God.

The corporate identity of the church, not individual rights or personal power and position, provides a more fitting perspective for understanding gender. The goal of the church as Christ's body and bride is to be wholly dedicated to him and through the Spirit to live in holiness and in loving and sacrificial relationships with one another. The orientation is not simply toward the benefits or rights of women and men in the new age. Rather believers are called to become a community that pursues holiness, submission, and devotion to God through the Spirit in imitation of Christ.

# Afterword

Lynn H. Cohick,
Professor of New Testament,
Wheaton College

Few topics can raise the temperature of the room like "the women's issue." This inadequate and inelegant phrase attempts to capture our society's concern with cultural and familial shifts in gender expectations and roles. Michelle Lee-Barnewall offers a new approach that brings more light than heat to the conversation. Categorizing today's growing number of positions is not easy. Some use the question of women's church leadership (either for or against it) as their shibboleth to establish a person's bona fides on right understanding of the biblical text. Others express frustration with the two opposing options of complementarianism or egalitarianism. They nuance their position along a spectrum of hard to soft complementarianism and a less political to more political egalitarianism. For example, some identify themselves as a "soft complementarian," a label that draws aspects of the egalitarian view into the complementarian position. This unsteady state of the debate is related to changes both in ideas about gender and in hermeneutical approaches to the Bible. Readers are well served by Lee-Barnewall's historical review. Her argument then pushes through the decades-long accumulation of verbal deadwood, opening a better path forward.

My own research on historical women in the Greco-Roman period disclosed a world as complex and multifaceted as our own.[1] In the ancient world, a woman's wealth, ownership of slaves, or membership in the senatorial or equestrian class often played a greater role in her social influence than her femaleness. Then as now, identity was shaped not only by gender but also by ethnicity, wealth, education, and employment. And as I explore Christian women's lives in the early centuries, I am repeatedly struck by the importance of the faithful discipleship—even to the point of martyrdom—that trumped their identity as women. This emphasis flows naturally from the New Testament's focus on carrying one's cross. In my work on Ephesians and Philippians,[2] I see Paul repeatedly stressing the need for faithful service in the body of Christ: service that does not insist on one's own privileges but looks instead for the good of others.

## Lee-Barnewall's Argument

Lee-Barnewall's starting point is the kingdom of God, the meta-theme or controlling construct that shapes the reader's understanding of love, unity, community, and holiness. Kingdom values often conflict with prevailing cultural norms, so reversal is necessarily a prominent theme in exegesis. Additionally, Lee-Barnewall encourages theological and ethical reading with an eye to social-justice concerns. She rightly worries that discussions about male and female, or masculine and feminine, can become abstract and disengaged from real life. Her answer is not to give detailed instructions on what men and women can and cannot do but to engage the church's imagination. Rather than begin with the principles of equality, rights, and power/authority that govern debates in the public square, she hopes to create a new mind-set reflecting the value of the kingdom of God, especially unity based on love of community. This focus makes individual rights a secondary concern.

Lee-Barnewall's first section, which sketches the historical landscape of the debate over the last century, underscores that every stance on gender is conditioned by social events and cultural arguments. No position can be transcultural in its reading of Scripture, for cultural norms and contextual assumptions permeate every position. Her second section examines key biblical texts, focusing on the kingdom of God and its vision of a church united in

1. Cohick, *Women in the World of the Earliest Christians*.
2. Cohick, *Ephesians*; Cohick, *Philippians*.

love. Using historical and literary methods, as well as attending to theological emphases, she is alert to the principle of reversal.

Starting points matter, and that Lee-Barnewall chose the kingdom of God as her foundation indicates that she sees the question of men and women's relationship in the church and home as rooted in ecclesiology and connected with eschatology. These two doctrines are often ignored in the current discussion, and Lee-Barnewall is right to put them back on the table. She links discussions of kingdom of God with mission and holiness, a needed emphasis because it reaches the younger and newer members of the church who take for granted that social advocacy is normative and social justice is a noble goal.

Her discussion of Gen. 1 and 2 exemplifies her approach. She considers the detail of Adam's being created first, before Eve. She recognizes that explanations of this detail draw on wider convictions about the nature of God, the nature of humanity, and the concepts of order and purpose. Lee-Barnewall wants unity and love to be the primary foci of the discussion. She argues that Adam's obedience, which is an aspect of love of God, comes to the fore, as does the overarching call for unity between Adam and Eve. The proper question is not "Who's in charge here?" or "How is Eve equal to Adam?" Instead, the questions revolve around kingdom values of unity and love. Moreover, applying the principle of reversal alerts the reader to a possible critique of existing Israelite culture. Likewise, her discussion about marriage and Eph. 5 draws on the principle of reversal. She demonstrates that Paul's command to the husband to offer self-sacrificial love to his wife challenged the definition of masculinity in his day.

## Where We Can Go from Here

I am sympathetic to Lee-Barnewall's decision not to offer too much practical advice. She is asking for a paradigm shift at the level of mind-set or worldview, not adjustments to existing ideas or practices. It makes sense to ask readers to sit a bit with these new ideas and let them infuse their entire outlook. She also invites the reader to study further, to explore the new vistas that open up when one privileges the kingdom of God, its call for love and unity, and its challenge to cultural norms.

Her argument invites further investigation in several different directions. I suggest at least five avenues of inquiry. First, Lee-Barnewall sets the stage for further inquiry on the kingdom of God and gender in the individual Gospels. We can study each Gospel's literary and theological emphases and elucidate its picture of historical women and men. Her focus on the reversal principle, as evidenced by women announcing Jesus's resurrection to the male disciples, deserves closer study. Given women's testimony to the resurrection, how should we express the virtue of holiness and the centrality of community? Are men being asked to imitate women?

Second, Lee-Barnewall's historical review invites us to discover how economic realities correlate with perceptions of gender in the church and in the home. Second wave feminists who advocated equal pay for equal work were rightly accused of speaking only for white, middle-class women. Immigrant and African American women have worked in low-paying, low-skill jobs throughout this country's history, often due to unfair labor practices and racism. To state that "a woman's place is in the home" is to assume an upper-middle-class socioeconomic position. (Sojourner Truth's 1851 address at the Women's Rights Convention in Akron, Ohio, can be a powerful pointer to this truth.) In the first-century church, with slaves comprising perhaps 20 percent or more of each local congregation, wealthy women enjoyed greater prestige than did male slaves. Gender was not the only consideration in the social configuration of the early churches.

Third, Lee-Barnewall rightly points to the fundamental New Testament concern for Jew-gentile unity. As we focus on unity within the body of Christ as a touchstone for gender studies, we come face to face with anti-Jewish rhetoric. Too often Jesus, portrayed as the proto-feminist who advocated for women, is contrasted with Jewish teachers, depicted as misogynists who ignored and devalued women. Further study can begin with Gal. 3:28, which Lee-Barnewall cites several times. Table fellowship (2:12) and circumcision (2:1–5) are the key practical issues threatening to undo the unity of the body of Christ in the Galatian churches. Paul rejects any functional distinction or role differentiation between Jew and gentile within the life of the church. That means both Timothy (Jewish) and Titus (gentile) may lead churches. Titus is not compelled to be circumcised; his life in the Spirit and in community with other members of the body of Christ is sufficient and complete (2:3).

In Rom. 14 Paul deftly allows expression of cultural identity—Jewish believers may continue observing dietary laws and Sabbath rest, because those practices are rooted in the word of God and express their heritage—while disallowing ethnic superiority on the part of either Jew or gentile. In the same way, I would argue, sexism is unacceptable within the church. As we read the Scriptures, we must not define maleness as the normative humanity over against which femaleness is either greater or lesser.

In Ephesians Paul focuses on unity in the body: Jew and gentile become "one new humanity [*anthrōpos*]" in Christ (2:15 NRSV). Later he speaks of these Jews and gentiles submitting to each other in Christ (5:21) and then uses body language metaphorically to speak of the unity of husband and wife. Lee-Barnewall's careful discussion of these verses allows the reader to continue along one possible trajectory. Paul speaks of reciprocity between the two bodies, husband and wife, as he enjoins the husband to see his wife as his own body, giving her the same careful attention he gives to himself. Within this statement is the implied reciprocal relationship wherein the wife treats her husband's body as her own.

The theme of reciprocity becomes explicit in 1 Cor. 7:1–4, where the wife has authority (*exousia*) over her husband's body in the most intimate and the most patriarchal of settings in the ancient world—the bedroom. Paul mentions circumcision as well as slavery here, signaling that these pairs (husband/wife or male/female; Jew/gentile; slave/owner) constituted the social landscape and presented a challenge to the working out of the gospel's call for functional unity and mutual submission. The dominant person in each pair had to give up a lot: the Jew had to rethink notions of purity and holiness; the (male or female) slave owner had to rethink notions of power and serve his/her slave (perhaps literally in the Communion meal); and husbands/men had to rethink notions of female inferiority and social second-class-ness as they relinquished sole authority in the bedroom and grew accustomed to the female voice in prayer and prophesying (1 Cor. 11:5). Such reversals are beautifully demonstrated by Peter's "conversion" as he watches Cornelius, a gentile, receive the Holy Spirit. Stunned, Peter confesses that he now sees that God shows no partiality (Acts 10:34). Paul makes a similar observation about God's impartiality to slave owners, warning them of the danger inherent in their position of (absolute) power (Eph. 6:9).

Fourth, Lee-Barnewall opens the way to talk about what I think is at the heart of the current debate: the definition of masculinity. By reframing the argument, Lee-Barnewall helps us to see that this is not about "women's issues"; questions of identity arise as much for men as for women. Our culture tends to define maleness in two interlocking ways. First, it defines male as that which is not female. The reverse is not entirely true, for a girl can be a tomboy and a woman can be a strong athlete without diminishing her identity as a female. Second, it defines a male as having more of something than a female, namely, authority. The ancient world's view of male and female shares similarities with our own. The reversal principle evident in the kingdom of God provides a lens through which to observe and critique our culture's constructions of masculinity.

In Rom. 8:17–25, for example, Paul warns those who claim an inheritance with Christ that they must also share in Christ's suffering, which involves the virtue of endurance. Paul uses the term *hypomonē* (endurance) in 8:25. Lest the reader make his call to suffer abstract, Paul uses the image of childbirth. He describes creation as groaning in the present age like a woman in labor, and then connects further with believers' own groaning. Ancient believers were well aware of the stock expression that connected the concept of endurance with the pain endured in childbirth, making endurance a feminine virtue. Indeed, the virtues in general were mapped across a gendered, hierarchical terrain in the first-century world. Traits and qualities that involved freedom of choice were labeled as masculine, and traits deemed passive were assigned a feminine label. Endurance was viewed as a second-order virtue for men and a first-order virtue for women, for several reasons. First, endurance is passive; thus for a free male to endure was viewed as even morally wrong or misguided. Seneca and Epictetus value bravery and manly courage but recognize that at times men must endure suffering; thus endurance could be useful if it was in the service of a greater virtue. For example, an athlete endures training so as to be victorious, to gain honor as the victor through courageous acts of valor. And a gladiator who has endured his opponent's superior abilities could gain honor for himself by killing himself. Endurance as an end in itself, however, is passive and thus suitable for those who are acted upon, such as slaves, women, and conquered armies. Second, endurance was needed only in adversity. For free men, endurance was temporary and occasional, a situation entered into by choice, while for women, endurance was a natural state. Seneca points to childbirth as a ready example of feminine endurance—passive acceptance of pain while uncontrollable forces consume the body (*Ep.* 24.14). Third, endurance is put in the service of self-control, the key virtue for many philosophers. Self-control allows one to endure that which is indifferent or unimportant in the cultivation of reason. Self-control and *andreia* (manly courage), public voice and action—these defined masculinity. Being wounded, silenced, and passive—these were feminine images, suitable only for women and slaves.

Paul, however, argues that this "feminine" virtue is of primary importance for both women and men in Christ. Romans 8:25 issues a countercultural mandate that defies the elite culture's hierarchy of virtues by promoting endurance as a first-order male virtue. Paul challenges the *telos* of elite male Roman society, which was domination and power unto death, by affirming bodily resurrection. Thus the virtue of endurance went hand in hand with the claim of resurrection. So if endurance is about passivity in the face of torture, affliction, and abuse, how should it shape our understanding of masculinity and femininity? Is this an example of the principle of reversal that Lee-Barnewall argues is characteristic of life in the kingdom of God? We are tempted to make endurance active in some way—choosing to endure or enduring to earn a greater good—but these spins put self in the center. Endurance in the ultimate sense is about humility and surrender and passivity, about the goal of an immortal, raised body—not earned but given through Christ.

Finally, questions surrounding sexual identity hold center stage today in the public square, and Christians have the opportunity to offer a robust biblical understanding of human sexuality. Lee-Barnewall's argument encourages further discussion about the role of transformation in light of the eschatological promises of the kingdom of God. The church is convinced that at the resurrection, believers will inherit a new, glorified body that is immortal, complete, and well suited for life in the new heavens and new earth. As we declare that Christ has a real human body now, resurrected and glorified, and existing in male form, so too we must think about our own raised bodies. This new body will be male or female, which means our sexuality is in some way eternal. But this sexuality does not include romantic attraction or desire in its resurrected state, for there is no marriage or procreation in the new resurrected life. How do our choices today reflect this eschatological reality?

The kingdom of God is about life today and life eternal. Lee-Barnewall's work rightly highlights the centrality of the kingdom of God, with its call to unity in love, as foundational for right belief today. The kingdom of God is also about tomorrow, the new heavens and new earth, and our embodied life with Christ for all eternity. Many thanks to Lee-Barnewall for reminding us of our destination, even as she helps us navigate the journey now.

# Bibliography

Achtemeier, Paul J. *1 Peter*. Hermeneia. Minneapolis: Fortress, 1996.

Adewuya, J. Ayodeji. *Holiness and Community in 2 Cor. 6:14–7:1*. Studies in Biblical Literature 40. New York: Peter Lang, 2001.

Alter, Robert. *The Art of Biblical Narrative*. New York: Basic Books, 1981.

Anderson, Janice Capel. *Matthew's Narrative Web: Over, and Over, and Over Again*. Journal for the Study of the New Testament Supplement Series 91. Sheffield: Sheffield Academic Press, 1994.

Anonymous editorial. *Eternity*, May 1956, 11.

Arnold, Clinton E. *Ephesians*. Zondervan Exegetical Commentary on the New Testament. Grand Rapids: Zondervan, 2010.

———. "Jesus Christ: 'Head' of the Church (Colossians and Ephesians)." Pages 346–66 in *Jesus of Nazareth: Lord and Christ*. Edited by Joel B. Green and Max Turner. Grand Rapids: Eerdmans, 1994.

Aune, David E. *Prophecy in Early Christianity and the Ancient Mediterranean World*. Grand Rapids: Eerdmans, 1983.

Babbitt, Frank Cole, et al., trans. *Plutarch: Moralia*. Loeb Classical Library. Cambridge, MA: Harvard University Press, 1927–69.

Bailey, Faith Coxe. "Texas Grows a GIANT Bible Class." *Moody Monthly* 55, June 1955, 17–19, 43–45.

Balch, David L. *Let Wives Be Submissive: The Domestic Code in I Peter.* Society of Biblical Literature Monograph Series 26. Atlanta: Scholars Press, 1981.

Balswick, Judith K., and Jack O. Balswick. "Marriage as a Partnership of Equals." Pages 448–63 in Pierce and Groothuis, *Discovering Biblical Equality*.

Barcus, Nancy. "A Milestone for Christian Women." Review of Letha Scanzoni and Nancy Hardesty, *All We're Meant to Be: A Biblical Approach to Women's Liberation. Eternity*, March 1975, 41.

Bar-Efrat, Shimon. *Narrative Art in the Bible*. London: T&T Clark, 2004.

Barker, Margaret. *The Gate of Heaven. The History and Symbolism of the Temple in Jerusalem*. London: SPCK, 1991.

Barnett, Paul. *The Second Epistle to the Corinthians*. New International Commentary on the New Testament. Grand Rapids: Eerdmans, 1997.

Barnhouse, Donald Gray. "The Bible Way to a Successful Marriage." *Eternity*, September 1960, 12–14, 33.

Bartchy, S. Scott. "Slavery (Greco-Roman)." Pages 65–73 in vol. 6 of *The Anchor Bible Dictionary*. Edited by David Noel Freeman. 6 vols. New York: Doubleday, 1992.

———. "Slaves and Slavery in the Roman World." Pages 169–87 in *The World of the New Testament*. Edited by Joel B. Green and Lee Martin McDonald. Grand Rapids: Baker Academic, 2013.

———. "Who Should Be Called Father? Paul of Tarsus between the Jesus Tradition and Patria Potestas." *Biblical Theology Bulletin* 33 (2003): 136.

Barton, Stephen C. "Dislocating and Relocating Holiness: A New Testament Study." Pages 193–213 in *Holiness: Past & Present*. Edited by Stephen C. Barton. London: T&T Clark, 2003.

Bauckham, Richard. *Gospel Women*. Grand Rapids: Eerdmans, 2002.

Beale, G. K. *Revelation*. New International Greek Testament Commentary. Grand Rapids: Eerdmans, 1999.

———. *The Temple and the Church's Mission*. Downers Grove, IL: InterVarsity, 2004.

Beck, James R., and Craig L. Blomberg, eds. *Two Views of Women in Ministry*. Counterpoints. Grand Rapids: Zondervan, 2001.

Bedale, Stephen. "The Meaning of Κεφαλή in the Pauline Epistles." *Journal of Theological Studies* 5 (1954): 211–15.

Belleville, Linda L. "Ἰουνίαν . . . ἐπίσημοι ἐν τοῖς ἀποστόλοις: A Re-examination of Romans 16.7 in Light of Primary Source Materials." *New Testament Studies* 51 (2005): 231–49.

———. "Women in Ministry: An Egalitarian Perspective." Pages 21–103 in *Two Views on Women in Ministry*. Edited by Stanley N. Gundry. Grand Rapids: Zondervan, 2005.

———. *Women Leaders and the Church: 3 Crucial Questions*. Grand Rapids: Baker Academic, 2000.

Bendroth, Margaret Lamberts. "Fundamentalism." Pages 439–47 in vol. 1 of *Encyclopedia of Women and Religion in North America*. Edited by Rosemary Skinner Keller and Rosemary Radford Ruether. 3 vols. Bloomington: Indiana University Press, 2006.

———. *Fundamentalism and Gender: 1875 to the Present*. New Haven: Yale University Press, 1993.

———. "The Search for 'Women's Role' in American Evangelicalism, 1930–1980." Pages 122–34 in *Evangelicalism and Modern America*. Edited by George Marsden. Grand Rapids: Eerdmans, 1984.

Berg, Barbara J. *The Remembered Gate: Origins of American Feminism*. Oxford: Oxford University Press, 1978.

Berger, Brigitte, and Peter L. Berger. *The War over the Family: Capturing the Middle Ground*. Garden City, NY: Doubleday, 1984.

Best, Ernest. *One Body in Christ*. London: SPCK, 1955.

Bilezikian, Gilbert. *Beyond Sex Roles*. 2nd ed. Grand Rapids: Baker, 1985.

———. "Biblical Community versus Gender-Based Hierarchy." *Priscilla Papers* 16 (2002): 3–10.

Bittlinger, A. *Gifts and Graces: A Commentary on 1 Cor. 12–14*. Translated by H. Klassen. Grand Rapids: Eerdmans, 1968.

Bloch, Ruth H. "The Gendered Meanings of Virtue in Revolutionary America." *Signs* 13 (1987): 37–58.

Blomberg, Craig L. "Gender Roles in Marriage and Ministry: A Possible Relationship." Pages 48–62 in *Reconsidering Gender: Evangelical Perspectives*. Edited by Myk Habets and Beulah Wood. Eugene, OR: Pickwick, 2011.

———. "Neither Hierarchicalist nor Egalitarian: Gender Roles in Paul." Pages 283–326 in *Paul and His Theology*. Edited by Stanley E. Porter. Leiden: Brill, 2006.

———. "Not beyond What Is Written: A Review of Aída Spencer's *Beyond the Curse*." *Criswell Theological Review* 3 (1988): 403–21.

———. "Women in Ministry: A Complementarian Perspective." Pages 121–84 in *Two Views on Women in Ministry*. Edited by Stanley N. Gundry. Grand Rapids: Zondervan, 2005.

Bock, Darrell L. *Luke*. 2 vols. Baker Exegetical Commentary on the New Testament. Grand Rapids: Baker Academic, 1996.

Borland, James A. "Women in the Life and Teachings of Jesus." Pages 113–23 in Piper and Grudem, *Recovering Biblical Manhood and Womanhood*.

Braude, Ann. "Religions and Modern Feminism." Pages 11–23 in vol. 1 of *Encyclopedia of Women and Religion in North America*. Edited by Rosemary Skinner Keller and Rosemary Radford Ruether. 3 vols. Bloomington: Indiana University Press, 2006.

———. "A Religious Feminist—Who Can Find Her? Historiographical Challenges from the National Organization for Women." *Journal of Religion* 84 (2004): 555–72.

Breines, Wini. *Young, White, and Miserable: Growing Up Female in the Fifties*. Boston: Beacon Press, 1992.

Brown, Schuyler. *Apostasy and Perseverance in the Theology of Luke*. Rome: Pontifical Biblical Institute, 1969.

Brownson, Carleton L., et al., trans. *Xenophon*. 7 vols. Loeb Classical Library. Cambridge, MA: Harvard University Press, 1914–23.

Carson, D. A. "1 Peter." Pages 1015–45 in *Commentary on the New Testament Use of the Old Testament*. Edited by G. K. Beale and D. A. Carson. Grand Rapids: Baker Academic, 2007.

———. *The Gospel according to John*. Pillar New Testament Commentary. Grand Rapids: Eerdmans, 1991.

Cary, Earnest, trans. *Dionysius of Halicarnassus: Roman Antiquities*. 7 vols. Loeb Classical Library. Cambridge, MA: Harvard University Press, 1943–56.

Cervin, Richard. "Does Κεφαλή Mean 'Source' or 'Authority Over' in Greek Literature? A Rebuttal." *Trinity Journal* 10 (1989): 85–112.

Chafe, William Henry. *The American Woman: Her Changing Social, Economic, and Political Roles, 1920–1970*. New York: Oxford University Press, 1972.

Charlesworth, James H., ed. *The Old Testament Pseudepigrapha*. 2 vols. New York: Doubleday, 1983–85.

Charter of the National Organization for Women. http://feminist.org/research/chronicles/early1.html.

Chaves, Mark. *Ordaining Women: Culture and Conflict in Religious Organizations*. Cambridge, MA: Harvard University Press, 1997.

Cherlin, Andrew J. *Marriage, Divorce, Remarriage*. Rev. ed. Cambridge, MA: Harvard University Press, 1992.

Chilton, Bruce, and J. I. H. McDonald. *Jesus and the Ethics of the Kingdom*. Grand Rapids: Eerdmans, 1987.

Clarke, Andrew D. *A Pauline Theology of Church Leadership*. London: T&T Clark, 2008.

———. *Secular and Christian Leadership in Corinth*. Milton Keynes, UK: Paternoster, 2006. Repr., Eugene, OR: Wipf & Stock, 2006.

———. *Serve the Community of the Church: Christians as Leaders and Ministers*. Grand Rapids: Eerdmans, 2000.

Clines, David J. A. *What Does Eve Do to Help? and Other Readerly Questions to the Old Testament*. Journal for the Study of the New Testament Supplement Series 94. Sheffield: Sheffield Academic Press, 1990.

Clowney, Edmund P. *The Church*. Downers Grove, IL: InterVarsity, 1995.

Cochran, Pamela D. H. *Evangelical Feminism*. New York: New York University Press, 2005.

Cohick, Lynn H. *Ephesians: A New Covenant Commentary*. New Covenant Commentary Series. Eugene, OR: Cascade, 2010.

———. *Philippians*. Story of God Bible Commentary. Grand Rapids: Zondervan, 2013.

———. *Women in the World of the Earliest Christians*. Grand Rapids: Baker Academic, 2009.

Collins, John N. *Diakonia*. New York: Oxford University Press, 1990.

Collins, Raymond F. *First Corinthians*. Sacra Pagina. Collegeville, MN: Liturgical Press, 1999.

Colson, F. H., and G. H. Whitaker, trans. *Philo*. 12 vols. Loeb Classical Library. Cambridge, MA: Harvard University Press, 1929–62.

Combes, I. A. H. *The Metaphor of Slavery in the Writings of the Early Church*. Journal for the Study of the New Testament Supplement Series 156. Sheffield: Sheffield Academic Press, 1998.

Coontz, Stephanie. *A Strange Stirring: The Feminine Mystique and American Women at the Dawn of the 1960s*. New York: Basic Books, 2011.

———. *The Way We Never Were: American Families and the Nostalgia Trap*. New York: Basic Books, 1992.

Corley, Kathleen E. "The Egalitarian Jesus: A Christian Myth of Origins." *Forum* 1–2 (1998): 291–325.

Crosby, H. Lamar, et al., trans. *Dio Chrysostom*. 5 vols. Loeb Classical Library. Cambridge, MA: Harvard University Press, 1932–51.

Cutter, Barbara. *Domestic Devils, Battlefield Angels: The Radicalism of American Womanhood, 1830–1865*. DeKalb: Northern Illinois University Press, 2003.

Dantuma, Angelyn. "If I Were a Mother." *Moody Monthly* 45, May 1945, 478–79.

Davids, Peter H. *The First Epistle of Peter*. New International Commentary on the New Testament. Grand Rapids: Eerdmans, 1990.

Dawes, Gregory W. *The Body in Question: Metaphor and Meaning in the Interpretation of Ephesians 5:21–33*. Leiden: Brill, 1998.

Dayton, Donald W. *Discovering an Evangelical Heritage*. New York: Harper & Row, 1976.

Dearman, J. Andrew. *The Book of Hosea*. Grand Rapids: Eerdmans, 2010.

DeBerg, Betty A. *Ungodly Women: Gender and the First Wave of American Fundamentalism*. Macon, GA: Mercer University Press, 2000.

Degler, Carl N. *At Odds: Women and the Family in America from the Revolution to the Present*. Oxford: Oxford University Press, 1980.

Deidun, T. J. *New Covenant Morality in Paul*. Analecta Biblica 89. Rome: Biblical Institute Press, 1981.

deSilva, David A. *Honor, Patronage, Kinship & Purity*. Downers Grove, IL: InterVarsity, 2000.

Dicker, Rory. *A History of U.S. Feminisms*. Berkeley: Seal, 2008.

Dodd, C. H. *The Apostolic Preaching and Its Developments*. London: Hodder & Stoughton, 1944.

Drake, Larry. "The Reversal Theme in Luke's Gospel." PhD diss., Saint Louis University, 1985.

Drury, John. *Tradition and Design in Luke's Gospel*. Atlanta: John Knox, 1976.

Dubbert, Joe L. *A Man's Place: Masculinity in Transition*. Englewood Cliffs, NJ: Prentice-Hall, 1979.

DuBois, Ellen Carol. *Woman Suffrage and Women's Rights*. New York: New York University Press, 1998.

Duling, Dennis C. "'Egalitarian' Ideology, Leadership, and Factional Conflict within the Matthean Group." *Biblical Theology Bulletin* 27 (1997): 124–39.

Du Mez, Kristin Kobes. *A New Gospel for Women: Katharine Bushnell and the Challenge of Christian Feminism*. New York: Oxford University Press, 2015.

Dunn, James D. G. *The Epistles to the Colossians and to Philemon*. New International Greek Testament Commentary. Grand Rapids: Eerdmans, 1996.

Earhart, Mary. *Frances Willard*. Chicago: Chicago University Press, 1944.

Elliott, John H. *The Elect and the Holy*. Leiden: Brill, 1966.

———. *1 Peter*. Anchor Bible 37B. New York: Doubleday, 2000.

———. *A Home for the Homeless*. Philadelphia: Fortress, 1981.

———. "The Jesus Movement Was Not Egalitarian but Family-Oriented." *Biblical Interpretation* 11 (2003): 173–210.

———. "Jesus Was Not an Egalitarian: A Critique of an Anachronistic and Idealist Theory." *Biblical Theology Bulletin* 32 (2002): 75–91.

———. "Ministry and Church Order in the NT: A Traditio-Historical Analysis." *Catholic Biblical Quarterly* 32 (1970): 367–91.

Enlow, David R. "Ministries on Your Doorstep." *Moody Monthly* 60, October 1959, 20–22.

Epstein, Barbara Leslie. *The Politics of Domesticity: Women, Evangelism, and Temperance in Nineteenth-Century America*. Middletown, CT: Wesleyan University Press, 1981.

Evans, Craig A. *Mark 8:27–16:20*. Word Biblical Commentary 34B. Nashville: Nelson, 2001.

———. "The Prophetic Setting of the Pentecost Sermon." Pages 212–24 in *Luke and Scripture: The Function of Sacred Tradition in Luke-Acts*. Minneapolis: Fortress, 1993.

Evans, Mary J. *Woman in the Bible*. Downers Grove, IL: InterVarsity, 1983.

Fee, Gordon D. *The First Epistle to the Corinthians*. New International Commentary on the New Testament. Grand Rapids: Eerdmans, 1987.

———. "Hermeneutics and the Gender Debate." Pages 364–81 in Pierce and Groothuis, *Discovering Biblical Equality*.

———. "Male and Female in the New Creation: Galatians 3:26–29." Pages 172–85 in Pierce and Groothuis, *Discovering Biblical Equality*.

———. "Praying and Prophesying in the Assemblies: 1 Corinthians 11:2–16." Pages 142–71 in Pierce and Groothuis, *Discovering Biblical Equality*.

Ferguson, Everett. *The Church of Christ*. Grand Rapids: Eerdmans, 1996.

Finley, Thomas. "The Relationship of Woman and Man in the Old Testament." Pages 49–71 in *Women and Men in Ministry*. Edited by Robert L. Saucy and Judith K. TenElshof. Chicago: Moody, 2001.

Fitzmyer, Joseph A. "Another Look at Κεφαλή in 1 Corinthians 11.3." *New Testament Studies* 35 (1989): 503–11.

———. *First Corinthians*. Anchor Bible 32. New Haven: Yale University Press, 2008.

Fitzwater, P. B. *Woman: Her Mission, Position, and Ministry*. Grand Rapids: Eerdmans, 1949.

Fletcher, Holly Berkley. *Gender and the American Temperance Movement of the Nineteenth Century*. New York: Routledge, 2008.

Foster, B. O., et al., trans. *Livy: History of Rome*. 14 vols. Loeb Classical Library. Cambridge, MA: Harvard University Press, 1919–59.

Foster, J. Ellen. "Work for Women." *The Christian Workers Magazine* 9, 1909, 483.

Frank, Douglas W. *Less than Conquerors*. Grand Rapids: Eerdmans, 1986.

Friedan, Betty. *The Feminine Mystique*. New York: Norton, 2001.

Fung, Ronald Y. K. "Some Pauline Pictures of the Church." *Evangelical Quarterly* 53 (1981): 89–107.

Gallagher, Sally. *Evangelical Identity and Gendered Family Life*. New Brunswick, NJ: Rutgers University Press, 2003.

García Martínez, Florentino, ed. *The Dead Sea Scrolls Translated: The Qumran Texts in English*. Translated by G. E. Watson. 2nd ed. Grand Rapids: Eerdmans, 1996.

Garland, David E. *1 Corinthians*. Baker Exegetical Commentary on the New Testament. Grand Rapids: Baker Academic, 2003.

Garnsey, Peter, and Richard Saller. *The Roman Empire: Economy, Society and Culture*. Berkeley: University of California Press, 1987.

George, Timothy. "Egalitarians and Complementarians Together? A Modest Proposal." Pages 266–88 in *Women, Ministry and the Gospel*. Edited by Mark Husbands and Timothy Larsen. Downers Grove, IL: InterVarsity, 2007.

———. *Galatians*. New American Commentary 30. Nashville: Broadman & Holman, 1994.

Gombis, Timothy G. "A Radically New Humanity: The Function of the *Haustafel* in Ephesians." *Journal of the Evangelical Theological Society* 48 (2005): 317–30.

Goppelt, Leonhard. *A Commentary on I Peter*. Edited by Ferdinand Hahn. Translated by John E. Alsup. Grand Rapids: Eerdmans, 1993.

Graebner, William. *The Age of Doubt: American Thought and Culture in the 1940s*. Prospect Heights, IL: Waveland, 1998.

Granberg, Lars. "Husbands Hold the Key to Happy Homes." *Eternity*, May 1961, 11–35.

Green, Joel B. *1 Peter*. Two Horizons New Testament Commentary. Grand Rapids: Eerdmans, 2007.

Greenleaf, Robert K. *The Servant as Leader*. Peterborough, NH: Windy Row, 1973.

Grenz, Stanley J., with Denise Muir Kjesbo. *Women in the Church*. Downers Grove, IL: InterVarsity, 1995.

Grimké, Sarah. *Letters on the Equality of the Sexes and Other Essays*. Edited by Elizabeth Ann Bartlett. New Haven: Yale University Press, 1988.

Groothuis, Rebecca Merrill. *Good News for Women*. Grand Rapids: Baker, 1997.

———. *Women Caught in the Conflict*. Eugene, OR: Wipf & Stock, 1997.

Grudem, Wayne. *Countering the Claims of Evangelical Feminism*. Colorado Springs: Multnomah, 2006.

———. "Does Κεφαλή ('Head') Mean 'Source' or 'Authority Over' in Greek Literature? A Survey of 2,336 Examples." *Trinity Journal* 6 (1985): 38–59.

———. *Evangelical Feminism & Biblical Truth*. Sisters, OR: Multnomah, 2004.

———. "The Meaning of *Kephalē* ('Head'): A Response to Recent Studies." Pages 425–68 in Piper and Grudem, *Recovering Biblical Manhood and Womanhood*.

Gummere, Richard M., et al., trans. *Seneca*. 10 vols. Loeb Classical Library. Cambridge, MA: Harvard University Press, 1917–72.

Gundry, Patricia. *Neither Slave nor Free*. San Francisco: Harper & Row, 1987.

———. *Woman Be Free*. Grand Rapids: Suitcase Books, 1977.

Gundry-Volf, Judith M. "Beyond Difference? Paul's Vision of a New Humanity in Galatians 3:28." Pages 8–36 in *Gospel and Gender: A Trinitarian Engagement with Being Male and Female in Christ*. Edited by D. A. Campbell. London: T&T Clark, 2003.

Gunn, David M., and Danna Nolan Fewell. *Narrative in the Hebrew Bible*. Oxford: Oxford University Press, 1993.

Gurin, Gerald, Joseph Veroff, and Sheila Feld. *Americans View Their Mental Health: A Nationwide Interview Survey*. New York: Basic Books, 1960.

Halsey, A. H. "Equality." Pages 260–63 in *The Social Science Encyclopedia*. Edited by Adam Kuper and Jessica Kuper. London: Routledge, 1989.

Hardesty, Nancy A. "Women and Evangelical Christianity." Pages 65–79 in *The Cross & the Flag*. Carol Stream, IL: Creation House, 1972.

———. *Women Called to Witness: Evangelical Feminism in the Nineteenth Century*. 2nd ed. Knoxville: University of Tennessee Press, 1999.

———. *Your Daughters Shall Prophesy: Revivalism and Feminism in the Age of Finney*. New York: Carlson, 1991.

Hardesty, Nancy, and Letha Scanzoni. *All We're Meant to Be*. Waco: Word, 1974.

Harris, Barbara J. *Beyond Her Sphere: Women and the Professions in American History*. Westport, CT: Greenwood, 1978.

Harris, Murray J. *Slave of Christ*. Downers Grove, IL: InterVarsity, 1999.

Harrison, Beverly Wildung. "The Early Feminists and the Clergy: A Case Study in the Dynamics of Secularization." *Review and Expositor* (Winter 1975): 41–52.

Hartmann, Susan M. *The Home Front and Beyond: American Women in the 1940s*. New York: Twayne, 1995.

———. "Prescriptions for Penelope: Literature on Women's Obligations to Returning World War II Veterans." *Women's Studies* 5 (1978): 223–39.

Hassey, Janette. "Evangelical Women in Ministry a Century Ago." Pages 39–57 in Pierce and Groothuis, *Discovering Biblical Equality*.

———. *No Time for Silence: Evangelical Women in Public Ministry around the Turn of the Century*. Minneapolis: Christians for Biblical Equality, 1986.

Hauser, Alan Jon. "Genesis 2–3: The Theme of Intimacy and Alienation." Pages 383–98 in *"I Studied Inscriptions from before the Flood": Ancient Near Eastern, Literary, and Linguistic Approaches to Genesis 1–11*. Edited by Richard S. Hess and David Toshio Tsumura. Winona Lake, IN: Eisenbrauns, 1994.

Hays, Richard B. *The Moral Vision of the New Testament*. San Francisco: HarperSanFrancisco, 1996.

Hearn, Virginia. *Our Struggle to Serve*. Waco: Word, 1979.

Hellerman, Joseph H. *The Ancient Church as Family*. Minneapolis: Fortress, 2001.

———. *Embracing Shared Ministry: Power and Status in the Early Church and Why It Matters Today*. Grand Rapids: Kregel, 2013.

———. *Reconstructing Honor in Roman Philippi*. Society for New Testament Studies Monograph Series 132. Cambridge: Cambridge University Press, 2005.

Hengel, Martin. *The Cross of the Son of God*. London: SCM, 1986.

———. *Crucifixion in the Ancient World and the Folly of the Message of the Cross*. Philadelphia: Fortress, 1977.

Hess, Richard S. "Equality with and without Innocence: Genesis 1–3." Pages 79–95 in Pierce and Groothuis, *Discovering Biblical Equality*.

Hestenes, Roberta. "Culture, Counterculture and Christian Transformation." Pages 278–82 in *Women and the Ministries of Christ*. Edited by Roberta R. Hestenes and Lois Curley. Evangelical Women's Caucus Southwest Chapter. Pasadena, CA: Fuller Theological Seminary, 1979.

Hill, Patricia R. *The World Their Household: The American Woman's Foreign Mission Movement and Cultural Transformation, 1870–1920*. Ann Arbor: University of Michigan Press, 1985.

Hoehner, Harold W. *Ephesians*. Grand Rapids: Baker Academic, 2002.

Holmberg, Bengt. *Paul and Power: The Structure of Authority in the Primitive Church as Reflected in the Pauline Epistles*. Coniectanea Biblica: New Testament Series 11. Lund, Sweden: CWK Gleerup, 1978.

Holmes, Michael W., ed. and trans. *The Apostolic Fathers: Greek Texts and English Translations*. 3rd ed. Grand Rapids: Baker Academic, 2007.

House, H. Wayne. *The Role of Women in Ministry Today*. Grand Rapids: Baker, 1995.

Howard, Walden. "What Right Has a Woman?" *Moody Monthly* 48, May 1948, 633.

Howe, Karen. "Husbands, Forget the Heroics!" *Eternity*, December 1974, 11–13.

Hubbard, David Allan. *Hosea: An Introduction and Commentary*. Tyndale Old Testament Commentaries. Leicester, UK: Inter-Varsity, 1989.

Hull, Gretchen Gaebelein. *Equal to Serve*. Grand Rapids: Baker, 1987.

Hunter, James Davison. *Evangelicalism: The Coming Generation*. Chicago: University of Chicago Press, 1987.

Hurley, James B. *Man and Woman in Biblical Perspective*. Grand Rapids: Zondervan, 1981.

Hutchison, John C. "Servanthood: Jesus' Countercultural Call to Christian Leaders." *Bibliotheca Sacra* 166 (2009): 53–69.

Iber, Gerhard. "Zum Verständnis von I Cor. 12:31." *Zeitschrift für die neutestamentliche Wissenschaft und die Kunde der älteren Kirche* 54 (1963): 43–52.

Ilan, Tal. *Jewish Women in Greco-Roman Palestine*. Peabody, MA: Hendrickson, 1995.

Ingersoll, Julie. *Evangelical Christian Women*. New York: New York University Press, 2003.

Ironside, H. A. "The Ministry of Women." *Our Hope* 56 (1950): 653–58.

Jacobsen, Margaret. "Marriage—A Career?" *HIS* 5, January 1945, 5–7.

Jeremias, Joachim. *Jerusalem in the Time of Jesus*. Philadelphia: Fortress, 1969.

Jewett, Paul K. *Man as Male and Female*. Grand Rapids: Eerdmans, 1975.

Jobes, Karen H. *1 Peter*. Baker Exegetical Commentary on the New Testament. Grand Rapids: Baker Academic, 2005.

Johnson, S. Lewis. "Role Distinctions in the Church: Galatians 3:28." Pages 154–64 in Piper and Grudem, *Recovering Biblical Manhood and Womanhood*.

Kassian, Mary A. *Women, Creation and the Fall.* Westchester, IL: Crossway, 1990.

Keener, Craig S. *Acts: An Exegetical Commentary.* Vol. 1, *Introduction and 1:1–2:47.* Grand Rapids: Baker Academic, 2012.

———. *Paul, Women & Wives.* Peabody, MA: Hendrickson, 1992.

———. "Women in Ministry: Another Egalitarian Perspective." Pages 205–57 in *Two Views on Women in Ministry.* Edited by Stanley N. Gundry. Grand Rapids: Zondervan, 2005.

Keller, Rosemary Skinner. *Georgia Harkness: For Such a Time as This.* Nashville: Abingdon, 1992.

Kennedy, George A., trans. *Aristotle: On Rhetoric.* New York: Oxford University Press, 1991.

Kerber, Linda K. *Women of the Republic.* Chapel Hill: University of North Carolina Press, 1980.

Kiel, Luetta. "Just a Housewife . . . What Can I Do?" *Moody Monthly* 55, June 1955, 14–15, 36–37.

Kimball, Cynthia Neal. "Nature, Culture and Gender Complementarity." Pages 464–80 in Pierce and Groothuis, *Discovering Biblical Equality.*

Kline, Meredith G. *Images of the Spirit.* Grand Rapids: Baker, 1980.

Knight, George W., III. "Husbands and Wives as Analogues of Christ and the Church: Ephesians 5:21–33 and Colossians 3:18–19." Pages 165–78 in Piper and Grudem, *Recovering Biblical Manhood and Womanhood.*

———. *The Role Relationship of Men & Women.* Chicago: Moody, 1985.

Kraditor, Aileen S. *The Ideas of the Woman Suffrage Movement, 1890–1920.* New York: Doubleday, 1971.

———. *Up from the Pedestal: Selected Writings of the History of American Feminism.* Chicago: Quadrangle Books, 1968.

Kroeger, Catherine Clark. "The Classical Concept of *Head* as 'Source.'" Pages 267–83 in Hull, *Equal to Serve.*

Kruse, Colin. *2 Corinthians.* Tyndale New Testament Commentaries. Leicester, England: Inter-Varsity, 1987.

Kvalbein, Hans. "'Go Therefore, and Make Disciples': The Concept of Discipleship in the New Testament." *Themelios* 13 (1988): 48–53.

Ladd, George Eldon. *A Theology of the New Testament.* Rev. ed. Grand Rapids: Eerdmans, 1998.

Lambert, W. G., and A. R. Millard. *Atra-Ḫasīs: The Babylonian Story of the Flood.* Oxford: Clarendon, 1969.

Larkin, William J., Jr. *Acts.* IVP New Testament Commentary Series. Downers Grove, IL: InterVarsity, 1995.

Larson, Jennifer. "Paul's Masculinity," *Journal of Biblical Literature* 123 (2004): 91.

Lee, Michelle V. *Paul, the Stoics, and the Body of Christ*. Society for New Testament Studies Monograph Series 137. Cambridge: Cambridge University Press, 2006.

Lee-Barnewall, Michelle. "Turning Κεφαλή on Its Head: The Rhetoric of Reversal in Eph. 5:21–33." Pages 599–614 in *Christian Origins and Classical Culture: Social and Literary Contexts for the New Testament*. Edited by Stanley E. Porter and Andrew W. Pitts. Early Christianity in Its Hellenistic Context 1. Leiden: Brill, 2013.

Leeman, Richard. *"Do Everything" Reform: The Oratory of Frances E. Willard*. New York: Greenwood, 1992.

Lerner, Anne Lapidus. *Eternally Eve: Images of Eve in the Hebrew Bible, Midrash, and Modern Jewish Poetry*. Waltham, MA: Brandeis University Press, 2007.

Lerner, Gerda. *The Creation of Feminist Consciousness*. New York: Oxford University Press, 1993.

Levine, Baruch A. *Leviticus*. JPS Torah Commentary. Philadelphia: Jewish Publication Society, 1989.

Lewis, Clifford. *God's Ideal Woman*. Grand Rapids: Zondervan, 1941.

Liefeld, Walter L. "The Nature of Authority in the New Testament." Pages 255–71 in Pierce and Groothuis, *Discovering Biblical Equality*.

———. "Women, Submission and Ministry in 1 Corinthians." Pages 134–54 in *Women, Authority & the Bible*. Edited by Alvera Mickelson. Downers Grove, IL: InterVarsity, 1986.

Lincoln, Andrew T. *Ephesians*. Word Biblical Commentary 42. Dallas: Word, 1990.

Lindley, Susan Hill. *"You Have Stept Out of Your Place": A History of Women and Religion in America*. Louisville: Westminster John Knox, 1996.

Longenecker, Richard N. *Galatians*. Word Biblical Commentary 41. Dallas: Word, 1990.

———. *New Testament Social Ethics for Today*. Grand Rapids: Eerdmans, 1984.

Longman, Tremper, III. *Literary Approaches to Biblical Interpretation*. Grand Rapids: Zondervan, 1987.

———. "The Literary Approach to the Study of the Old Testament: Promise and Pitfalls." *Journal of the Evangelical Theological Society* 29 (1985): 385–98.

Lutz, Cora E., trans. *Musonius Rufus: "The Roman Socrates."* Yale Classical Studies 10. New Haven: Yale University Press, 1947.

Mack, Burton L. *Rhetoric and the New Testament*. Minneapolis: Fortress, 1990.

Malbon, Elizabeth Struthers. "Fallible Followers: Women and Men in the Gospel of Mark." *Semeia* 28 (1983): 29–48.

Malherbe, Abraham J. *Social Aspects of Early Christianity*. Baton Rouge: Louisiana State University Press, 1977.

Marsden, George M. "From Fundamentalism to Evangelicalism: A Historical Analysis." Pages 122–42 in *The Evangelicals*. Edited by David F. Wells and John D. Woodbridge. Nashville: Abingdon, 1975.

———. *Fundamentalism and American Culture*. Oxford: Oxford University Press, 2006.

———. *Religion and American Culture*. 2nd ed. Fort Worth: Harcourt College Publishers, 2001.

Martin, Dale. *The Corinthian Body*. New Haven: Yale University Press, 1995.

———. *Slavery as Salvation: The Metaphor of Slavery in Pauline Christianity*. New Haven: Yale University Press, 1990.

———. "Tongues of Angels and Other Status Indicators." *Journal of the American Academy of Religion* 59 (1991): 547–89.

Martin, Ralph P. *Reconciliation: A Study of Paul's Theology*. Atlanta: John Knox, 1981.

———. *The Spirit and the Congregation: Studies in 1 Corinthians 12–15*. Grand Rapids: Eerdmans, 1984.

Mather, Cotton. *Ornaments for the Daughters of Zion*. Delmar, NY: Scholars Facsimiles and Reprints, 1978.

Matthews, Glenna. *The Rise of Public Woman: Woman's Power and Woman's Place in the United States, 1630–1970*. New York: Oxford University Press, 1992.

Matthews, Kenneth A. *Genesis 1:1–11:26*. New American Commentary 1A. Nashville: Broadman & Holman, 1996.

Matthews, Victor H., and Don C. Benjamin. *Old Testament Parallels: Laws and Stories from the Ancient Near East*. New York: Paulist Press, 1991.

May, Elaine Tyler. *Homeward Bound: American Families in the Cold War Era*. New York: Basic Books, 2008.

McDannell, Colleen. *The Christian Home in Victorian America, 1840–1900*. Bloomington: Indiana University Press, 1986.

McKelvey, R. J. *The New Temple: The Church in the New Testament*. Oxford: Oxford University Press, 1969.

McKeown, James. *Genesis*. Two Horizons Old Testament Commentary. Grand Rapids: Eerdmans, 2008.

Mead, Margaret. "The Women in the War." Pages 274–89 in *While You Were Gone: A Report on Wartime Life in the United States*. Edited by Jack Goodman. New York: Simon & Schuster, 1946.

Mettinger, Tryggve N. D. *The Eden Narrative: A Literary and Religio-Historical Study of Genesis 2–3*. Winona Lake, IN: Eisenbrauns, 2007.

Meye, Robert P. *Jesus and the Twelve: Discipleship and Revelation in Mark's Gospel*. Grand Rapids: Eerdmans, 1968.

Meyerowitz, Joanne, ed. *Not June Cleaver: Women and Gender in Postwar America, 1945–1960*. Philadelphia: Temple University Press, 1994.

Mezerik, A. G. "Getting Rid of the Women." *Atlantic Monthly* 175, June 1945, 79–82.

Michaels, J. Ramsey. *1 Peter*. Word Biblical Commentary 49. Waco: Word, 1988.

Mitchell, Margaret. *Paul and the Rhetoric of Reconciliation*. Louisville: Westminster/John Knox, 1991.

Mollenkott, Virginia Ramey. "The Women's Movement Challenges the Church." *Journal of Psychology and Theology* 2 (1974): 298–310.

Montagu, Ashley. "The Triumph and Tragedy of the American Woman." *Saturday Review* 41, September 27, 1958, 13–15, 34–35.

Moo, Douglas J. *The Letters to the Colossians and Philemon*. Pillar New Testament Commentary. Grand Rapids: Eerdmans, 2008.

———. "What Does It Mean Not to Teach or Have Authority over Men?" Pages 179–93 in Piper and Grudem, *Recovering Biblical Manhood and Womanhood*.

Morris, Leon. *The Gospel according to John*. New International Commentary on the New Testament. Grand Rapids: Eerdmans, 1995.

Neill, Stephen. *A History of Christian Missions*. Rev. ed. Harmondsworth, UK: Penguin, 1964.

Nelson, Peter. "The Flow of Thought in Luke 22:24–27." *Journal for the Study of the New Testament* 43 (1991): 113–23.

Newton, Michael. *The Concept of Purity at Qumran and in the Letters of Paul*. Society for New Testament Studies Monograph Series 53. Cambridge: Cambridge University Press, 1985.

Nickelsburg, George W. E., and Michael E. Stone. *Faith and Piety in Early Judaism*. Philadelphia: Fortress, 1983.

Noll, Mark. *One Nation under God?* San Francisco: Harper & Row, 1988.

Nolland, John. *Luke*. 3 vols. Word Biblical Commentary 35A–C. Dallas: Word, 1993.

Oakes, Peter. *Philippians: From People to Letter*. Society for New Testament Studies Monograph Series 110. Cambridge: Cambridge University Press, 2001.

O'Brien, Peter T. *Colossians, Philemon*. Word Biblical Commentary 44. Waco: Word, 1982.

———. *The Letter to the Ephesians*. Pillar New Testament Commentary. Grand Rapids: Eerdmans, 1999.

Ortlund, Raymond C., Jr. "Male-Female Equality and Male Headship: Genesis 1–3." Pages 95–112 in Piper and Grudem, *Recovering Biblical Manhood and Womanhood*.

———. *Whoredom: God's Unfaithful Wife in Biblical Theology*. Grand Rapids: Eerdmans, 1996.

Osborne, Grant R. "Women in Jesus' Ministry." *Westminster Theological Journal* 51 (1989): 259–91.

Osiek, Carolyn. "Slavery in the Second Testament World." *Biblical Theology Bulletin* 22 (1992): 174–79.

Parker, Michael. *The Kingdom of Character: The Student Volunteer Movement for Foreign Missions (1886–1926)*. Lanham, MD: American Society of Missiology and University Press of America, 1998.

Patterson, Richard D., and Andrew E. Hill. *Minor Prophets: Hosea–Malachi*. Cornerstone Biblical Commentary 10. Carol Stream, IL: Tyndale House, 2008.

Payne, Philip B. *Man and Woman, One in Christ*. Grand Rapids: Zondervan, 2009.

Perrin, Bernadotte, trans. *Plutarch: The Parallel Lives*. 11 vols. Loeb Classical Library. Cambridge, MA: Harvard University Press, 1914–26.

Perrin, Norman. *Jesus and the Language of the Kingdom*. Philadelphia: Fortress, 1976.

Peterson, David G. *The Acts of the Apostles*. Pillar New Testament Commentary. Grand Rapids: Eerdmans, 2009.

Pierce, Ronald W., and Rebecca Merrill Groothuis, eds. *Discovering Biblical Equality*. Downers Grove, IL: InterVarsity, 2005.

Piper, John, and Wayne Grudem. *Fifty Crucial Questions: An Overview of Central Concerns about Manhood and Womanhood*. N.p.: Council on Biblical Manhood and Womanhood, 1992.

———, eds. *Recovering Biblical Manhood and Womanhood*. Wheaton: Crossway, 1991.

———. "A Vision of Biblical Complementarity." Pages 31–59 in Piper and Grudem, *Recovering Biblical Manhood and Womanhood*.

Porterfield, Amanda. *Mary Lyon and the Mount Holy Missionaries*. New York: Oxford University Press, 1997.

Quebedeaux, Richard. *The Worldly Evangelicals*. New York: Harper & Row, 1978.

Raymond, Maud Wotring. *The King's Business: A Study of the Increased Efficiency for Women's Missionary Societies*. Boston: Central Committee on the United Study of Foreign Missions, 1913.

Rengstorf, K. "Die neutestamentliche Mahnungen an die Frau, sich dem Manne unterzuordnen." Pages 131–45 in *Verbum Dei manet in Aeternum*. Edited by W. Foerster. Witten: Luther-Verlag, 1953.

Renwick, David. *Paul, the Temple and the Presence of God*. Brown Judaic Studies. Atlanta: Scholars Press, 1991.

Resseguie, James L. *Narrative Criticism of the New Testament*. Grand Rapids: Baker, 1994.

Rice, John R. *The Home—Courtship, Marriage, and Children*. Wheaton: Sword of the Lord Publishers, 1945.

Routledge, Robin. *Old Testament Theology: A Thematic Approach*. Downers Grove, IL: IVP Academic, 2012.

Ryken, Leland. *How to Read the Bible as Literature*. Grand Rapids: Zondervan, 1985.

———. *Words of Delight*. Grand Rapids: Baker, 1992.

Ryrie, Charles Caldwell. *The Place of Women in the Church*. New York: Macmillan, 1958.

Santos, Nancy F. *Slave of All: The Paradox of Authority and Servanthood in the Gospel of Mark*. Journal for the Study of the New Testament Supplement Series 237. Sheffield: Sheffield Academic Press, 2003.

Saucy, Robert L. *The Church in God's Program*. Chicago: Moody, 1972.

Saucy, Robert L., and Judith K. TenElshof. "The Complementary Model of Church Ministry." Pages 311–38 in *Women and Men in Ministry: A Complementary Perspective*. Edited by Robert L. Saucy and Judith K. TenElshof. Chicago: Moody, 2001.

———. "Conclusion." Pages 339–42 in *Women and Men in Ministry: A Complementary Perspective*. Edited by Robert L. Saucy and Judith K. TenElshof. Chicago: Moody, 2001.

———. "A Problem in the Church." Pages 19–31 in *Women and Men in Ministry: A Complementary Perspective*. Edited by Robert L. Saucy and Judith K. TenElshof. Chicago: Moody, 2001.

Savage, Timothy B. *Power through Weakness*. Society for New Testament Studies Monograph Series 86. Cambridge: Cambridge University Press, 1996.

Scanzoni, Letha. "The Feminists and the Bible." *Christianity Today*, February 1973, 10–15.

Schlesinger, Arthur, Jr. "The Missionary Enterprise and Theories of Imperialism." Pages 336–73 in *The Missionary Enterprise in China and America*. Edited by John K. Fairbank. Cambridge, MA: Harvard University Press, 1974.

Schlier, Heinrich. *Der Brief an die Epheser.* Düsseldorf: Patmos, 1957.

Schreiner, Thomas R. "The Valuable Ministries of Women in the Context of Male Leadership." Pages 209–24 in Piper and Grudem, *Recovering Biblical Manhood and Womanhood*.

———. "Women in Ministry: Another Complementarian Perspective." Pages 265–322 in *Two Views on Women in Ministry*. Edited by Stanley N. Gundry. Grand Rapids: Zondervan, 2005.

Scudder, C. W. *The Family in Christian Perspective*. Nashville: Broadman, 1962.

Seifrid, Mark A. "Romans." Pages 607–94 in *Commentary on the New Testament Use of the Old Testament*. Edited by G. K. Beale and D. A. Carson. Grand Rapids: Baker Academic, 2007.

Shaw, Luci Deck. "Finding Time for God's Best." *Moody Monthly* 55, January 1955, 22, 67–68.

Skinner, John. *A Critical and Exegetical Commentary on Genesis*. 2nd ed. International Critical Commentary 1. Edinburgh: T&T Clark, 1930.

Smith, Elizabeth Oakes. *Woman and Her Needs*. New York: Fowlers & Wells, 1851.

Speiser, E. A. *Genesis*. Anchor Bible 1. Garden City, NY: Doubleday, 1964.

Spencer, Aída Besançon. *Beyond the Curse*. Peabody, MA: Hendrickson, 1985.

———. "Jesus' Treatment of Women in the Gospels." Pages 126–41 in Pierce and Groothuis, *Discovering Biblical Equality*.

Stansell, Christine. *The Feminist Promise: 1792 to the Present*. New York: Modern Library, 2011.

Stegemann, H. Ekkehard, and Wolfgang Stegemann. *The Jesus Movement: A Social History of Its First Century*. Minneapolis: Fortress, 1999.

Stendahl, Krister. *The Bible and the Role of Women*. Philadelphia: Fortress, 1966.

Sternberg, Meir. *The Poetics of Biblical Narrative*. Bloomington: Indiana University Press, 1985.

Stienstra, Nelly. *YHWH Is the Husband of His People*. Kampen: Kok Pharos, 1993.

Storkey, Elaine. *What's Right with Feminism*. Grand Rapids: Eerdmans, 1985.

Stuart, Douglas. *Hosea–Jonah*. Word Biblical Commentary 31. Waco: Word, 1987.

Sumner, Sarah. *Men and Women in the Church*. Downers Grove, IL: InterVarsity, 2003.

Sweazy, Carl M. "The Christian Home." *Baptist Bulletin* 10, March 1945, 2–3.

Sweeney, Douglas A. *The American Evangelical Story*. Grand Rapids: Baker Academic, 2005.

Tannehill, Robert C. "The Disciples in Mark: The Function of a Narrative Role." *Journal of Religion* 57 (1977): 386–405.

———. *The Sword of His Mouth*. Philadelphia: Fortress, 1975.

Tannen, Deborah. *The Argument Culture*. New York: Random House, 1998.

Thackeray, H. St. J., et al., trans. *Josephus*. 10 vols. Loeb Classical Library. Cambridge, MA: Harvard University Press, 1926–65.

Thielman, Frank. *Ephesians*. Baker Exegetical Commentary on the New Testament. Grand Rapids: Baker Academic, 2010.

———. *Paul & the Law*. Downers Grove, IL: InterVarsity, 1994.

Thiselton, Anthony C. *The First Epistle to the Corinthians*. New International Greek Testament Commentary. Grand Rapids: Eerdmans, 2000.

Thomas, Gordon J. "A Holy God among a Holy People in a Holy Place: The Enduring Eschatological Hope." Pages 53–69 in *"The Reader Must Understand": Eschatology in Bible and Theology*. Edited by K. E. Brower and M. W. Elliott. Leicester, UK: Apollos, 1998.

Thompson, James W. *Moral Formation according to Paul*. Grand Rapids: Baker Academic, 2011.

Tidball, Derek. *The Message of Holiness*. Downers Grove, IL: InterVarsity, 2010.

Tredennick, Hugh, et al., trans. *Aristotle*. 23 vols. Loeb Classical Library. Cambridge, MA: Harvard University Press, 1926–91.

Trueblood, Elton, and Pauline Trueblood. *The Recovery of Family Life*. New York: Harper & Brothers, 1953.

Tucker, Ruth A. *Guardians of the Great Commission: The Story of Women in Modern Missions*. Grand Rapids: Academie Books, 1988.

Verhey, Allen. *The Great Reversal*. Grand Rapids: Eerdmans, 1984.

Walton, John H. *Genesis*. NIV Application Commentary. Grand Rapids: Zondervan, 2001.

Watt, David Harrington. *A Transforming Faith*. New Brunswick, NJ: Rutgers University Press, 1991.

Webb, William J. "A Redemptive-Movement Hermeneutic: The Slavery Analogy." Pages 382–400 in Pierce and Groothuis, *Discovering Biblical Equality*.

Wells, Jo Bailey. *God's Holy People: A Theme in Biblical Theology*. Journal for the Study of the Old Testament Supplement Series 305. Sheffield: Sheffield Academic Press, 2000.

Welter, Barbara. "The Cult of True Womanhood, 1820–1860." Pages 21–41 in *Dimity Convictions: The American Woman in the Nineteenth Century*. Edited by Barbara Welter. Athens: Ohio University Press, 1976.

Wenham, Gordon J. *Genesis 1–15*. Word Biblical Commentary 1. Nashville: Nelson, 1987.

———. "Sanctuary Symbolism in the Garden of Eden Story." Pages 399–404 in *"I Studied Inscriptions from before the Flood": Ancient Near Eastern, Literary, and Linguistic Approaches to Genesis 1–11*. Edited by Richard S. Hess and David Toshio Tsumara. Winona Lake, IN: Eisenbrauns, 1994.

Whitehead, Barbara Dafoe, and William Blankenhorn. "Man, Woman, and Public Policy." *First Things* 15 (August–September 1991): 28–35.

Wilkins, Michael J. "Disciples." Pages 176–82 in *Dictionary of Jesus and the Gospels*. Edited by Joel B. Green, Scot McKnight, and I. Howard Marshall. Downers Grove, IL: IVP Academic, 1992.

———. *Following the Master*. Grand Rapids: Zondervan, 1992.

———. *Matthew*. NIV Application Commentary. Grand Rapids: Zondervan, 2004.

———. "Women in the Teaching and Example of Jesus." Pages 91–112 in *Women and Men in Ministry: A Complementary Perspective*. Edited by Robert L. Saucy and Judith K. TenElshof. Chicago: Moody, 2001.

Wischmeyer, O. *Der höchste Weg: Das 13. Kapitel des 1. Korintherbriefes*. Gutersloh: Gutersloher Verlaghaus, 1981.

Witherington, Ben, III. *Women in the Ministry of Jesus*. Cambridge: Cambridge University Press, 1984.

Witherington, Ben, III, with Darlene Hyatt. *Paul's Letter to the Romans: A Socio-Rhetorical Commentary*. Grand Rapids: Eerdmans, 2004.

Wolff, Hans Walter. *Hosea*. Hermeneia. Philadelphia: Fortress, 1974.

"Women as Ministers." *Baptist Bulletin* 22, July 1956, 5.

Wood, Gordon S. *The Creation of the American Republic*. Chapel Hill: University of North Carolina Press, 1998.

Wuthnow, Robert. *The Restructuring of American Religion*. Princeton, NJ: Princeton University Press, 1988.

York, John O. *The Last Shall Be First: The Rhetorical Reversal in Luke*. Journal for the Study of the New Testament Supplement Series 46. Sheffield: Sheffield Academic Press, 1991.

# Index of Scripture and Other Ancient Sources

## Old Testament

### Genesis



### Exodus



### Leviticus



### Numbers



### Deuteronomy



### Judges



### 1 Samuel



### 2 Samuel



### 2 Kings

# Index of Modern Authors

# Index of Subjects